Waqf in Islamic Economics and Finance

Waqf is emerging globally as a distinctive institution, serving as a vital bridge between societal and economic needs, and resource allocation. *Waqfs* functioning in some parts of the world, of a variety of assets such as cash, stocks, securities, intellectual property rights, and other financial instruments by individual, institutional, and corporate *wāqifs*, are paving the way for financial and social inclusion. This book explains how the system of *awqāf* leads to welfare in society by facilitating financial and social intermediation.

It describes *waqf* in accessible terms, focusing on how it helps people, communities, and nations, and how it can help make societies equitable, peaceful, efficient, and more prosperous. It comprises eight key themes, including a brief overview of the historical role of *waqf* in various periods in Muslim societies in socioeconomic sectors; the evolutionary aspects of *waqf* as an institution; the role of *waqf* in promoting entrepreneurship; the role of *awqāf* system in an economy by facilitating financial and social intermediation; potential options for using *waqf* as financial intermediation; an overview of the management and regulation of *waqf* entities; the organizational and legal framework for the institution of *waqf*; and key findings and recommendations for realizing the capacity of *waqf* in the pursuit of socioeconomic welfare. Specifically, the book takes Pakistan as a case study.

This research-oriented book is tailored to readers interested in understanding the fundamental concepts of Islamic finance and social welfare, without requiring a background in the discipline. It caters to academics, researchers, policymakers, and those keen on exploring the transformative potential of *waqf* to achieve societal welfare and shared economic growth.

Muhammad Ayub is Professor of Islamic Economics and Finance, Riphah Center of Islamic Business, Riphah International University, Islamabad, Pakistan.

Khurram Khan is Professor of Management and Finance at the Faculty of Management Sciences, Riphah International University, Islamabad, Pakistan.

Muhammad Ismail is Assistant Professor of Finance and Islamic Finance, Iqra National University, Peshawar, Pakistan.

Islamic Business and Finance Series
Series Editor: Ishaq Bhatti

There is an increasing need for western politicians, financiers, bankers, and indeed the western business community in general to have access to high-quality and authoritative texts on Islamic financial and business practices. Drawing on expertise from across the Islamic world, this new series will provide carefully chosen and focused monographs and collections, each authored/edited by an expert in their respective field all over the world.

The series will be pitched at a level to appeal to middle and senior management in both the western and the Islamic business communities. For the manager with a western background the series will provide detailed and up-to-date briefings on important topics; for the academics, postgraduates, business communities, manager with western and an Islamic background the series will provide a guide to best practice in business in Islamic communities around the world, including Muslim minorities in the west and majorities in the rest of the world.

The Islamic Economic System
Cultural Context in a Global Economy
Muhammad Awais, Ali Osman Ozturk, Omar Khalid Bhatti and Nazima Ellahi

Islamic Finance, Governance and Regulation
Global Perspectives
Hakimah Yaacob, Razali Mat Zin and Qaisar Ali

Waqf in Islamic Economics and Finance
An Instrument for Socioeconomic Welfare
Muhammad Ayub, Khurram Khan and Muhammad Ismail

For more information about this series, please visit: www.routledge.com/Islamic-Business-and-Finance-Series/book-series/ISLAMICFINANCE

Waqf in Islamic Economics and Finance

Waqf is emerging globally as a distinctive institution, serving as a vital bridge between societal and economic needs, and resource allocation. *Waqfs* functioning in some parts of the world, of a variety of assets such as cash, stocks, securities, intellectual property rights, and other financial instruments by individual, institutional, and corporate *wāqifs*, are paving the way for financial and social inclusion. This book explains how the system of *awqāf* leads to welfare in society by facilitating financial and social intermediation.

It describes *waqf* in accessible terms, focusing on how it helps people, communities, and nations, and how it can help make societies equitable, peaceful, efficient, and more prosperous. It comprises eight key themes, including a brief overview of the historical role of *waqf* in various periods in Muslim societies in socioeconomic sectors; the evolutionary aspects of *waqf* as an institution; the role of *waqf* in promoting entrepreneurship; the role of *awqāf* system in an economy by facilitating financial and social intermediation; potential options for using *waqf* as financial intermediation; an overview of the management and regulation of *waqf* entities; the organizational and legal framework for the institution of *waqf*; and key findings and recommendations for realizing the capacity of *waqf* in the pursuit of socioeconomic welfare. Specifically, the book takes Pakistan as a case study.

This research-oriented book is tailored to readers interested in understanding the fundamental concepts of Islamic finance and social welfare, without requiring a background in the discipline. It caters to academics, researchers, policymakers, and those keen on exploring the transformative potential of *waqf* to achieve societal welfare and shared economic growth.

Muhammad Ayub is Professor of Islamic Economics and Finance, Riphah Center of Islamic Business, Riphah International University, Islamabad, Pakistan.

Khurram Khan is Professor of Management and Finance at the Faculty of Management Sciences, Riphah International University, Islamabad, Pakistan.

Muhammad Ismail is Assistant Professor of Finance and Islamic Finance, Iqra National University, Peshawar, Pakistan.

Islamic Business and Finance Series
Series Editor: Ishaq Bhatti

There is an increasing need for western politicians, financiers, bankers, and indeed the western business community in general to have access to high-quality and authoritative texts on Islamic financial and business practices. Drawing on expertise from across the Islamic world, this new series will provide carefully chosen and focused monographs and collections, each authored/edited by an expert in their respective field all over the world.

The series will be pitched at a level to appeal to middle and senior management in both the western and the Islamic business communities. For the manager with a western background the series will provide detailed and up-to-date briefings on important topics; for the academics, postgraduates, business communities, manager with western and an Islamic background the series will provide a guide to best practice in business in Islamic communities around the world, including Muslim minorities in the west and majorities in the rest of the world.

The Islamic Economic System
Cultural Context in a Global Economy
Muhammad Awais, Ali Osman Ozturk, Omar Khalid Bhatti and Nazima Ellahi

Islamic Finance, Governance and Regulation
Global Perspectives
Hakimah Yaacob, Razali Mat Zin and Qaisar Ali

Waqf in Islamic Economics and Finance
An Instrument for Socioeconomic Welfare
Muhammad Ayub, Khurram Khan and Muhammad Ismail

For more information about this series, please visit: www.routledge.com/Islamic-Business-and-Finance-Series/book-series/ISLAMICFINANCE

Waqf in Islamic Economics and Finance

An Instrument for Socioeconomic Welfare

Muhammad Ayub, Khurram Khan, and Muhammad Ismail

Routledge
Taylor & Francis Group
LONDON AND NEW YORK

First published 2025
by Routledge
4 Park Square, Milton Park, Abingdon, Oxon OX14 4RN

and by Routledge
605 Third Avenue, New York, NY 10158

Routledge is an imprint of the Taylor & Francis Group, an informa business

British Library Cataloguing-in-Publication Data
A catalogue record for this book is available from the British Library

ISBN: 978-1-032-76205-0 (hbk)
ISBN: 978-1-032-76206-7 (pbk)
ISBN: 978-1-003-47754-9 (ebk)

DOI: 10.4324/9781003477549

Typeset in Sabon
by Newgen Publishing UK

Contents

Foreword

Waqf is considered one of the most important components of Islamic social finance architecture with its increasing scope, fulfilling the basic needs of society, and acting as sustainable investment entity for socioeconomic development. It is a unique institution within the Islamic economy for intergroup resource sharing that caters to both short- and long-term needs of those who need support in consumption, production, businesses, or job opportunities in Micro, Small, and Medium Enterprise (MSME) sectors as well as large-scale industries.

Waqf is increasingly being seen as a socioeconomic financial intermediary tool for the welfare of society. It played a crucial role in the Ottoman era, Mughal India, and the Malay region. It served as an institution for the equitable distribution of wealth in society to support production, businesses, education, capacity building, and rehabilitation from any calamities.

Waqf is emerging globally as a distinctive institution, serving as a vital bridge between societal and economic needs. It can be an effective tool for Islamic financial institutions to realize the objectives of Islamic ethical and social finance. Islamic social finance, including *waqf*, fintech, and digital economy, could be termed as the Key Economic Growth Activities (KEGA) for those countries that are facing the challenges of increasing debt burden, fiscal and balance of payment deficits, and the widening gap between the poor and the rich, including the OIC member countries.

The concept of cash *waqf* resolved many problems enabling the institution to play a multifaceted role in the socioeconomic growth of economies and societies. It turned the *waqf* into a kind of socioeconomic financial intermediary through which smaller amounts of charities were channeled into many subsystems of socioeconomic welfare in education, healthcare, hospitality, and other sectors.

Linking the globally emerging concept of corporate social responsibility (CSR) to *waqf* institutions could also be instrumental in the endeavor for the welfare of the public. The funds allocated by the corporate bodies, particularly by the banking and finance companies, may relate CSR funds to the *waqf*-based community development programs.

The potential of *waqf* in the 21st century has been recognized globally as a social-sector institution that can be used to realize socioeconomic objectives. Islamic banks and finance institutions (IBFIs) can play their role in this perspective. It will also promote shared prosperity by promoting financial and social inclusion, concepts that are not only central to the teachings of the divine law but also part of CSR and Sustainable Development Goals (SDGs).

It may be worth mentioning that Accounting and Auditing Organization for Islamic Financial Institutions (AAOIFI) has issued the revised Sharī'ah Standard No. 60 on *waqf*, Financial Reporting by *waqf* institutions (FAS 37), and *waqf* governance standard (GS 13). FAS 37 elucidates different types of *waqfs*, along with the addition of concepts such as the "*Statement of Service Performance*" and the "*Ghallah Statement*" (for charity box). The standard also requires reporting on the impact that a *waqf* has created, utilization of *ghallah*, statement of changes in *waqf* equity, and disclosures in the statement of *ghallah*, among others. Further, the robust governance of *waqf* cannot be overemphasized which is important for the sustainability and integrity of *waqf* system, and to achieve its objectives.

The International Working Group on *Waqf* which represented experts from the Islamic Development Bank Institute (formerly IRTI), Bank Indonesia, and many *waqfs* operating in various parts of the world suggested in 2018 the 29 *Waqf* Core Principles (WCPs) for optimal *waqf* management. Applying AAOIFI's standards and the WCPs would maximize the benefits to human societies inclusively and enhance public confidence in the *waqf* system. The authors have referred to all these sources for the contemporary application of *waqf*.

Waqfs are also functioning presently in some parts of the world in the form of cash, stocks, securities, intellectual property, and other financial instruments by individuals and institutions (corporate *wāqifs*). Over the last few decades, it played a contributory role in enhancing sustainability in terms of environmental hazards and bridging infrastructural deficits. The *awqāf* system must therefore be promoted to create *waqfs* for socioeconomic purposes, by individuals, banks, NBFCs, and other entities in public or private sectors.

The book delves deeper into the historical origins of *waqf*, explaining its role in various cultures in Islamic history. Based on the historical role, the book provides insights into the contemporary application of the *waqf* system and offers a clear, and practical approach with a global perspective. This approach makes it a valuable resource for the readers.

The book comprises eight chapters on key aspects of *waqf* and its role in socioeconomic welfare in modern societies. The themes discussed and analyzed in the book include (i) an overview of the historical role of *waqf* and its evolution as an institution, (ii) *waqf* for promoting entrepreneurship by facilitating financial and social intermediation, (iii) management and regulation of *waqf* entities, and (iv) the organizational and legal frameworks for the institution of *waqf*.

The book also includes different practices of *waqf* operations from historical perspectives and deliberations with *waqf* experts from Türkiye, Malaysia, Indonesia, and Pakistan. It thus reflects the global wisdom of contemporary jurists, researchers, and Islamic finance professionals. Further, the role of fintech and digitalization has also been discussed which can play an enabling role in mobilizing and spending *waqf* funds.

As mentioned by the former Governor of Bank Negara Malaysia, H.E. Ms. Shamsiah Mohd Yunus in her address at the GIFF 2018, the Islamic finance industry must embody and exemplify the value of *iḥsān*, continuously striving for the attainment of excellence. It implies attaining efficiency with equity while implementing the "*Adl* and *Iḥsān*" equation as discussed in detail in the AAOIFI's Code of Ethics for the Islamic Finance Professionals. It requires "*value-based growth*" that is balanced, progressive, sustainable, and inclusive. The potential of *waqf* has to be realized in this context.

Banking and nonbanking finance players need to create value-based products to achieve efficiency with equity. In this way, they will help their respective governments and societies achieve goals set out under the United Nations (UN) SDGs.

Social inclusion, as discussed in the book, would require financing to underserved segments of society and entrepreneurs. Islamic banks and investors should realize that returns on investments should not be measured solely by financial yardstick but also by the social impact they create. Besides, as part of the CSR, IBFIs are encouraged to use social institutions like *zakāt* and *waqf* increasingly.

The book is a valuable contribution of the Riphah Center of Islamic Business (RCIB) toward providing analytical research material and helping strengthen curricula on the Islamic socioeconomic system of faculties of universities and business schools. It is recommended that the philosophy, approach, and principles of Islamic finance which are distinct from that of conventional finance be made compulsory subjects for bachelors-level students of social sciences and business faculties in universities and business schools.

The book will be useful for researchers, policymakers, and other stakeholders keen on exploring the transformative potential of *waqf* as a means to achieve societal welfare and shared economic growth. It is also crucial in providing theoretical, operational, managerial, regulatory, and legal guidance for developing the *waqf* system anywhere in the world, particularly in the OIC member countries. It is a welcome addition to the literature on *waqf* and its role in the past, the present, and the future. Authored by an accomplished scholar Dr. Muhammad Ayub and the co-authors, I sincerely hope that this book will be insightful.

Omar Mustafa Ansari
Secretary-General
Accounting and Auditing Organization for Islamic Financial Institutions (AAOIFI)
Fellow Member of the Institute of Chartered Accountants of Pakistan (ICAP)

Preface

Commercial capitalism and mercantilism emerging from Europe and spreading to the whole world in the 19th and 20th centuries led to the accumulation of capital and wealth in certain groups and persons. Islamic finance was institutionalized in the second half of the 20th century in many OIC member states to resolve the problem of increasingly inequitable income distribution due to exploitation tools of *ribā* and *gharar* and the resultant financialization. It also evolved in other countries and was adopted by mega-conventional financial institutions as a business proposition. Practically, of course, it has failed, at least so far, in realizing the objective of equity and justice mainly because it pursued the paradigm of conventional finance and ignored the objectives and tools of Islamic social finance.

Banking and nonbanking finance players need to introduce value-based products to achieve efficiency with equity and reach sustainability goals. In this way, they will be helping the respective governments to achieve the conditions and to avoid the carbon tax that could be levied in the future in the case of noncompliance. The achievement so far is unsatisfactory as the latest UN Global Sustainable Development Report, 2023, gives a stark warning – at the halfway point to 2030, the world is not on track to achieve the SDGs.

Waqf being the most effective institution in the beyond-market segment of the Islamic economy can be an effective tool for Islamic financial institutions in realizing the objectives of Islamic economics and social finance. It is a unique institution for intergroup resource sharing to take care of both short- and long-term needs of those in the society who might need support for their instant consumption requirements, or production and business process/job opportunities. Particularly the cash *waqf* played its role, as a ribā-free system, particularly in Ottoman Europe to meet the basic needs of the society. It fulfilled the financial needs of priority sectors of economy like that of farmers, craftsmen, entrepreneurs, producers, and merchants through Islamic contracts and practices. It, thus, worked as a financial intermediary in socioeconomic sectors as a tool for the general welfare. It could be the most effective tool for poverty alleviation and sustainability for the present-day economies with

Muslim populations that are facing the challenges of increasing debt burden, trade and budgetary deficits, and an increasingly widening gap between the poor and the rich.

While the institution of *waqf* is being revived in some parts of the world to play its historic role in socioeconomic development, little work has been done in Islamic countries like Pakistan, to revive/promote *waqfs* for realizing the social and economic objectives. Among the challenges being faced in developing the *awqāf* system, one serious challenge is the lack of awareness and proper knowledge about the scope and potential of *waqf* in social and economic fields not only among the public but also among the academia and researchers. The policymakers, state functionaries, and common people think of *waqf* as limited to *masjid*, *madrasah*, and *mazārāt* (shrines). Although the regulators, some financial market players, and researchers have been talking about financial inclusion, no one has thought of an effective model of financial inclusion leading to social inclusion with the crucial role of *waqf*.

Keeping in view the need for research, the authors submitted a research proposal to the Higher Education Commission (HEC), Pakistan for a detailed study about the potential role of *waqf* for socioeconomic welfare and shared growth in Pakistan, which was approved. The research on the project culminated in a comprehensive report covering all conceptual, operational, organizational, and legal aspects for evolving the system of *awqāf* to play its multifaceted role in the welfare of any Muslim society, and particularly the people of Pakistan. This book is based on that report while generalizing the findings and recommendations for promoting the system of *awqāf* in Islamic countries today.

Waqf as an institution of social welfare preceded the modern institution of "trust". The West learned about *waqf* as charitable endowments during the Crusades. The 20th-century "*welfare states*" popularized this trend of *waqf*-like institutions in their quest to mitigate the impact of the capitalistic economy that increasingly widened the gap between the poor and the rich. Accordingly, many charitable trusts are running universities and other educational institutions. Hence, while the West adopted "trust" in their perspective, nonprofit organizations (NPOs), trusts, charities, and other philanthropies emerged also in the Islamic world, while ignoring the sanctity and role of the *waqf* system.

Since the beginning of the 21st century, of course, the potential of *waqf* has been increasingly recognized as an institution that can be used to realize social and economic objectives. Many types of *waqfs* are being created of fixed and liquid assets such as cash, stocks, securities, intellectual property rights, and other financial instruments by individual, institutional, and corporate *wāqifs*. Initiatives taken over the last decade have made *waqf* studies more relevant for resolving socioeconomic problems like poverty, hunger, lack of education, and health and civic facilities in Muslim societies. At the policymaking level, *waqf* is becoming a contributory tool for bridging infrastructural deficits in developing economies.

The conceptual, operational, managerial, regulatory, and legal frameworks for *awqāf* have been suggested in the book based on the interpretative and qualitative research methods. The report for the HEC was prepared by document analysis and the information gathered through interviews, focus group discussions, and observations of the experts. Primary data was gathered from around 60 experts belonging to charity or NPOs, welfare organizations, companies' personnel involved in CSR activities, officials of *awqāf*, and the researchers on the potential and role of *waqf*. The perceptions, perspectives, and understandings of the research participants have been analyzed to derive various frameworks required for the revival of *awqāf* in present-day Islamic societies. For the purpose of brevity, however, the details about the methodology of this research have not been included in the book.

Based on the discussions and content analysis, a format for *waqf* law has been suggested enabling/requiring different institutions to establish *awqāf* to which the well-to-do at the micro level may also contribute to social causes. The funds allocated by the corporate bodies, particularly, by the banking and finance companies, oil and gas companies, etc. may relate CSR funds to the *waqf*-based community development programs.

This book comprises eight chapters that discuss all conceptual as well as operational and supervisory aspects of the institution of *waqf* for playing an effective role in the socioeconomic development of Islamic societies. Chapter 1 gives a brief overview of the historical role of *waqf* in various periods in Muslim societies. It also discusses the importance of *infāq* or spending for the benefit of others. It also analyzes the available material on *waqf* to suggest frameworks for the operation of *waqf* institutions.

Chapter 2 discusses the evolutionary stages of *waqf* as an institution for the longer-term benefit of the poor and the needy. Immovable properties such as land, fields, farms, or buildings such as mosques, schools, hospitals, or basic infrastructures such as bridges, roads, water supply, etc. were the form of *waqf* in early Islamic history. But later, other movable, financial, and intangible assets were included to facilitate cash and liquid assets endowments. The concept of cash *waqf* led to a micro-level formalized philanthropy system enabling *awqāf* to play a multifaceted role in the socioeconomic growth of economies and societies. It turned the *waqf* into a kind of social finance intermediary through which smaller amounts of charities were channeled into many subsystems of socioeconomic activities in education, healthcare, hospitality, and other infrastructural sectors.

The role of *waqf* in promoting entrepreneurship is discussed in Chapter 3. Entrepreneurship for micro-production units and businesses is the growth engine in any market economy and the best tool for broad-based and shared growth by integrating the interests of all stakeholders in any society. The chapter explains how entrepreneurship can be promoted in Islamic countries and the Muslim community by adopting a nonaccumulative paradigm for a formal but discretional system of wealth sharing and thus realizing the objective of financial and social inclusion.

Chapter 4 is the crux of the whole study that elaborates on how the *awqāf* system may lead to welfare in society by facilitating financial and social intermediation. It compares the capitalistic paradigm with the Islamic perspective of market economy where the institution of *waqf* would be functioning for sharing the wealth by the affluent with those who might not get needed resources due to any incapacity or market functioning. It deliberates on various facets of socioeconomic development, the role of consumer behavior in shaping the social sector in the economy, and the potential and role of donations and charity making for instant and long-term requirements for the community's welfare. It discusses the role of *waqf* in poverty alleviation, education, and health sectors, and the realization of *maqāsid al sharī'ah* in the context of UNDP's SDGs 2030.

Chapter 5 discusses the opportunities for intermediation including cash *waqf*, *waqf-takaful*, *waqf sukuk/al khair sukuk*, *al khair* bank accounts, *qarḍ hassan*, *waqf* for financing infrastructure projects and public finance, and use of fintech for *waqf*-related collections and financing. By involving the community at micro levels, financial institutions can provide affordable finance and address the banes of inequity and injustice being meted out currently. It also suggests the ways of sustainability of philanthropic activities through various social venture management schemes.

Chapter 6 provides a detailed background and scheme for the management of *waqf* entities, and their supervision and regulation. Good governance is a success factor for *waqfs* where the *waqf* board, *mutawalli*, administrator, and the board of trustees share many of the responsibilities. The chapter also suggests the regulatory framework of *waqf* organizations.

The organizational and legal frameworks for the institution of *waqf* have been discussed in Chapter 7. The interviews and deliberations with *waqf* experts from Pakistan, Türkiye, Malaysia, and Indonesia have enabled the authors to suggest related frameworks. The laws, provisions of law, court monitoring, and conflict resolution in the operations of *waqf* institutions have been elaborated.

Chapter 8 is on findings and recommendations on realizing the potential of *waqf* for welfare. It suggests a framework to provide education, health, and other civic amenities for the public in general and the poor, small farmers, small traders, and home-based businesses, in particular. It also includes establishing vocational training centers for capacity building of human resources in the lower income groups in society. It is to enhance entrepreneurship and provide opportunities for self-employment. In this way, it will contribute toward the upward social mobility of the beneficiaries.

The inability of the state institutions to provide necessary civic, health, and education facilities to the public is causing serious harm to the balance of society that could be devastating in the long run to all groups including the rich. The book highlights that the development of *awqāf* on the emerging trends for broad-based social and economic development would lessen the burden on the government which is facing huge budgetary and trade deficits.

Greed, extravagance, and pride in one's richness in societies with a capitalistic mindset need to be replaced with the welfare of all human beings through cooperation, benevolence, and sacrifice for others. All these features constitute the cornerstone of Islam's socioeconomic system and social finance. Therefore, *waqf*-related laws and rules must not only make philanthropy easy but also involve all members of society by way of wealth sharing for financial and social inclusion.

The primary readers of this book could be the researchers, graduate and postgraduate students in Islamic economics and finance, Islamic social finance, public finance, development economics, fintech, and crowdfunding. Similarly, the book also provides valuable material for development agencies, NGOs, and financial institutions and offers detailed guidelines for policymakers for poverty alleviation. For policymakers, it offers a more comprehensive and practical approach, encompassing historical, contemporary, legal, operational, managerial, and socioeconomic dimensions.

Finally, this research-oriented book is tailored for readers interested in knowing about *waqf* as the prime institution of Islamic finance for social welfare, without requiring a background in the discipline. It caters to academics, researchers, policymakers, and general readers keen on exploring the transformative potential of *waqf* to achieve societal welfare and shared economic growth.

Muhammad Ayub
Professor, Islamic Economics and Finance
Riphah Centre of Islamic Business (RCIB)
Riphah International University
Islamabad

Acknowledgments

All Praise to ALLAH, the most merciful and most gracious, "The Master of the Day of Judgment". His infinite munificence enabled us to accomplish this task despite our limitations.

Credit for this book goes primarily to the Higher Education Commission (HEC), Pakistan, which accepted our research proposal and approved the grant for the research on the potential role of *waqf* for socioeconomic development in Pakistan. At our level, it would not have been possible to involve many specialists in *waqf* from different parts of the world, particularly Türkiye, Malaysia, Indonesia, and many areas in Pakistan. The research project enabled us to explore the historical and innovative role of *waqf* from the related organizational and legal frameworks of *waqf* operating in other countries, published reports of many *waqfs*, and material published in academic journals and books. I take this opportunity, on our behalf and on behalf of the Chancellor, Vice Chancellor, and the Management of Riphah International University, to pay gratitude to the HEC for granting the research project to Riphah under its flagship research initiative – National Research Program for Universities (NRPU).

Credit for the successful completion of this study also goes to our academic and sectoral collaborators. While renowned academic institutions including the Centre of Excellence in Islamic Finance (CEIF) Institute of Business Administration (IBA) and Malaysia-based International Sharī'ah Research Academy for Islamic Finance (ISRA) provided us with wide-ranging academic support, the Securities and Exchange Commission of Pakistan (SECP) helped us in getting extremely useful information about the legal and organizational framework of *waqf* system to be evolved. I pay rich gratitude to Datuk Prof. Dr. Mohamad Akram Laldin, Executive Director of ISRA, Malaysia, for facilitating us in getting research material on *waqf* from Malaysia and Indonesia. Dr. Irum Saba, Associate Professor at IBA (SBS and CEIF) Karachi facilitated in conducting the focus group meeting (FGM) at IBA with many *waqf* specialists and researchers from Karachi.

Mr. Bilal Rasul, Executive Director/Secretary to the SECP/Policy Board, and Mr. Tariq Naseem, Head of the Islamic Finance Department of the SECP deserve our special gratitude for providing insights regarding the possible legal and organizational framework of *waqf* in Pakistan. Mr. Tariq Naseem also added much value by participating in the final FGM held in Islamabad to discuss the draft of the research report. It would not have been possible to complete the study without their support. We record our deep appreciation to SECP officials.

For the completion of this qualitative research project, many senior researchers, economists, heads of trusts/NPOs, social welfare practitioners, philanthropy specialists, banking and finance regulators, and Sharīʿah scholars provided us with extremely useful information about the historical and potential role of *waqf*. It helped us to get insights on conceptual, legal, organizational, and operational aspects helpful in suggesting a model for promoting *awqāf* to play an effective role in socioeconomic development in Pakistan or other Muslim societies. Many specialists from Malaysia, Indonesia, and Pakistan added value by participating in the FGMs. We are deeply obliged to all of them.

From a historical perspective, Türkiye is a country having a long history of successfully operating welfare *awqāf*. We visited Istanbul, Ankara, and Konya to study the legal and operational frameworks, and fund management of *awqāf* while ensuring sustainability and good governance. Research participants from Türkiye included Dr. Necmettin Kızılkaya, Dr. Necdet Sensoy, Dr. Kadir Yaman, General Secretary of MAVERA, Dr. Mehmet Koca, Mutavelli, "Karzi Hasen Vakfi", Dr. Yusuf Bilgin of IHH Humanitarian Relief Foundation, Dr. Ozan Marasli of Zam University Istanbul, Dr. Cem Korkut of Turkish Academy of Sciences, and Waqf "Ankara Centre for Thought and Research", Dr. Kamola Bayram, Dr. Huseyn, and Mr. Sinan of Karatay Universitesi, Konya; and director of Regional Foundation Directorate of *awqāf* at Konya. We feel humbled and deeply obliged to all of them for their warm hospitality and the diverse information they shared about *waqf* and its historic role. We are also grateful to Mr. Hassan Muhammad Khan, Chancellor of Riphah International University, Islamabad, for taking a personal interest in the research project and funding our visit to Türkiye.

Within Riphah International University, we record our appreciation to Prof. Dr. Khurram Shahzad, Dean, FMS, Riphah; Dr. Rahila Yasmeen, Dean/Director, ORIC and RARE; Mr. Muhammad Irfan, Manager, ORIC; and officials of the Finance Department for their support in smooth execution of the project. We are also indebted to Dr. Zeshan Ghafoor, Mr. Irfan Mazari of the Graduate Research Office of FMS, and other colleagues at FMS and RCIB who extended us support when needed for any task relating to the project.

Finally, we are obliged to the reviewers of the manuscript for publication in the form of a book. We also record our deep appreciation to Prof. Dr. Ishaq Bhatti, Series Editor for Routledge, Ms. Cristina, Editorial Assistant, and others for their facilitation and support in the publication of the book.

Muhammad Ayub
Riphah Centre of Islamic Business (RCIB)
Riphah International University
Islamabad

Figures

Tables

Boxes

Acronyms

Acronym	*Definition*
ABA	Al Khair Bank Accounts
AGM	Annual General Meeting (of Companies)
AH	After Hijrah
AMCs	Asset Management Companies
APIF (of IsDB, Jeddah)	*Awqāf* Properties Investment Fund
BISP	Benazir Income Support Program (Pakistan)
CCI	Council of Common Interest (Pakistan)
CEIF-IBA	Centre for Excellence in Islamic Finance at Institute of Business Administration Karachi
CII	Council of Islamic Ideology
CIV	Collective Investment Vehicle
CSR	Corporate Social Responsibility
CWCs	Cash *Waqf* Certificates
DC	Discipline Committee
EAD	Economic Affairs Division (Pakistan)
EFP	Entrepreneurial Factors of Production
ESG	Environment, Social values and Governance
FC	Finance Committee [of the Waqf Board]
FGM	Focus Group Meeting
FPCCI	Federation of Pakistan's Chambers of Commerce and Industry
FSC	Federal Sharī'ah Court
GDP	Gross Domestic Product
HFP	Hired Factors of Production
HLIs	Higher Learning Institutions
IBFIs	Islamic Banks and Financial Institutions
ICIS	Islamic Collective Investment Schemes
IFS	*Infāq fi Sabeel Allah*

Acronym	*Definition*
IFSB	Islamic Financial Services Board (KL, Malaysia)
IIFA	International Islamic Fiqh Academy
IIFC	International Islamic Fiqh Academy [of the OIC, at Jeddah]
IPR	Intellectual Property Rights
ISRA	International Sharī'ah Research Academy for Islamic Finance (KL, Malaysia)
IWB	Indonesian *Waqf* Board
IWD	Indonesian Waqf Deposits
IWG	International Working Group
IWSD	International Waqf for Sustainable Development
KEGA	Key Economic Growth Activities
KiTS	Karachi Internet Trading System
LOFW	Legal and Organizational Framework for *Waqf*
MAINS	Islamic Religious Council of Negeri Sembilan
MFF	Microfinance Foundation
MMEs	Micro and Medium Enterprises
NBFIs	Nonbanking Financial Institutions
NPO	Nonprofit Organizations
NRSP	National Rural Support Program
OECD	The Organisation for Economic Co-operation and Development
OGDC	Oil and Gas Development Corporation, Pakistan
PAF	Pakistan Audit Foundation
PBA	Pakistan Banks Association
PCI	Per Capita Income
PCP	Pakistan Centre for Philanthropy
PIPO	Pakistan Institute of Public Opinion
PPAF	Pakistan Poverty Alleviation Fund
PPC	Pakistan Peace Collective
PWB	Provincial *Waqf* Boards
PWTF	Pakistan Waqf Takaful Foundation
RAA	Radiyallahu Anhum (Salutation to the Companions of Prophet, PBUH)
REITs	Real Estate Investment Trusts
SAP	Social Action Program
SBP	State Bank of Pakistan (the Central Bank)
SDGs	Sustainable Development Goals
SECP	Securities and Exchange Commission Pakistan
SESRIC	Statistical, Economic, and Social Research and Training Centre for Islamic Countries
SIBL	Social Investment Bank Limited

Acronym	*Definition*
SMEDC	Small and Medium Enterprises Development Corporation
SMEs	Small and Medium Enterprises
SPDC	Social Policy and Development Centre
SRI	Socially Responsible Investment
SRP	Social Responsibility Protocol
TOR	Terms of Reference
TREC	Trading Right Entitlement Certificate
UNDP	United Nations Development Program
UNICEF	United Nations International Children's Emergency Fund
VBI	Value-Based Intermediation
VC	Venture Capital (entities)
WBP	Waqf Board Pakistan
WCO (Iran)	*Waqf* and Charity Organisation
WCP	*Waqf* Core Principles
WDF	*Waqf* Development Foundation

1 Introduction and Historical Perspective of *Waqf*

1.1 Introduction

Human beings are the most sublime masterpieces of the universe created by Allah Tā'la. The whole universe is obedient to His commands and protocols (Qur'an, 13:2; 41:11) that constitute the "Natural Law" to be observed by all His creatures. Man,[1] as vicegerent to Allah, is authorized to employ all resources of the universe while remaining within the laws of nature (rules prescribed by the Creator of the universe). As all human beings, their future generations, and other creatures on the planet have an equal right to benefit from the resources endowed by nature, man has been required to remain within the discipline suggested as the divine guidelines.

Man is designed to live in a society and, therefore, the rules applicable to it for the peaceful coexistence of all human beings pertain to virtue and benevolence, cooperation for broad-based risk-reward sharing, social and ethical values, and ownership and exchange related laws and protocols. While commercial and exchange laws are applicable to the production and distribution of wealth – goods and services, business, and transfer of ownership as per market forces of demand and supply; the rules pertaining to benevolence, sacrifice for others, and cooperation are tools for maintaining the natural balance and peaceful survival of the human societies.

Based on the capitalistic mindset, the human being is being increasingly divided into two extremes of poor and the rich. According to the Oxfam International Report 2019, "*The world's billionaires, 2,208 in number, are growing $2.5 billion richer every day, while the poorest half of the global population is seeing its net worth dwindle*". The report that calls for attention to the growing gap between rich and poor indicates that the combined fortunes of the world's 26 richest individuals reached $1.4 trillion in 2018 – the same amount as the total wealth of the 3.8 billion poorest people.[2]

The institution of "*waqf*" is the tool belonging to the latter category that fulfills an in-built instinct in human beings engrained by nature for

DOI: 10.4324/9781003477549-1

broad-based welfare and happiness of human societies. It helps human beings in peaceful coexistence by assisting those in society who might remain behind in terms of fulfilling any of their basic and genuine needs. Such acts are part of nature's overall Social Responsibility Protocol, a part of which has been recently adopted by the UNDP under the term "CSR".

The divine protocol requires that all human beings must do the following: (i) honor the rights and ownership of others by avoiding immoral and prohibited acts or contracts to exploit fellow human beings, and (ii) help one another in resolving the issues faced at an individual, communal and the global levels. The latter type of accomplishment is bifurcated into three categories: (i) compulsory, (ii) relatively necessary in a social context and not transgressing the equally legitimate needs of other species, and (iii) recommended or desirable (*mustahab*) in terms of helping or spending for others. The institution of *waqf* is the subject of this book, which explores the potential of the second part of the divine protocol suggested by nature regarding social and shared welfare and sustainable development of OIC member countries' economies and societies.

1.2 Objectives of the Book

Waqf, as suggested and made by the Prophet of Islam (PBUH) himself, is a tool for the community's welfare by the well-off in any society. It is a historical, religious, and cultural system of endowments for the welfare of any specified group or society. Notwithstanding the principles of Islamic law of contracts covering mainly the "exchange part", the main theme of the Islamic socioeconomic system revolves around socioeconomic justice and care for the poor and the indigent. The institution of *waqf*, in this context, is a crucial part of that system and had been the main provider of education, healthcare, and water resources in Islamic societies.

In many OIC member countries like Pakistan, Indonesia, Malaysia, Saudi Arabia, Kuwait, the UAE, Oman, Qatar, and others huge amounts of charity are given to the needy and the social sectors, but that charity must be formalized in a proper manner to make it effective for welfare of the society. *Waqf* is a crucial part of the "beyond market sector" of the Islamic economy, and a civil societal institution that could play a crucial role in formalizing charity giving for broader-level benefits of poverty alleviation, and social and financial inclusion. It is one of the traditional Islamic institutions based on philanthropy, the others being *zakāh* and *infāq* (spending as gratitude to Allah while seeking His blessings) in general.

The primary objective of this book is to suggest a *waqf*-based practical and sustainable model involving the rich and philanthropists, the State institutions, and banking and nonbanking financial institutions particularly in Islamic countries. It is to provide education, health, and other civic amenities to the public in general and the poor, and the indigent, in particular. In

Islamic history, *waqf*-based institutions have been rendering all such social and economic services.

Under the above main objective, the scope of the research is as follows:

- To explore the role of *waqf* as an instrument for a sustainable system of social welfare in Pakistan as a case study.
- To indicate the areas crucial in the revitalization of the institution of *waqf* for the welfare of society and the economy by involving banking and nonbanking financial institutions (NBFIs) in the fintech age. In this context, the role of State institutions like the M/O Finance, central banks, Securities Commissions, and banking and nonbanking companies, particularly Islamic banks and financial institutions (IBFIs) have also been explored by way of focal group meetings and structured and semistructured interviews with the stakeholders.
- To explore the importance of disciplined virtuous giving for others, the current scenario of *awqāf* and charity in society, and the potential role of *waqf* in the reduction of poverty. It also discusses how *waqf* can contribute to social welfare programs that cannot be undertaken by the State institutions due to lack of funds, or by the private sector because of commercial nonviability. Some specific suggestions have also been given for the development of *waqf* for shared and general welfare-based growth.
- To explore and suggest a *waqf*-based welfare-based framework to provide education, health, and other civic amenities for the public in general and the poor, small farmers, small traders, home-based businesses, and SMEs, in particular.
- To suggest measures for promoting entrepreneurship at the micro level based on *waqf*. The *awqāf* model will also include establishing vocational training centers for capacity building of human resources in the lower income groups in society. It is to enhance entrepreneurship and provide opportunities for self-employment. In this way, it will contribute toward the upward social mobility of the beneficiaries.
- To suggest a framework of specific *waqf* law to be promulgated by the Government of Pakistan, as a case study, enabling/requiring different institutions to establish *awqāf* to which the well-to-do will be contributing to making the system sustainable.

1.3 Problem Statement

Many Islamic countries have been experiencing a high incidence of poverty. In Pakistan, as a case study, poverty estimates by an SPDC research report for the year 2016 show that close to 38% population of Pakistan was living below the poverty line during the year 2015–16. The percentage of rural poor is higher (41%) as compared to urban poverty incidence which is estimated at 32%. Similarly, the depth and severity of rural poverty are relatively higher as compared to urban areas. The unemployment rate is 6% while about 60% population of Pakistan is considered literate (Labor Force Survey, 2012–13). The same is the case of many other countries in almost all parts of the world.

1.3.1 Macro Issues Facing Pakistan's Economy as a Case

The major issues facing Pakistan's economy are huge budget and trade deficits, low levels of savings, investments, and capital formation, and lack of economic and social infrastructure particularly with respect to high cost but still insufficient energy. This, coupled with a lack of consistent and long-term taxation, monetary and exchange rate policies, increasingly uneven income distribution, and neglecting capacity building, has led to capital flight abroad, high incidence of indirect taxation, and resultant lack of export competitiveness and import substitution. Thus, Pakistan has become a "Consumption economy". Its consumption in 2021–22 was almost 100pc of the GDP. Since GDP is a sum of consumption, investment, and net exports, the impact of the investment-to-GDP ratio of 15.1pc is fully offset by the negative gap between exports and imports in national income accounts (Riazuddin, 2022).

The public sector in Pakistan has heavy debt servicing obligations rendering it almost impossible to spare resources for the welfare of the common man. Pakistan's total debt and liabilities at the end of June 2021 stood at Rs. 47. 8 trillion (100.3% of GDP). Total public debt from external resources amounted to $95.2 billion which also included debt taken from IMF ($7.4 billion). Public foreign debt including that of PSEs amounted to $102.2 billion (SBP, 2021).[3]

The high rates of borrowing and the speed of increasing debt-servicing obligations are issues of even more serious concern. Domestic public debt taken from the banks increased to Rs. 15.4 trillion on March 30, 2022, from Rs. 8.9 trillion in December 2019 (SBP). A more serious issue is the high cost of public sector borrowing from the money market, while SBP has been prohibited by an amendment in its autonomy act (2021) to lend directly to the government. In July 2023, the per annum T - Bills rate rose to around 22%.

A major part of the remaining banks' financing goes to the corporate sector, thus crowding out the SMEs, micro businesses, agriculture and agri-based value-adding industries, and the potential entrepreneurs in emerging areas of renewable energy, software industry, and high-tech services. As a result of all these problems, the most serious issue of concern regarding all economies like that of Pakistan is the widening gap between the rich and the poor making it increasingly difficult for the latter who are having a hard time making both ends meet.

1.3.2 Potentials in Pakistan's Economy

But still, Pakistan's economy has considerable economic potential in terms of socioeconomic growth based on its geographic position, rich natural resources, a culture of mutual help and benevolence, and the globally accepted talent of its hardworking and enthusiastic population. In addition to the fact that it serves as a transit route for global trade for almost half of the world's population, fertile tracts of land, the huge irrigation system, the mountains, and the towns and cities of Pakistan offer great potential to be realized.

Helping others at times of distress is an instinct ingrained in human beings as we witness philanthropy, humane behavior, and welfare activities in all societies of the world. But for Muslim societies, spending for the cause of Allah and His creatures (*infāq-fi-Sabeelillah* – a distinct institution of Islamic beyond market economy) is a part and parcel of the belief to be pious (*muttaqi*) and virtuous (*mohsin*). From the social and cultural perspective, therefore, Pakistan's society with a 97% Muslim population is well equipped with social norms of sacrifice for others, spending for others for sharing Allah's bounties, and cooperative risk mitigation at community and national levels.

In Islamic perspectives, broadly, there are five types of social initiatives or activities: (i) compulsory spending for others (*zakāh* and *'ushr*), (ii) voluntary spending for others (*sadaqāt*), (iii) spending as a social obligation, (iv) cooperative risk and reward sharing for mutual survival, and (v) *awqāf*. The above means and institutions tend to ensure that equity – equal opportunities to all, also including those who might remain behind due to sickness/any inability, or malfunctioning of the market, and social harmony – are integral parts of prosperity. Faith, accountability, belief in every human's ultimate encounter with Allah, and cooperation leading to shared prosperity of human societies are the cardinal pillars of an economy that cherishes the above initiatives.

While Pakistan is the only country in the modern world where a well-defined system of *zakāh* and *'ushr* was established in 1980, although grossly mismanaged, but still works and could become a means of social welfare to the extent of entitled beneficiaries, if revived with proper care and management. Spending for the welfare and benefit of others, over and above *zakāh* and *'ushr*, is also ingrained in Muslim societies. A huge amount of funds is spent individually and collectively for humane causes. The affluent have a tendency to contribute to the welfare of the poor. According to a study conducted by Pakistan Peace Collective (PPC), Pakistanis give an estimated Rs. 650 billion in charity every year to mosques, seminaries, poor and homeless people, needy relatives, victims of terrorism, and hospitals (Zibago, 2015).

One such institution that has a rich historical perspective for an impactful role in the welfare of society is "*waqf*". Starting from the earlier period of Islam, *waqf* played a crucial role in Islamic civilization that had an impact on Western civilizations as well where many "endowments" played a visible role in social sectors of education and health. *Waqf* is a crucial part of the "beyond market sector" of the Islamic economy that served as the main provider of education, healthcare, and water resources in Islamic history, particularly in the Ottoman period. Recently, the earliest *waqf* legacy in the world was deciphered in two villages in Palestine with complete and oldest inscriptions for the description of *waqf* rules[4] (Schuster, 2021).

In principle, a *waqf* is perpetual, irrevocable, and unconditional. Of course, many jurists allowed a temporary *waqf* as well. Accordingly, the present unanimous view is that time-bound *waqfs* of liquid assets like cash, deposits, *ṣukūk*, or profits on any investment could be the subject of *waqf*, as we have discussed in different chapters quoting mainly from the AAOIFI's Sharīʼah Standard on *waqf* (No. 60), and the International Working Group on Waqf Core Principles (IWG-2018) that represented experts from IRTI of IsDB Jeddah, Bank Indonesia, and many *waqfs* operating in various parts of the world.

1.3.3 Uniqueness of Waqf *as a Welfare Institution*

The continuity of reward of a virtuous act is of utmost importance as per the Islamic belief system. This sublime objective can best be achieved by creating perpetual endowments for social and national causes and for the benefit of human beings. *Waqf* that fits in the best in this paradigm is driven by a firm belief in Allah and the day hereafter, social justice, and personal satisfaction of its creator (donor) and is purposely meant to provide key essential services like health and education to improve the welfare of the people in the society at little cost to the government. The prophet (PBUH) suggested *waqf* for the donation of Orchards and used it to finance the State economy and weaponry in times of war via the fruits from Orchards left by Mukhayriq (Lawal, 2018).

Over the period, *waqf* evolved to take care of the wider scale of the needs of people and the environment. To take this institution to the micro level, cash *waqf*s (*al-waqf al nuqud* –movable *waqfs* established with liquid money) were established to serve many areas like education, health, public services, culture, trade, finance, and so forth (Bulut, 2021).

Cash *waqf*, generally considered an Ottoman innovation, is a multidimensional tool of Islamic finance for social and financial inclusion and economic development (Madni, 2022). It served as a financial intermediary like modern banking and nonbanking institutions working under the principles of Sharīʼah. The managers of the *waqf* funds (*mutawalli*) collected the funds from the donors (*wāqifs*) and invested the money in micro, small, and medium-sized ventures and/or other Sharīʼah compliant investment opportunities. Accordingly, researchers indicate that the *waqf* system can be used for essential services in health, education, and municipal sectors and may contribute significantly to modern economies leading to a reduction in public sector expenses, resulting in a smaller budget deficit and a lower need for government borrowing.

A visible revival of the institution of *waqf* has been witnessed over the last two decades, particularly in countries like Indonesia, Malaysia,

South Africa, Jordan, and other parts of the world. But, in many countries like Pakistan, neither the "*waqf*" is playing its historical role of socio-economic uplift, nor deep research has been conducted to activate the movement for its revival. Many trusts, endowments, NPOs/NGOs, societies, and entities are working to help the poor and the needy in sectors like health, education, civic facilities, catering to emergencies or calamities, employment generation/women entrepreneurship, housing for the poor and environment for sustainable future of mankind. At the corporate level, many entities are allocating voluntary funds for CSR under section 42 of the Companies Act, 2017, while some companies are doing social welfare functions as a part of regulatory requirements as in the case of oil and gas companies (e.g., OGDC, Mari Petroleum Company, etc.). In addition to the well-known names of Edhi Trust, Indus Hospital Trust, many memorial hospitals and universities/education centers working under various trusts, many NPOs/NGOs are operating to serve the social and economic cause in the society.

However, the entities listed above have failed to create a visible impact in ameliorating the sufferings of the poor across the country and contributing to shared growth of the economy by creating business opportunities and increasing production for consumption and value-added exports. Further, the public has not wholeheartedly supported some of the NGOs working for social and political rights. A sort of negative impression developed about such NGOs due to foreign funding and the perception that they might be working for the support of the Western agenda. There are, however, some organizations in Pakistan that have earned good names, such as Akhuwat Foundation, Edhi Welfare Trust, Ansar Barney Trust, Shaukat Khanam Trust, Hamdard Foundation, and Anjuman Himayat-e-Islam. To name a few more NPOs:

(1) Pakistan Poverty Alleviation Fund (PPAF) – an apex institution for community-driven development and poverty alleviation – set up under section 42 of the Companies Act, 2017
(2) NRSP – National Rural Support Program
(3) Baluchistan Rural Support Program
(4) Goth Seengar Foundation
(5) HANDS Pakistan
(6) SABAWON Urban WASH and Thardeep Rural Development Programme
(7) Pakistan Space Science Education Centre

Many NGOs and CSR-related entities are helping the government in providing support to the low and middle classes in the society in health, and education sectors, and mitigating the loss due to calamities like earthquakes, floods, and terrorist activities. During the worst flood (2022) in Pakistan's history which affected over 33 million people in all provinces of the country, formal and informal welfare activities by almost all groups in the society enabled the State, to some extent, to revive the economy at micro and macro levels.

Despite all welfare and social activities as listed above, the objective of achieving broad-based general welfare and growth of economy is not likely to be realized. It is in the interests of national development, therefore, that the voluntary charity sector is reorganized, developed, strengthened, and made viable through the re-emerging institution of *waqf*. According to a study by the Pakistan Centre of Philanthropy (PCP) (2015), 69% of charity in Pakistan is given in the form of money. If some of the compulsory (*zakāh*) and voluntary charity (*infāq*) were channeled through *waqfs* to provide employment to those who have some capacity to do business, it could bring about a social revolution in society and contribute to sustainable development.

In light of the issues facing Pakistan's economy and its potential, the inability of the State institutions and nonprofit entities to work for the welfare of certain groups in the society, and the role of the re-emerging institution of *waqf*, the problems this research-based book explores are:

(1) How the historical institution of *waqf*, as emerging in various parts of the world, could be evolved as a tool to alleviate poverty, develop social capital, increase financial and social inclusion, and provide employment opportunities through promoting entrepreneurship?
(2) What could be the legal, operational, and regulatory frameworks for the *waqf* system keeping in view the good governance principles? How various provisions of law could enable the independent but minutely regulated functioning of various *awqāf* at micro, macro, public, and corporate levels?
(3) How would the proposed institution work on a sustainable basis as per the principles of Islamic law and what would be the transfer/alienability principles for *awqāf*?
(4) How the charity giving would be easy and safe – donations for different *awqāf* could be given, based on their performance and socioeconomic impact, with ease without violating the rules applicable at the domestic and the global level?
(5) How the effective oversight and governance of the *waqf* institutions could be ensured to maintain the credibility of the noble system of *awqāf*?
(6) What would be the role of related State functionaries at provincial and Federal levels, the auditors, and the financial market regulators?

1.4 Significance of the Research for the Book

The failure of government-sponsored programs in alleviating poverty in developing countries like Pakistan indicates the need for developing and implementing an effective system and programs to ensure visible improvement in the socioeconomic conditions of the poor on a sustainable basis.

Islamic institution of *waqf*, along with other institutions like *zakāh*, mutual *takaful*, and *qard hasan* based microfinance for agriculture, small businesses, and SMEs has the potential to provide a strong basis for developing a comprehensive system ensuring social justice, equity, and peace by enabling the state to fulfill the basic needs of society (Zarqa, 1988; Siddiqi, 2004).

The study will help to reduce poverty and empower the poor through the institution of *waqf* which has an excellent historical record in social development. Application of the proposed system could reduce inequality over time among a lower and upper group of society. Coincidently, the system of Islamic banking and finance is being evolved in around 120 countries of the world, also including Pakistan. However, despite its visible growth over the last two decades to cover 20% of the banking system in the country since 2002, Islamic banking has failed to realize its objectives due mainly to the credibility gap. That, in turn, is because the change is in form, not substance, as many products are mere replicas of conventional products.

IBFIs are considered entities whose social goals are at least (if not more) as important as making a profit (Hannifa & Hudaib, 2007). The World Bank's 2030 agenda for sustainable development seeks to eradicate poverty in all its forms and emphasizes Islamic finance to promote responsible and risk sharing based finance. It is a recognition of the core principles of Islamic finance, a form of Socially Responsible Investment providing mechanisms for redistribution to address imbalances that may occur during the wealth production and distribution cycle in any market economy (Solimán, 2017). Through proper linkage between the real sector and finance, the investors contribute to the growth process. It is, however, a serious issue that the IBFIs have not so far been able to move toward achieving the goal of social and socioeconomic inclusion. This book makes a case for persuading the IBFIs to adopt *qarḍ hassan* and other financing techniques through *waqf*. It also suggests innovative instruments like al-*khair ṣukūk* for socioeconomic development and addresses environmental, social, and ethical safeguards, side by side with the business for profits.

In other words, there is a need to provide a way to expand the scope of banking or financial intermediation, enabling banking companies to serve the social cause, in addition, to doing business for profit. IBFIs will be giving a helping hand in the revival of the historical institution established by the Prophet (PBUH) himself and operated for centuries in many parts of the world. The book provides the combined and feasible framework for the joint working of the *awqāf*, the Islamic tradition, and trusts, the British tradition. With the suggested framework of *waqfs*, the lacuna in the operation of trusts could be reduced to minimum, if not removed.

During the interviews and the focus group meetings a few of the participants expressed the view that while many trusts are operating in Pakistan, there might not be any need to develop (new) institutions of *waqf*. But the view was strongly opposed by majority of the research participants on the ground that by giving an out-of-the-way edge to the trust, not only the "*sunnah* of *waqf*" is being erased[5] but also the true potential of *waqf* is not utilized. Introduction and application of welfare-oriented *waqf* law could be helpful in removing the lacuna in the running of trusts in the country, thus enhancing their efficiency as per their trust deeds.

The current law based on the colonial rules dealing traditionally with *masjid*, *madrasa*, and *mazār* has no link with present-day socioeconomic realities and requirements. It does not have the potential to provide for the introduction and evolution of *waqf* as an institution for the socioeconomic growth of the economy and society.

1.5 Spending as an Inspiring Part of Belief in the Islamic Paradigm

Spending for others is a sublime part of the Islamic belief system. Reward for charitable giving in the *hereafter* and its inspiration is of much more value for the Muslims than the possible benefit of community welfare in the secular structure. A crucial condition for virtuous giving is that the giver must avoid taunting and hurting (Qur'an: 2:264). All wealth belongs to Allah, and one should be grateful for being given and enabled to spend it, so one should be thankful and spend for the sake of Allah what belongs to Him, for *barakah* in this world and reward in the *hereafter*.

Giving to one's relatives, orphans, the wayfarer, beggars, and for the salvation of the poor debtors helps in building a cohesive society. Qur'an (107: 1–7) warns that

> those who are not kind to the orphan, do not urge others to feed the poor, they are hypocrites not performing their *salāt* (prayer) properly, do any good deeds only to be seen, and withhold (simple) assistance to fellow beings.

Qur'an and Sunnah of the Prophet (PBUH) cherish the act of spending for others which helps in building a case for a society where spending by way of *waqf* could be a common characteristic of the well-off, philanthropist, and the institutions involved in socioeconomic development.

The very first few verses of Al-Baqarah indicate that Qur'an is a book of guidance for those pious and mindful believers in Allah and the Day of Judgment who donate from what Allah has provided for them (2:2–4). While spending with moderation is liked by Islam even for own family, spending for others as a way to please Allah (SWT) fetches manifold rewards by Allah, based on the level of sincerity of the donor which according to Islamic law is very well known by Allah. While defining the virtue and piety, Qur'an declares,

> ... true righteousness consists in believing in Allah and the Last Day, ----, and in giving away one's property in love of Him to one's kinsmen, the orphans, the poor and the wayfarer, and to those who ask for help, and in

freeing the necks of slaves, and in establishing Prayer and dispensing the Zakāh (2: 177).

More importantly, spending for others should be from the goods or properties that are quite dear to one as Qur'an declares, "*By no means shall you attain Al-Birr (piety, righteousness), unless you spend (in Allah's Cause) of that which you love; and whatever of good you spend, Allah knows it well*" (3:92). The Prophet (PBUH) also emphasized spending for others. Following *ahādith* are particularly important in the context of helping others:

(1) The example of the believers in their affection, mercy, and compassion for each other is that of a body. When any limb aches, the whole body reacts with sleeplessness and fever (*Sahih* Al-Bukhari).
(2) The believer for another believer (in a community) is like that of a well-compacted building where one part of the building strengthens the other (*Sahih* Al-Bukhari).
(3) No one of you becomes a true believer until he likes for his brother what he likes for himself (*Sahih* Al-Bukhari).
(4) If someone shows no compassion (to people) he will not be shown any compassion (by Allah) (*Sahih* Al-Bukhari).

Islam accepted the instinct of self-interest as the basis of the market economy but made others' interests competitive to self-interest by commanding some prohibitions, and by putting a divine reward of spending for others more than 700 times the worldly reward (Qur'an; 2:261, *Hadith*; *Sahih* Bukhari, 6126). A Muslim is not expected to go on increasing its eating expenses without any limit just because of an increase in income. "*He is not a believer whose stomach is filled while the neighbor to his side goes hungry*", warned Prophet Muhammad (PBUH) (*Albāni*, *Sahih al Jamie*, 5382). Accordingly, an Islamic economy is to ensure sufficient food for all by prohibiting overeating and a lavish style of consumption. It implies that all well-to-do in an Islamic society are responsible for ensuring that all in one's society are fed. The Prophet (PBUH) highlighted in one of his sayings:

> The one who looks after and works for a widow and for a poor person (dependent), is like a warrior fighting for the cause of Allah, or like a person who fasts during the day and prays throughout the night.

While *zakāh* and *'ushr* are obligatory, optional *infāq* by the well-to-do could be informal in the form of spending to ameliorate the life of others in the society, and formal that may take the form of *waqf* and any cooperative arrangements for mitigating the losses of others. Spending to help others through the formal means of *waqf* had been the most effective institution for socioeconomic activities in Islamic history.

Spending for others only for pleasing Allah promotes a mutual help and brotherhood culture, a beneficence approach, and a cooperative environment. It tends to redefine "profitability", and real success for human beings, and that is by helping the poor and fulfilling social responsibilities. It highlights how the institution of *waqf* and donating to the general welfare may play a crucial role in the socioeconomic growth of Muslim societies.

1.5.1 **Maqāṣid al Sharī'ah** ***and Their Relevance with*** **Awqāf**

Waqf is an institutional tool that helps in realizing the higher purposes of Sharī'ah. *Maqāṣid al Sharī'ah* for development and human rights as postulated by Jasser Auda (2015) could best be realized by developing *waqf* as a tool for socioeconomic development and sustainable growth. All three levels of human needs, i.e., *ḍarūriyyāt* (essential), *hājiyyāt* (complimentary), and *taḥsiniyyāt* (tertiary) (Zaprulkhan, 2018), of all members of a society can be fulfilled in case the carefully evolved system of *waqf* is in the application.

The *maqāsid*, general or specific, are related to the life of mankind. Fulfilling the fundamental and essential needs of all human beings is a social obligation that must be fulfilled by the State or by the well-off in society. The Prophet (PBUH) is reported to have said, "Any community, whosoever they are, if a person among them became hungry; they will be removed from the protection of Allah Almighty" (Hanbal, 2001, p. 482).

Maqasid also include *jināyat* which refer to *al-amr bi al-ma'rūf and al-nahy 'an al-munkar* (commanding good and righteous behavior and discourage vice and immorality). Auda (2015) reconstructs *maqāṣid al-Sharī'ah* by offering six features: cognitive nature, wholeness, openness, interrelated hierarchy, multidimensionality, and purposefulness. He uses the approach of system philosophy and indicates the contribution of *maqāsid* to the development of Islamic law and human rights. This approach views the world and the functions of nature and its components in the context of a holistic system comprising infinite subsystems having interactive, open, hierarchical, and purposeful natures (Auda 2015, Zaprulkhan, 2018). Hence, *awqāf* have to be evolved for all activities ranging from fulfilling the basic needs of all to commanding good deeds and preventing immorality and evil in any form.

1.6 The Concept of *Waqf* and Its Historical Role

Waqf (plural: *awqāf*), literally means "to hold" a property, hence also termed as *habus* (withheld property) in North Africa. Technically, *waqf* refers to tying up by someone a property in perpetuity for any virtuous purpose or for benefit of any specified group of persons. In other words, *waqf* involves retention of a property by someone for the benefit of a charitable or humanitarian objective, or for a specified group of people such as any charity institution or the members of the donor's family. The purpose of all such spending is pleasing Allah. *Irsād* that is a variant form of *waqf*, where the assets used to be set aside by the State or the government to cater to identified social needs also served for the social needs of some societies (IRTI, 2014). *Waqf* as a religious charity was also in pre-Islam era. A rich person used to assign a property to a temple, and monks used that property or its income for the temple expenses.

The Hanafi Jurist Al-Kasani (d. 587/1189) defined *waqf* as a continuous charitable act for the sake of Allah Almighty. IRTI's Islamic Social Finance study (2014) says, "The institution of *waqf* implies holding or setting aside certain physical assets by the donor and preserving it so that the asset benefits continuously to a specified group of beneficiaries or community". It implies that once declared as *waqf*, the maker relinquishes all his property rights, transforming it into Allah's name, an inalienable "claim of Allah". Hence, *waqf*, governed by the fundamental principles of perpetuity, inalienability, and irrevocability has the potential to create robust not-for-profit entities that may address the education, healthcare, and other social needs in Muslim societies.

One of the well-known *awqāf* in Islamic history is by the Second Caliph Umar (RA) who acquired a land at Khyber. He came to the Prophet (PBUH) and said: "Allah's Messenger, I have acquired land in Khyber; I have never acquired property more valuable for me than this, so what do you command me to do with it?" The Prophet said: "If you like, you may keep the corpus intact and give its produce as *sadaqah*". So Umar (RA) gave it as *sadaqah* declaring that the property must not be sold or inherited or given away as a gift. He devoted the produce to the poor, to the nearest kin, and the emancipation of slaves, etc.; there is no sin for one who administers it, if he eats something from it in a reasonable manner, or if he feeds his friends and does not hoard up goods (for himself).

The importance of *waqf* as a long-term or perpetual *sadaqah* is proven by the Prophet Muhammad (PBUH) as he said,

> Among acts and good deeds for which a believer is rewarded after death, a piece of knowledge he has taught and diffused, a virtuous progeny he has brought up, a mosque or a wayfarer's house he has constructed, a river he has caused to stream or alms he has handed out of his riches while still healthy and alive so that he benefits therefrom in the afterlife.
>
> (Ibn Majah)

A traditional example of *waqf* is that of donating or setting aside land for the construction of a mosque, a school, or a hospital. According to the *waqf* regulations developed in the 3rd-century *hijrah*, *waqf* is established by a legal deed that names the owner of the endowed property, the substance of the endowment (*'ayn* or *'asb)*, and the beneficiary of its income.

Executing a *waqf*, like ordinary *sadaqah*, but unlike *zakāh*, is a voluntary act. *Waqf* is distinct from ordinary *sadaqah* in the sense that the benefits flowing from *waqf* are by default sustainable. Like ordinary *sadaqah*, *waqf* is flexible in the sense that its beneficiaries need not be restricted to Muslims. And unlike ordinary *sadaqah*, *zakāh* and *infāq* that are usually in the nature of specific financial flows, *waqf* provides for flow of benefits on a sustained basis. The mechanism of *waqf* should result in a corpus that is either intact or growing. It has a legal identity separate from its manager and, therefore, it is most suitable for the creation of an institution in the voluntary or not-for-profit sector. The trustee manager is described as *mutawalli* or *nāzir*.

According to Abattouy and Al-Hassani (2013), the subjects of *waqf* included properties such as agricultural land, farms, gardens, as well as apartment buildings, houses, hotels, warehouses, shops, baths, mills, bakeries, looms, soap works, paper works, oil and sugar presses, stables, and post houses. They also indicated that in Islamic history, *waqf* had been relied upon for the comprehensive development of the community, ranging from various social institutions such as hospitals and schools to religious objects like mosques, and welfare schemes like highway facilities and water supply. Historically, *waqf* endowments were insulated from imperial/state authority (Joseph, 2014).

As indicated by Kahf (2003), *waqfs* have been traditionally established for immovable property such as land, fields, farms, or buildings like mosques, schools, hospitals, or basic infrastructures such as bridges, roads, water supply, etc. and movable property like books, cattle, crops, and shares. But the cash *awqāf* have been equally important for welfare objectives. Many studies have argued that cash *waqf* can pool more resources and ensure wider participation of individual donors (Sadeq, 2002;Salman Sheikh, et. Al.,2017). If movable assets like books and cattle can serve a good purpose as far as they exist, cash also can be used for sustainable welfare objectives with proper investment and risk-management plans. One may donate the benefits of a fund, any individual asset, or a pool of assets. The idea of perpetual corporate entities that are based on share capital/equity has also been accepted by the Sharīʿah scholars.

White (2006) has classified *waqf* into three types: Religious *Waqf*, Family *Waqf*, and Philanthropic *Waqf*. But to qualify as a charitable institution, the ultimate purpose of the *waqf* must be of the nature of virtue and piety (Çizakça, 1998). It is the reason that *waqf* must be irrevocable, perpetual, and inalienable. According to Çizakça (1998) and Abattouy and Al-Hassani (2013), the *awqāf* system has remarkable resilience, and many *awqāf* had survived even for more than a millennium and some considerably longer than half a millennium. But, if any *waqf* is terminated due to any reason, its assets have to be given to charity.

White (2006) mentions the following elements of *waqf*:

a) A declaration of *waqf* by the legal owner of any asset (*waqf* deed);
b) The specific purpose of *waqf* should be stated – the beneficiaries be clearly defined;
c) *Waqf* needs to be managed as per criteria set by the maker;
d) *Mutawalli* (trustee) needs to be appointed along with his successors;

e) Fiduciary duties of the *mutawalli*;
f) Employees, if required to assist the *mutawalli*;
g) Judicial oversight of *mutawalli* and the work.

Regarding the management of *waqf*, Sharīʿah provides for the institution of *nāzir* or *mutawalli* as the trustee-manager of *waqf* assets. The State plays a supervisory role devoid of actual ownership or direct management of *waqf* assets. Presently, in some Islamic countries like Pakistan, there is concentration of authority in the hands of the State due mainly to the reason that *awqāf* generally pertains to graveyards (*mazārs*) and masques (IRTI, 2014) with chances of corruption.

1.6.1 Waqf *in Historical Perspective*

The history of *awqāf* in the Muslims' era is very rich with prominent achievements in enhancing welfare in general and serving the poor. Muslims established various kinds of *awqāf* for education and research, healthcare, and other public utilities. *Awqāf* for education also covered scientific research, including research in astronomy, mathematics, pharmacology, physiology, etc. (Ahmed, 2007). Abattouy and Al-Hassani (2013) indicated that in Islamic history, *waqf* had been relied upon for the comprehensive development of the community, ranging from various social institutions such as hospitals and schools to religious objects like mosques, and any welfare schemes.

Waqf played a crucial role during the Ottoman Empire, covering Türkiye, the Middle East, and Eastern Europe. *Awqāf* used to have immovable assets, such as production facilities, residences, shops, and other public/social facilities. It used to provide consumption goods such as operating commuter ships, delivering water to a local area, supporting retired sailors, defending a town, paying neighborhood taxes, etc. In the mid-9th century, three-fourths of lands in the Ottoman Empire were established as *waqf* lands. Similarly, *waqf*-related agricultural land constituted one-third of Tunisia and half of the size of Algerian land. In the mid-20th century, one-eighth of Egyptian land belonged to *awqāf*.

The introduction of cash *waqf* by the Ottoman was a game-changer in the institutional history of *awqāf*. It had been playing a role in providing employment and promoting entrepreneurship in Ottoman Europe and some other Muslim societies (Bulut, 2021).

The term "cash *waqf*" refers to the historical institutions of the Ottoman Empire (15th century). It was used for public services like education and healthcare. Common people used to contribute funds with the stipulation that the principal sum will remain intact while its return (over investment into projects/modes of financing, allowed by Sharī'ah) shall be utilized for the benefit of the public. These peculiar endowments were an innovation of the Turks against customary "foundations of immovable property". Wealthy people could save their original assets in such initiatives. The idea of cash *waqf* has recently been highlighted by almost all Islamic economists.

The cash *waqf* model is an avenue to improve and establish public properties under *waqf* institutions. Since cash *waqf*, once established, is financial in nature it is a logical consequence to manage it under an organization that may look like a financial institution or bank. It covers activities of mobilizing funds and distributing them in productive activities/projects. In addition, it includes the activity of distributing income generated from investment placement.

Cash *waqf* is considered a trust fund established with money to support services to mankind in the name of Allah. Others may contribute to such Funds at the micro level. Cash *waqf* and *waqf ṣukūk*, or the certificates, can be used to mobilize capital for *awqāf*. Through cash *waqfs*, Islamic banks can provide finance to smallholders for tools/machinery at a lower rent.

The *waqf* went beyond meeting the immediate needs of the poor to provide means for long-term amelioration and welfare. It played a role in developing various aspects of society and the economy in the sense of modern economies (Zuki, 2012). Çizakça (1998) indicated that from the Atlantic to the Pacific, all over the vast Islamic world, *awqāf* system financed and maintained, for centuries, magnificent works of architecture as well as a myriad of services vitally important for society. *Awqāf* worked for different social sectors including:

Awqāf for Health Facilities

Awqāf has been used in the past for health services, covering the expenses of patients as well as the provision of physicians and training, besides the construction of hospitals. In addition to the construction of male and female bathrooms in hospitals, *waqf* provided food and special clothes to the patients. In women's *awqāf*, health services received the lion's share and many hospitals had been established offering medical education and free treatment to poor patients.

Hospitals and medicines had been the most famous subsectors of *awqāf* (Ahmed, 2007). In 88 *Hijrah*, Caliph Walid ibn Abd al-Malik was the first who built a hospital or *bimaristan* and appointed doctors and paid for them to care for the sick and for quarantine of the lepers. The revenue of *waqf* would pay for the maintenance and running costs of the hospital, and sometimes even small stipends to the patients upon discharge. Such hospitals in the 3rd Islamic century were spread all over the Islamic world and were a source of happiness for the Muslim community because the patient received treatment, care, food, and clothing. Additionally, many of these hospitals performed the function of a medical education center along with treating patients.

Mannan (2005) and Hasan (2006) indicated that an important beneficiary of Muslim *awqāf* had been the health and hygiene sector. In Egypt, Ibn

Tulun built the first hospital in 261 AH and endowed it with several *waqfs* to provide for its expenses. According to Abattouy and Al-Hassani (2013), in every town of reputation in the Islamic world, particularly Cairo, Baghdad, Makkah, Madinah, Aleppo, Tunis, Ray, Granada, and Marrakech, there had been at least one *waqf* hospital.

Al-Nuri Hospital was built on *waqf* land in Damascus in AD 1145. It remained in operation for seven centuries and was one of the first hospitals to adopt medical records. Doctors were paid from the endowed funds and the *waqfs* covered all expenses on food, lodging, medicine, and treatment of the patients. In the early 20th century, *awqāf* healthcare centers and hospitals were established in Türkiye. A special children's hospital was built in Istanbul out of the *waqf* fund.

In Spain, hospital facilities were available for both Muslims and non-Muslims alike. The well-known Qalāwūn Complex built by Sultan Al-Nasir Muhammad Ibn Qalāwūn in AD 1284–85 in Cairo included a hospital, a school, and a mausoleum. It was once the most impressive hospital of its time and functioned throughout the late Ottoman period, till 1910. In the Complex, medicines were prepared in addition to the research and teaching facilities. Hospitals provided medicine, food, clothing, and shelter to the sick and poor. Pharmaceutical drugs were also produced for medical treatment.

Awqāf for Basic and Professional Education

Human resource development is the pivotal factor in the success of any poverty-alleviation and social development programs. The provision of basic and professional education funded through *waqf* can enhance the income-earning potential of the beneficiaries.

In many Islamic countries, with a very large segment of the young population, it is vital to educate all members of society and provide them with professional and technical training, particularly the matter relating to information technology and artificial intelligence. For an effective role in socio-economic and sustainable development, the focus has to be on *waqf*-based human development and finance institutions providing technical training and microfinance to farmers and small enterprises. Awareness and orientation regarding the role of *awqāf* for *qarḍ hassan* based microfinance as the case of "*akhuwat*" in Pakistan is also necessary.

Education is the second most important social activity attracted by the *awqāf* in Islamic history. *Waqf* had been the source of funds for the establishment of schools and universities. *Awqāf* also supported medical education and research and preparation of medicines. Along with schools and hospitals, medical education was also offered in mosques and universities such as Ai-Azhar. In Syria, a number of *waqfs* financed a large number of educational institutions such as *madāris*, *maktab*, *Dār al-Qurān*, and *Dār al-Hadīth*. *Awqāf* also stipulated the curricula for these institutions (Frenkel, 2009).

Al-Azhar University, the best-known place of learning in the Islamic world, was founded in AD 972 in Cairo with the endowment of a charitable trust and financed by its *waqf* revenues until 1812 when the government of Muhammad Ali took control over the *awqāf*. Financing from *waqf* covered expenses on books, libraries, stipends to students, and salaries of teachers and other staff. Other significant education related to *awqāf* included: (i) Nizāmiyya school established in Baghdad in 459 H; (ii) Mustansiriya school established in 623 H from the endowment by Abbasid Caliph Al-Muntasir Billah; supplemented in 631 H it was the best school in the world at that time; (iii) Al-Bashiriya school and library established in 1255 in Baghdad; (iv) Al-Zahiriyya School established in Damascus in 678/1279, its library contained books on all sciences; and (v) In Makkah, Sultan Qaitbay School established in 884 H was endowed from *awqāf* funds. Besides, there were many schools in Egypt, Syria, Yemen, and other areas.

In the Ottoman period, the number of institutions of higher education built by the *waqfs* stood at over 500 after conquering Constantinople (Istanbul) until the 19th century (Babacan, 2011). *Waqf* funds were also used to establish libraries, reading rooms, labs for research activities, and translation of valuable materials. With the support of the *waqf* funds, Muslim scholars and scientists either wrote or translated many books. Research using scientific and empirical methods was also encouraged and supported by *waqf* funds.

Awqāf also provided support for education in different parts of South Asian Muslim areas where schools (*madāris*) or orphanages had been getting sufficient *waqf* funds in Muslim communities. Thousands of *madāris* that also provided boarding facilities had been established, financed, and managed through *awqāf* funding in Pakistan, India, Bangladesh, Malaysia, and Indonesia. This system needs to be developed to include education and orientation in emerging areas of science and technology.

Awqāf for Shelter/Habitation and Protective Wear

Shelter with proper drinking water and sanitation facilities is the basic right of human beings for modesty and also as an adornment. Similarly, they need proper clothing for protection from severities of weather (Qur'an, 7:27). *Waqf* can provide the infrastructure and create a source of revenue for social welfare enhancing activities at family, community, and state levels. In the history of *awqāf*, the endowment documents many times included clauses for the distribution of clothing and provision of food (Frenkel, 2009). Hasan (2006) indicated that in modern times, *awqāf* could play a much greater role in providing shelters, arranging water to any locality, and supplying food to the poor and especially children.

Providing housing facilities and proper shelter to the poor is also a responsibility of the State and the well-off communities in any society. While the resources available in most of the States in the Muslim world might not be sufficient to provide shelter of a bare minimum standard to all, *awqāf* can provide a helping hand for providing simple habitation with the basic amenities of life like drinking water, sanitation, education, and basic health facilities.

Awqāf for Providing Economic Opportunities and Empowerment

A poor not having proper employment, food, education, or health facility cannot be a free and respectable member of any society. Cash *waqfs* can be a good source of revenue generation for charitable work, including *qarḍ hassan* for employment and poverty alleviation and also for start-up projects through the issuance of *ṣukūk*. Like the Ottoman *waqfs* that used *Ijārah* as one of their financing modes, the cash *waqfs* by Islamic banks could provide finance to the smallholders for tools/machinery at a lower rent.

Islamic banks, by dint of being Islamic institutions managing the wealth of the society, are required to play a role in realizing *maqāṣid al-sharīʿah* by serving the community through poverty alleviation and welfare activities for the common people. In this perspective, Islamic banks may establish *waqf*-based Islamic microfinance institutions (Ahmed, 2007).

For socioeconomic inclusion in OIC member countries, it is necessary that financing to the extremely poor and small farmers, businesses, and entrepreneurs be based on *qarḍ hassan* or trade-/lease-based modes at a lower cost. Credit cost combined with the increasing cost of other inputs work as a double-edged sword against small farmers, micro-level commodity-producing units, and SMEs. Any scheme that involves a market competitive charge to groups having small means would result in negative effects such as higher income inequality and soaring interest (Adams & Von Pischke, 1992).

Due to the overwhelming status of modern corporations and interest-based systems, the potential of *waqf* remained untapped over the last 200 years. Going forward, authors like Sadeq, Ahmed, Hasan, Manjoo, and others have presented the idea of *waqf*-based microfinance institutions for poverty reduction (SESRIC, 2015). A study by SESRIC (2015) indicated a consensus among the respondents from Malaysia, Indonesia, and Bangladesh that *waqf* could play a significant role in providing financing for human development programs related to microfinance and poverty alleviation.

1.7 *Waqf* Laws in British India and Countries Like Pakistan

If we discuss *waqf* laws in Pakistan, as a case study, it inherited both the *waqf* and trust laws as well as the *waqf* and trust organizations from the British colonial period. It was a legacy that has been lasting to date, of course with some changes. The Wakf Act 1923 did not impose any official supervision on *awqāf* but required the submission of the particulars of *awqāf* and their annual accounts with the state functionaries. Given the politically sensitive nature of the regulation of *awqāf*, the colonial administrators deemed it appropriate to delegate the issue of such regulations to provincial legislatures.

Therefore, various provincial legislatures such as Bengal, United Provinces, and Delhi established separate public bodies which were vested with wider administrative powers of supervision over *awqāf*.

After the creation of Pakistan in 1947, the Punjab Muslim *Awqāf* Act 1951 was passed to "provide for the proper administration of Muslim Awqāf in Punjab". The Act established a Board that had limited supervisory powers over *awqāf*. The main functions of the Board were limited to the registration of *awqāf*, conducting inquiries about the administration of *awqāf*, and appointment of *mutawallis*.

The Government revised the *waqf* laws and promulgated the West Pakistan Waqf Properties Ordinance 1959 and the West Pakistan Waqf Properties Rules of 1960 with the aim to curtail the powers of *peers* (spiritual guides) and *sajjadah-nashins* and to regulate the religious endowments under the apparatus of the state. The rationale behind this policy was that these shrines were being exploited by their administrators; therefore, the State took over their control. The Ordinance enabled an *awqāf* administrator to take over the control of *waqf* property. Hence, the authority of the shrine holder was replaced by the authority of *awqāf* administrator, who was a state official. The policy corresponded to the social and economic aims of the state, one of which was to control religious elements.

A statistical survey of Pakistan revealed that by the year 1984, 344 shrines, 648 mosques, 31,913 acres of culturable lands, 48,188 acres of unculturable lands, 2,215 shops, and 1,869 houses had been nationalized (Malik, 1990: 72).

Practically, the public *awqāf* in Pakistan are strictly regulated by the State because of their entrenchment with the politics of peers (spiritual guides). Private *awqāf*, though relatively lightly regulated, are economically inefficient. Therefore, most philanthropic activities in the country take place in the form of various English law institutions such as registered societies, trusts, and not-for-profit corporations. Of course, many *awqāf* properties exist belonging mostly to mosques, *madāris*, shrines (*dargahs*), and graveyards which continue to be established as *awqāf* (Abbasi, 2019).

1.8 Scheme of the Book

The research project for study on *waqf* that became the basis for the book adopted an specifically thought-out sequence based on the relevance and rationale of different aspects discussed in it. The first chapter details the objectives and scope, methodology, the problem statement, and importance of *infāq* (spending for the cause of Allah) as per Qur'an and Sunnah and its relevance to the institution of *waqf*, literal meaning and technical definition of the *waqf*, its establishment, consolidation, and various stages of the development of *waqf*. It also provides a historical role of *waqf* in various periods in socioeconomic sectors. The scheme of the other chapters of the book is as follows.

The second chapter figures out the evolutionary aspects of the *waqf* as an institution. It gives explanation of *waqf* as an institution. Besides, a debate is generated on stages of institutionalization of *awqāf*, both from an Islamic viewpoint and from the Western one. The future requirements for the institutionalization of *waqf* are also highlighted, keeping in view the UN's SDGs 2030. Categories of *waqf* are also explained.

The role of *awqāf* in promoting entrepreneurship is discussed in the third chapter. Here, the importance of entrepreneurship for economic development is elaborated. It also discusses Ottomans' manufacturing guilds, and their urban *waqf* arrangements. A scheme of collective capital accumulation is explained here as it can push humanity out of an individualistic capitalistic mindset into the new age of shared market economy. The importance of cash *waqf* for entrepreneurship is also discussed here.

The fourth chapter discusses key aspects of socioeconomic development by *awqāf*. Here basic concepts of socioeconomic development, the few scientific approaches developed so far, and their implications are included while stages of development in Islamic perspective are also detailed. The Ottoman model of capital accumulation and redistribution of wealth is covered here. The debate is generated for *maqāsid al sharī'ah* and the western conception of sustainable development where *waqf* can have a balancing role.

The fifth chapter is about the role of financial intermediation, fintech, and other technical developments regarding the potential of *waqf*. Fundraising strategies are also explained here. The use of various financial instruments and institutions including Islamic ones, which collect funds for *waqf*, are added. The focus of the chapter remains on the appropriateness of institutions and instruments for *waqf* in terms of compliance with Sharī'ah standards in Islamic finance. *Waqf*-based financial instruments include *ṣukūk*, cash *waqf*, *al Khair* deposits, *al-khair* (mutual) funds, and *takaful*. Methods and issues of financing, and so reviving, the old *waqf* properties, are also described. The chapter also works out the role of the financial regulators (central bank/SEC), along with accounts and audits in managing the *waqf*-specific instruments and institutions.

The sixth chapter deals with the management and governance issues of the *waqf* organizations. The latest approaches for the management of corporate firms and organizations are debated. The critical aspects of the role of trustees, the structure of the managing boards, and accountability/audit arrangements are detailed. The chapter looks at the aspects and extent of the interference of government departments. The Ottoman historical records for management are also discussed, where *Qādi* was an integral part.

The seventh chapter discusses the present legal frameworks at work in Pakistan for trusts and *awqāf* and also provides insights for the future. It also suggests the future legal requirements of the *awqāf*. Here, some taxation-related issues and restrictive methodologies of the state apparatus are described. The chapter explains how Sharī'ah-based legal structure of *waqf* emerged over time.

The last chapter is on recommendations for realizing the potential of *waqf* for shared growth and sustainable socioeconomic development. It also summarizes the aspects and the potential of *waqf* with focus on alleviating poverty, promoting entrepreneurship at micro level, and social inclusion.

1.9 Summary and Conclusion

The broader-level welfare schemes can be initiated through the revival of the institution of *waqf* as it evolved in Islamic societies in the historical perspective. Poverty-alleviation strategies need to be designed that may enhance social inclusion and cohesion in society. Many *waqf*-based humanitarian and infrastructural projects have been working in the Muslim world such as establishing orphan houses, springs development for providing water for public consumption, helping the handicapped and the poor, financing the marriage of young people, building and operating hospitals and universities, and building bridges and highways (Zuki, 2012). Perpetuity complemented by the profitability of the *waqf* asset could make the *waqf* institutions sustainable for a longer time to come. Therefore, *waqf* is more effective when compared to individual charities, in matching the social targets and providing sustainable sources of funds to the beneficiaries.

The concept of cash *waqf* provides innovative opportunities to involve the well-off at the micro level. A consensus has emerged among Muslim scholars about the legitimacy of cash *waqf* (Abbasi, 2019; Mohsin, 2013). The founders of cash *awqāf* could be individuals, institutions, companies, organizations, NGOs, and public or private sector corporations. Merging the institution of *waqf* with that of CSR funds and activities might also enhance the potential of the welfare schemes and activities of the companies.

Currently, the *awqāf* in Islamic countries like Pakistan is limited to mosques, shrines, and graveyards due to the traditional regulatory regime and the misconception about *waqf*. It is not surprising to note, therefore, that for the provision of welfare services, the institutions like trusts, registered societies and cooperatives, foundations, and not-for-profit companies (registered under section 42 of the Companies Act 2017) lack sanctity that is associated with the institution of *waqf* as was witnessed in historical perspective.

Banks and *takaful* companies can use *waqf* for social welfare, cooperative risk mitigation, and promoting entrepreneurship (Abbasi, 2019). Helping others is an in-built characteristic in the instinct of human beings. Belief in Allah and manyfold reward in this world and also the hereafter makes it possible that a *waqf* is developed as a grand system of mutual help and sacrifice for others for shared growth and welfare. Islamic philanthropic institution of *waqf* provides solutions to socioeconomic problems and it is requirement for peaceful co-survival. Financing as a way of kindness and sacrifice for others is what made the Islamic civilization a just, beautiful, lasting, and rich in all respects of human life.

Notes

1 "Man", as human being, refers to both male and female that have been created spiritually equal. The Qur'an says: "Those who do good, whether male or female, and have faith will enter Paradise and will never be wronged … ." (4:124). In the book, wherever used, "man" will mean any human being irrespective of gender, color and creed.

2 According to Forbes, most of the mega-wealthy are American, for example, Amazon's Jeff Bezos, Microsoft's Bill Gates, Berkshire Hathaway's Warren Buffett, and Facebook's Mark Zuckerberg, who collectively are worth $357 billion.

3 www.sbp.org.pk/reports/stat_reviews/Bulletin/2021/Sep/Domestic%20and%20External%20Debt.pdf

4 According to Abdeljaouad, the waqfiyya inscription says, "In the name of Allah, the Compassionate, the Merciful", the irrevocable inscription begins. Abu Salih Hayr al-Hadim (or al-Khadim) gave as alms his farm in Kafr Tabaria and all his land in Kafr Kana, by means of an inviolable *waqf*, which may not be sold or given or transferred in inheritance or damaged by usury, or modified, for better or worse. "It is permanently protected in accordance with its fundamental regulations and the shares assigned to the beneficiaries in whose favor it has been made a *waqf* forever …".

5 Dr. Usman of Hamdard University Karachi used the word *Sunnah*, for *waqf*, in Pakistan and in that manner, if *waqf*, as an institution, is substantially revitalized and utilized at mass scale, it would be akin to the revitalization of a Sunnah of the Prophet Muhammad (PBUH).

2 Evolution of *Waqf* as an Institution for Socioeconomic Growth

2.1 Introduction

As briefly indicated in the first chapter, the institution of *waqf* initiated from the persuasion by Quran that piety or righteousness could be achieved only by spending what one loves to please Allah Tā'la [for benefit of others (3:92)]. It was to remove the misconception of the Jews about righteousness based on legalistic approach of their jurists.[1] Quran declares that the righteousness is based on the love of Allah and spending in His way and giving one's loved assets or goods for ease and welfare of fellow human beings. When the Companions of Prophet (PBUH) started giving their valuable assets like orchards and date palms as *sadaqah*, Prophet's advice was that the corpus of the orchard(s) might be kept intact, and their produce be given as sadaqah to make it a continued source of helping others. Such first *waqf* by Prophet's Companion Abu Talha and his wife consisted of 600 date palms the product and proceeds of which were meant to help out Madina's poor (Khan, 2020).

Accordingly, the advice to make the charity perpetual served as the basis for evolving the formal institution of *waqf* (وَقْف), also termed as *hubous* (حُبوس), individually by the well-off Muslims, and collectively by the groups and the Islamic state. *Waqf* is considered a system of creating and managing an inalienable charitable endowment as per Islamic precepts of sacrifice for others for the sake of Allah (SWT) with an ingrained sense of reward from Allah and expecting reward from Him. The person making such an endowment on permanent basis is known as a *wāqif* (the donor).

Although the *waqf* system is believed to be initiated on Sunnah of the Prophet Muhammad (PBUH), there are instances, however, that similar system of donations also existed in the pre-Islamic cultures. Of course, the specific full-fledged Islamic legal form of endowments in the form of *waqf* emerged in AD 9th century.

Waqf as a discretionary part of the Islamic social finance system played a distinct role throughout the centuries in ensuring economic and social stability as well as financial stability. Commercial capitalism and mercantilism emerging from Europe and spreading to the whole world in the 19th and

DOI: 10.4324/9781003477549-2

20th centuries led to the accumulation of capital and wealth in certain groups and persons. In this backdrop, *waqf*, particularly the cash *waqf* continued to play its role, as a ribā-free system, particularly in Ottoman Europe to meet the basic needs of the society. It, thus, fulfilled the financial needs of priority sectors of the economy like that of farmers, craftsmen, entrepreneurs, producers, and merchants through Islamic modes and practices (Bulut, 2021)

Çizakça (1998) indicates that the real potential of *awqāf* lies in the cash *waqf*. Timur Kuran (2001) noted that income generated by the businesses by *awqāf* for hundreds of years provided for the maintenance of mosques, soup kitchens, and traveler and pilgrim inns. In Aleppo, during the 18th century, a *waqf* included ten houses, 67 shops, 4 inns for the traveler, 2 storerooms, several dyeing plants and baths, 3 bakeries, 8 orchards, 3 gardens, and agricultural land, Kuran added. *Waqf* thus served the objectives of socialization of the financial system for shared and peaceful growth of human societies and of Islamic civilization even during the period when the capitalist and the colonial mindset created an imbalance in the society.

This chapter discusses the elements that made the *waqf* an institution which, in turn, helped in socialization and institutionalization of the society. It also discusses how *waqf* evolved into a system of financial intermediation through the tool of cash *waqf*, or the money *waqf*.

The provision for cash *waqf* enables people to contribute for a *waqf* or to establish a *waqf* even if they do not own any real estate. The institution of *waqf* can be used effectively in the contemporary world if we distinguish the perpetuity of an object itself and the dedication of its benefits. It is important to note that in the case of a *waqf* only the value capital is to be preserved perpetually, whereas the investment capital could be transformed into different types of assets that might be considered suitable for maximizing the benefits from the *waqf* (Mohammad et al., 2006).

Further innovations over the last three decades in cash *waqf* in the form of different financial market instruments pertaining to charity giving have also been discussed. It also relates the tradition of charity to the pre-Islam religious traditions and compares it with the secular tradition of philanthropy of the Greek-Western civilization.

But let's first briefly discuss the Theory of Institution to discuss further and explain the institutionalization of *waqf*.

2.2 The "Theory of Institutions" and Assessment of *Waqf* as an Institution

North (1990) defines an institution as a humanly devised constraint that structures the political, economic, or social interactions. Accordingly, institutionalization can be further divided into sociological institutionalism, historical institutionalism, and political institutionalism (Amenta and Ramsey, 2010).

Waqf is an institution, if the definition by North (1990) is followed, as it pertains to both economic and social constraints applied and implemented by some person(s) on the properties or assets (termed as *hubous*, or detention of asset) as we discussed briefly in Section 2.1.[2] The *hubous* here is of a voluntary but permanent nature, which helps structure social and economic interactions, if not political ones,[3] by providing either immediate assistance for the poor or through community development projects. As this constraint is applied on a permanent basis, in most cases, over the donated assets, its impact on the social assets is long term and cumulative.

North (1990) pushes for the system of exchange and so for the market, though exchange can also be in voluntary giving and taking. Market-based institutions are important for development, but still, before the creation of profit-oriented institutions (market), there was something that helped establish the human settlements. *Waqf* is one such institution that involves both informal restraints (the tradition of donating for the sake of Allah on a voluntary basis) and formal rules that are devised to create order and reduce uncertainty (in exchange).[4] Beyond-market segment is an important part of economies, particularly in Islamic economy. Mutual cooperation and sacrifice for others or helping others had been a tradition in all human civilizations as was the tradition of "*al-nahad*" for mutual survival in times of trade caravans in Arab civilization (Ayub, 2022, Ch. 11).

Any institution involving cooperation reflects an important humanistic attitude that all revealed religions tried to inculcate among the people. The behavior of cooperation keeps prevailing among humans despite the invention and strengthening of market and all other institutions. As Islam orders to "keep cooperating for the acts of goodness and piety", so the religions assert for the humanistic inclination for cooperation and spending for others for communal survival.

Waqf can also be termed as an institution if analyzed from the angle of being an instrument of durable social interactions, as Bowles (2004) indicates. Interactions determined by *waqf* are long term and durable as *waqf* itself is a long-term phenomenon.

Further, it is important to look how the system of *waqf* evolved, if seen from the Western lenses of the theory of evolution of an institution. *Waqf* developed in Muslim society out of persistent practices, leading to the level of collective activity in the society, that acquired the level of a tradition and legal norm, whereby its specific laws were developed. The same stages for the evolution of institutions have been indicated by North (1990) and Hodgson (2006) that reflect the importance of "habit or customary practice" in rules formation.

Waqf is also relevant to the definition of rules. Greif and Laitin (2004) suggest that rules are "behavioral instructions" through which individuals choose behavior according to the situations. It is important to understand here that as per divine instructions only the Prophet(s) [Peace be upon all of them] can initiate habits or behavioral actions under divine guidance.[5] So, habit (in particular, if adopted by a group that can be documented and then made a rule, acceptable for all the society) is something important and its impacts must not be ignored. One such customary practice of Muslim society is creating *awqāf*.

Accordingly, *waqf*, a *Sunnah* initiated by the Prophet Muhammad (PBUH) is an institution that exhibits an element of institutionalization of "creating rules" (Stacey and Rittberger, 2003). *Waqf*, indeed, involves rules for many of the segments of society – the poor, donors, state authorities, lawmakers, financial institutions, religious leaders, and sometimes the nationals living abroad and the foreigners.

Such rules that helped create *waqf-like* institution did not exist before Islam, while *waqf* helped create, later, the same sort of institutions/laws in all parts of the world. Early jurists of Islamic law were from the third generation of the Companions and so, the theorizing of the *waqf* should have been quite near to the spirit of the practices of the Companions. In that manner, the *waqf's* early laws should provide an original spirit of Islamic civilization for any institution. So, the documentation and theorizing of the most natural and genuine tradition into a law means that the preservation of an institution provides the best possible way for the welfare and socioeconomic development of worldly beings.

Waqf is an important microeconomic and macroeconomic tool for poverty alleviation in Muslim societies (Azad, 2018). At macro level, two possible causes of poverty are low level of GNP, and uneven distribution of income. At micro level, a person may be poor because one is unemployed, handicapped, and so on or just one is born in a poor family and hence is deprived of equal social opportunities (Foyasal Khan, 2010). In this perspective, an institution that could be helpful in alleviating poverty at both micro and macro levels is *waqf*. Through *awqāf*, well-off people in Muslim societies take responsibility for providing basic needs and financial security for those who are devoid of resources while expecting to find a return from Allah (Qaradawi, 2008).

It's believed, therefore, that *waqf* or assets donated for community development ensure social interaction wherein people can utilize the most possible potential of the assets, besides other uses. The common wisdom should also suggest that a sincere and honest use of a collective asset with the objective of fulfilling social responsibilities should have higher level of utility. All this led to the formation of the *waqf* as a formal and impactful institution.

2.2.1 The Institutional Characteristics of Waqf

Sacrifice for others and cooperation are the salient characteristics of *waqf* that could play a role in mitigating the negative impact of the functioning of a market economy in terms of available opportunities and distribution of income. It is to replace the exploitative tools of *ribā*, *gharar*, and short selling for the benefit of the poorest segments of the Muslim society by changing the spending and consumption behavior of the rich. If it is proved that a *waqf* is a form of cooperation, the very basic institution that provided the understanding of the word "institution", then religion is the main game changer from the unhindered market trends based on self-centered approach of capitalism. It highlights the relevance of cooperation for the best social and economic outcome and sacrifice for others for welfare at a broader scale.

The spirit of cooperation, perpetuity, and inalienability of *waqf* also added to the understanding of the institutions for humankind. Hence, considering the very basic definitions and the characteristics that the earliest jurists attached to the *waqf*, these elements were quite important in defining the nature of *waqf*. Had it been the case that early jurists ignored these important elements, the *waqf* would not have been converted into an institution and most of the benefits would have remained limited and quite temporary.

In fact, the two properties of *waqf* (perpetuity and inalienability) ensure that the *waqf* becomes an institution for the perpetual benefit of society. *Waqf* properties cannot be used even for collateral for getting financing from banks. In Malaysia, according to Azad (2018), neither the *waqf* institutions are eager to use *waqf* land as collateral, nor are the banks willing to accept the *waqf* land because of potential legal problems caused by the feature of inalienability and perpetuity of *awqāf*.

Through *waqf*, the poor and the needy can be provided the most essential social services without any cost to the government (Çizakça, 1998). While banks and financial institutions might not provide, as part of their normal business, the interest-free loans or financing to the poor who could become good entrepreneurs, the institution of *awqāf* can provide an alternative by involving the well-off people and financing the micro businesses, SMEs and the strategic commodity sectors like agriculture, agro-based value-added products, and renewable energy sectors.

With the aforementioned characteristic, *waqf* looks like microfinance and the recently innovated "syndicated finance". But *waqf*-related financial support is different from conventional microfinance or similar other schemes in a number of ways. A crucial difference is regarding the source of funds, which, in the case of *waqf*, are perpetual endowments, while generally interest based, or commercial funding is in the case of conventional microfinance institutions. This institutional characteristic of *waqf* provides a basic solution for poverty alleviation and the creation of job opportunities by encouraging entrepreneurship, instead of jobseekers in the macro-level corporate sectors.

The study by SESRIC (2015) presents an "*Integrated Waqf-based Islamic Microfinance*" model comprising components like *waqf*, microfinance, human resources, *takaful*, project financing and poverty alleviation. In this model, *waqf* institution is the funding entity, while Islamic microfinance institution is the "implementing agency", which also provides *takaful* and human resources development programs. The microfinance institution would also provide project financing facilities through Islamic modes. For fostering the upgrading of knowledge and skills of the finance recipients, skill-development programs have been suggested as a requirement for additional financing. The report of SESRIC (2015) concludes that the model suggested by it can be a viable alternative tool for poverty alleviation. This model is shown in Figure 2.1.

One objective of the *waqf*, from sociopolitical angle, is the governance of community-related matters. The governance system had been at action in *waqf* since centuries along with its philosophies into the societies of the Muslim South Asia and Ottoman Europe. Hence, *waqf* can also help achieve the objectives of promoting good governance of community-related institutions.

A strength of Islamic social theory is clubbing the different communities and groups in terms of their religious values into one nation under the constitution. This opportunity may enable the state to serve the masses by improving governance without compromising on the basic objectives of the state. It is possible for Islamic countries, therefore, to realize the objective of a good institutional governance process by promoting *waqf* as a cooperative policy action.

Waqf as a beyond-market institution served as a main source of institutionalization of the Muslim society and hence to the civilization. As the benefactors of humankind involving sacrifice for others for the sake of Allah Almighty, *waqfs* should be distinguished from the institutions with the motive of profit, the market. This refers to the self-sustained and holistic accountability in *waqf* compared to the corporate or secular concepts of accountability in business and even the NGOs working in secular perspective, though with the objective of the welfare of certain groups.

Waqf, being the supportive institution for the State for promoting prosperity by reaching out to the poorest and by providing *ribā*-free access to finance, can have far-reaching impact on economy. Among others, it could

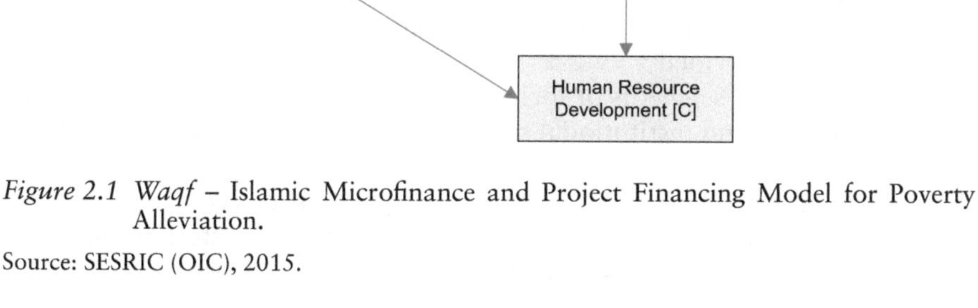

Figure 2.1 *Waqf* – Islamic Microfinance and Project Financing Model for Poverty Alleviation.

Source: SESRIC (OIC), 2015.

improve the behavioral and business ethics of the society because of spending for the welfare of the fellow being to please Allah. It will also improve the governance quality of the institutions by enhancing the acceptability, improving the cultural harmony, and providing long-term solutions to issues created by poverty.

2.2.2 Waqf *and Trust*

Waqf and the phrase trust (as used generally for welfare/social entities), apparently both are aimed at socioeconomic development. Wynen (1949) explains that the term "trust" was borrowed from the Islamic term "*waqfs*". Trust was to mitigate the intensity of problems created by capitalism that divided human societies into two groups – fewer rich by earning money from money and other exploitative tools, and the increasing poor. On the other hand, the economic and social infrastructure that developed under the institution of (cash) *waqf* was instrumental in sharing the rents of the *waqf* properties, fulfilling the consumption needs of the poor, promoting production, and providing the capital required by the bottom ranks in the societies for micro businesses.

The Western civilization, superimposed by self-interest and capitalistic paradigm, generated the quagmire of unemployment, abandoned children, chronic disability, and poverty with unequal wealth as indicated by Bremner (1956) and Rodgers (1998). It led to the creation of "trusts" in the West. Further, the concept of *waqf* is different from the formal or informal charity that is present in almost all civilizations. The main point of difference is the *waqf*'s link with its perpetual and manifold reward in the life *hereafter*, as we have discussed in the first chapter. With this objective and the main features of *waqf*, any term could be used for the institutions operating for the broader level and long-term welfare of the poor, needy, sick, jobless, or even for the progeny of the donor provided the objective is their welfare in socioeconomic perspective. One such term used for *waqf* is "Foundation" as operating in Türkiye. The acceptance of cash *waqf* as a valid form of *waqf* made it easy for foundations to undertake social-welfare activities all over the world where Muslims have a presence. The only requirement for such social spending to be covered under *waqf* is the urge to please Allah (SWT), and reward in the afterworld (Bulut, 2021).

The system of trusts worked side by side with increasing monopolization through the accumulation of wealth and richness in fewer hands. *Waqf*, on the other hand, provided a long-term and stable tool to spread wealth in the bottom ranks of all segments of society in an equitable manner with a unique economic, social, and institutional structure based on the concept of *balance* (Bulut, 2021).

Waqf, as a term, cannot be subordinated to the socioeconomic development, nor should its objectives be restricted merely to the western frameworks for development. It is because the trust, the main framework for mitigating the undesired results of the capitalistic system, is taken from the *waqf* and not vice versa. Yet, some comparison could be drawn for framework for socioeconomic development based on the principles of Islamic civilization. The question is whether the *waqf* still has something to offer to the civilization in the future that the trust could not yet offer.

The answer to the aforementioned question is in a positive direction. As indicated earlier, *waqf* as the new institution in human history emerged within the very 1st century of Islam under the guidance of the Prophet (PBUH) and his Companions (RAA). Its formal law was introduced during the lifetime of Imam Abu Yusuf (d. 113 AH). Çizakça (1998, indicated that the legal structure of *waqf* funds was established as a firm institution during the second half of the 2nd century AH, while Abdurrashid (2019) indicated that the legal formalities completed by the 3rd century or 250 AH with the "formative period" of *waqf*.

2.3 Evolution of *Waqf* in Terms of Activities Covered and Impact

Waqf is an institution for socioeconomic development that contributed to strengthening the Islamic civilization characterized by doing good with and sacrifice for others, and cooperation for the betterment of the fellow beings in the society. *Waqf* can, therefore, be explained by "socioeconomic development", the term used for the provision of food, health, education, and shelter besides widening the choices for economic opportunities in the economy.

Accordingly, in terms of objectives, *waqf* has two dimensions, i.e., religious dimension and socioeconomic dimension. Religious dimension means that *waqf* is regarded as giving one's property to others with the expectation of reward in the hereafter. As indicated by Affandi and Nufus (2010), people are motivated by religious aspects as they expect manifold rewards if they undergo some religious activities like *ibādah* including charity for *waqf* any time and especially during "Ramadan", the fasting month. The tradition of contributing more charity during Ramadan shows the relevance of religious factors.

Social dimension constitutes sacrifice for others, cooperation, assistance, and help to the needy as a social obligation. The primary priority of cash *waqf* prior to the 20th century was masques (management, maintenance, and running expenses), education (salary of teachers, provision of books, etc.), and the needy like orphan, poor, and detainees (Kahf, 2007). Mannan (2005) contends that *waqf* funds can be used to provide public (building infrastructure for public facility) or private goods (utilizing *waqf* funds for consumption by the public, as in the case of any natural calamity). According to Masyita et al. (2005, cf. Affandi and Nufus, 2010), cash *waqf* funds can be used for five sectors, namely, rehabilitation of poor, education and culture, victim of any natural disaster, social service facility, and health and cleanliness.

Within the framework of cash *waqf*, it may have further six schemes. First, in *waqf* shares scheme, in countries like Malaysia, Indonesia, and Kuwait, the trustee issues *waqf* shares and calls for public contributors who buy these shares. The amount collected is invested and then its generated revenue is channeled to the beneficiaries. This model financed many projects such as providing free medical services to the poor and needy, entrepreneurship development, and poverty-alleviation programs. Kuwait has established an International Islamic Charitable Organization (IICO) to provide global humanitarian aids. Through IICO, ten cash *waqf* schemes have been established including water wells scheme, educational scheme, orphans' scheme, and relief scheme.

Second, in Deposit Cash *Waqf* scheme, the founder contributes to a specific institution or a religious authority through a bank account. The bank then invests the money according to the agreement between the bank and the institution which acts as a trustee. The institution gives the revenues generated through such investment to the charitable beneficiaries. This kind of public *waqf* has been practiced largely in Singapore, Bahrain, and South Africa to fund a range of programs.

Third, in the compulsory cash *waqf* scheme, monthly compulsory contributions are made by Muslim employees depending on their monthly gross income. These contributions are deducted from their monthly salary by their employer which is then channeled to beneficiaries. This model is practiced in Singapore.

Fourth, in a corporate *waqf* scheme, the founder, which can be an individual or a public or private corporation, establishes an *Associated Waqf Institution* as the trustee. It then asks its subsidiaries to contribute part of their profits to the corporate *waqf* on a regular basis. The trustee then manages and invests the cash *waqf* accumulated from different founders, and the revenue is given off to different specified projects. This public *waqf* scheme has succeeded in providing different goods and services in Malaysia, Türkiye, and Bangladesh. Hamdard Waqf is a good example of corporate *waqf* which was established by a family member in India, and it reached Pakistan and Bangladesh.

Fifth, in the deposit *waqf* product scheme, a bank acts as a trustee. The founder deposits money as cash *waqf* in a specified bank account. The bank, as a trustee, collects and invests the amount through *mudarabah* contract. The revenue generated is utilized to provide services to beneficiaries. It is practiced by two banks in Bangladesh.

Sixth, cooperative *waqf* scheme has been practiced in Uzbekistan since 1992. Each district acts as a trustee where the citizens, acting as founders, contribute money to their districts. The trustee (district) manages and invests the collected funds, and the earnings are used for different development projects within the district. Hence, cash *waqf* is a powerful institution that collects funds from different founders to meet the crucial needs of society without depending on the government budget (Mohsin, 2013; Abbasi, 2012).

Regarding the socioeconomic impact of cash *waqf*, Affandi and Nufus, 2010) indicated that the potential of cash *waqf* in Indonesia could be in trillions annually, which could help the government boost the national economy and make enhanced allocation for the prosperity of society. It may also lead to better distribution of income and increase in the consumption level by the masses that, in turn, would boost production capacity in the economy. The cash received by *waqf* could be used for any productive activity, and the produce or return could be used for any social purpose as per the relevant *waqf* deed.

Abdurrashid (2019) explores origins and transformation of *waqf* and divides its evolution in five stages, namely:

(a) The formative period, till the start of Abbasid period;
(b) The post-formative period – from 250 AH/AD 864 to 648 AH/AD 1250);
(c) Maturing period – from 648 AH/AD 1250 to 1000 AH/AD 1592);
(d) The transformation period;
(e) The deterioration of the system of *awqāf* from the middle of the 19th century through World War I, when the interest-based system of lending and investment became a normal commercial activity in the world including the Muslim majority areas, many of which were colonized.

Briefly, during the formative period, the definition of the *waqf* was codified among various schools of Islamic thought. During the post-formative period, *waqfs* emerged out of cultural and terminological diversity. In the third period, *waqf* matured and affected a variety of places and beneficiaries in Muslim world. At this stage, Islamic societies developed mechanisms to cultivate an atmosphere of social and financial inclusion of marginalized segments for the first time in the history of mankind. In the transformation period (fourth period) issues of concreteness and perpetuity of *waqfs* began to be applied to cash, more mobile and useful for new world. The last and fifth period was of the deterioration of *waqfs*. In the following, we give some detail of these stages:

- In the formative period, the term *waqf* got codified across legal schools of Islam. It adopted concrete forms of mosques and *madrasas*. In early stages, terminological problem emerged, and jurists employed the terms such as *ḥubs*, *aḥbās*, *ṣadaqah*, *ṣadaqāt muḥarramāh*, and *ṣadaqāt mawqūfāh*. Mālikīs, early Shāfiʿīs, and Ẓāhirīs employed the terms *ḥabs* or *ḥubs* (to retain or detain). Imam Shāfiʿī preferred the *Sadaqāt muḥarramāt*, or inviolable charity, and explained that *hubs* is a term that meant *ṣadaqāt muḥarramāt*, a term for *waqf*. Later Shafie scholars followed that view and now universally employ the term *waqf*.

- Early Ḥanafī scholars also employed different terms and later settled on *waqf* as were Hanbalī scholars. Mālikī scholars retained *ḥubs* instead of *waqf* and so *ḥubs* became normative in North Africa and Al-Andalus. Shiah scholars employed both *ḥubs* and *waqf*, where *ḥubs* was not intended to extend into perpetuity. Islamic arts and sciences flourished in the same period. Major mosques, *madāris*, and libraries belonged to *awqāf*.
- In the evolution period, *waqf* expanded from *madrassa* mainly to many diverse forms. Many new types and facilities were developed. These included *sufi* lodges; construction and maintenance of tombs of scholars; travelers' inns; soup kitchens; public baths; famine relief centers, hospitals; veterinary services, animal fountains; prayer rooms along travel routes; libraries; public water fountains; orphanages; public baths cemeteries; kindergarten/primary schools founded independently adjacent to many mosques for the primary purpose of teaching Qur'an; institutions devoted to charitable causes such as feeding the poor, paying debts, the distribution of gifts on the two *eids*, and the preparation for burial of the deceased.
- Deterioration period of *waqf* started in the middle of the 19th century and lasted until World War I. *The waqf* system deteriorated due to the direct involvement of colonial powers and the evolution of interest-based finance and investments. Further, *waqfs* were gradually nationalized as the Muslim world began the transition to nationalism. Over time, this led to all *waqfs* becoming bankrupt and without any operational funding. The governments proved unable to meet the needs of the public and incapable of providing the same level of social services as that of *waqf* and this led to increasing impoverishment and general neglect.

2.3.1 Nationalization of Awqāf

The *awqāf* were traditionally administered by the trustees appointed by the creators of *awqāf* or any representatives of the beneficiaries. The shift of *waqf* management to government started with the establishment of *waqf* administration by the Ottoman Empire in 1826, which led to the liquidation of most Islamic *awqāf* of that time (Ihsan, H. 2007). Besides, under colonial rule in the 20th century, the *waqf* properties and their management were given under the colonial regimes or their representatives in most Muslim lands (Ihsan & Ayedh, 2015). Even after the independence of Muslim countries, *waqf* properties were controlled as part of the public sector in Syria, Egypt, and Türkiye (Al-Jaowhary, 2001).

Turkish attempt for nationalization may refer to the state's power and commitment toward the welfare of the citizens. Though there are too many opinions about the rights or wrongs of the nationalization, the post-colonial trend of state control by the Muslim rulers didn't show a good sign. It neither was a successful move nor was conducted by a commitment toward the development of society.

2.3.2 Continued Functioning of Awqāf

Looking at the speedy creation of *waqf* law (to start in the 1st century and maturation in the 3rd century AH) to take root as an informal (or a nongovernment) institution seems to be a miracle. It might be because of the in-built strength of the system initiated by the Prophet (PBUH) and practiced by the Companions (RAA) and the next generation(s). It was also due to a dominant trend in the society that Muslims were not only so generous and keen to do the volunteer and relief/rehabilitation work, but rather helped develop volunteer institutions. It was also an urge of the Muslims to assist the state functionaries for the welfare of the masses. Another reason could be that there were many wars in the early periods that rendered too many orphans, widows, and the disabled. It encouraged the Muslims to build an institution for permanent care for such segments of the society as *waqf* and develop its basic law.

The forms, management rules, and the role of *waqf* as an institution have been changing throughout Islamic history due mainly to the changes in the community's material and historical circumstances. However, *waqf* retained the substance of its sacred and spiritual imperative (Khan, 2020). It is believed, therefore, that in any form or status of evolution, *waqf* must fulfil the following requirements (Khan, 2020):

(a) The *wākif*, one who endows an asset, or the subsequent manager/*mutawalli*, uses the principal and its proceeds or produce to charity.
(b) The endowment be specifically and legally removed from commodification, that is, it is no longer "on the market" (for sales or transfer).
(c) The sole purpose be charitable, with the beneficiary group explicitly named.

In the earliest stage of evolution during the time of the Prophet (PBUH), the proceeds of the endowed orchards/gardens were used for feeding the poor. As time passed, the *waqf* activities covered increasing categories of almost all kinds of socioeconomic needs of the society. During the crusades, *waqf* dealt with war-related problems like nursing the injured and feeding and housing the displaced and orphan (Abdurrashid, 2019). While many hospitals and education centers were managed by *awqāf*, some commercial centers were also owned by different *waqfs*. The Haseki Sultan charitable complex in Jerusalem in the 16th century owned many shops, a covered bazaar, 2 soap plants, 11 flour mills, and bathhouses.[6]

Due to overwhelming status of modern corporations and interest-based systems, the potential of *waqf* remained untapped over the last 200 years. Going forward, many authors have presented the idea of *waqf*-based microfinance institutions for poverty reduction (SESRIC, 2015). A major milestone in this respect was evolving cash *waqf* in the current financial framework. While the cash *waqf* had been historically important in

Türkiye, the concept of cash *waqf*, stock, and other *waqf*-based securities has been implemented in Indonesia since 2004. Some of the *waqf*-related institutions and instruments established in Indonesia included Indonesian *Waqf* Deposit, *Centre for Justice and Caring of Ummah*, *Ummah Daarut Tauhid*, and many other cash *waqf* institutions (Affandi and Nufus 2010).

A study conducted for SESRIC (2015) indicated a consensus among the respondents from Malaysia, Indonesia, and Bangladesh that *waqf* could play a significant role in providing financing for human-development programs related to microfinance and poverty alleviation.

Syndicate finance is another option where finance-related *awqāf* could contribute for promoting start-ups and entrepreneurship for welfare of the lower- and middle-income groups of the society. Any cash *waqf* could serve as an arranger or become a part of a syndicate for financing any project of social or economic infrastructure. The responsibility of a lead arranger *waqf* can also be shared by more than one co-lead arranger as per the defined terms of reference of their respective mandate. Such *awqāf* dealing in syndicated finance will be subject to the governance and regulatory standards as applicable to Islamic finance institutions, and as per the respective regulatory rules in different markets. Further details about the microfinance and syndicated finance and SME financing models based on *waqf* have been discussed in Chapter 5.

2.4 Taking *Waqf* to Micro Level

Institutionalization of cash *waqf* resulted in taking *waqf* to the micro level enabling the middle-income groups in Muslim societies to charitable giving for long-term impact. Islam likes every act of kindness and help to others and manifold reward is promised for such acts of kindness. Specifically, spending for others does not only fulfill a religious obligation (*zakāh*) but also enables purification of the heart and the beautification of one's character. Charitable giving with intention to please Allah, whatever the amount could be, certainly resounds at the deeper level of the soul's salvation (Khan, 2020). It is based on saying of the Prophet (PBUH), "*Kind words, helping another across the road, removing litter from the street, showing affection towards spouse, feeding the poor, etc. are considered charitable in Islam*".

Based on the aforementioned philosophy of spending and sacrifice for others, cash *waqfs* could enhance the financial services for micro- and medium-sized enterprises (Lahsasna, 2010). Lahsasna adds that the cash *waqf* model can be used as a mechanism through its commercial and financial aspect to enhance the micro and medium enterprises (MMEs) and facilitate their business. As per Malaysian definition, Lahsasna (2010) included the following sectors in the MMEs: primary agriculture, manufacturing (including agro-based), manufacturing-related services (MRS), and services including information and communications technology.

Cash *waqf* has the potential to improve the economic growth of Pakistan economy and play a vital role in the socioeconomic development by allowing the SMEs, small enterprises (SE), and small and medium start-ups[7] to have access to the financial services. In Pakistan, for example, enterprises with annual sales turnover up to PKR 150 million are considered SEs while entities with annual sale turnover of PKR 150 million to PKR 800 million are the medium enterprises.

The well-to-do persons in the society may pool their funds to jointly create Corporate Cash *Waqfs* to create learning and capacity building centers, universities, hospitals, or the projects of civic amenities like creation of solar energy for the local population, providing drinking water and sanitary services. Currently, many such institutions are providing services, particularly in education and health sectors under the banner of "trusts" due mainly to the absence of law and legal and regulatory framework related to creation and operation of *waqfs* that certainly have the sense of sanctity and perpetuity.

2.5 Categories of *Waqf* Based on the Purpose or the Beneficiaries

Various categorizations of *waqf* have been mentioned by the researchers. White (2006) has classified *waqf* into three types: Religious *waqfs*, Family *waqfs*, and Philanthropic *waqfs*. Farfor (2001) categorized *waqf* based on purpose into (i) general or public *waqf*, (ii) family or posterity *waqf*, and (iii) the private or philanthropic *waqf*. Usufruct of a general purpose or public *waqf* is used for a wide range of public interests such as hospitals, schools, public restrooms, masques, etc. Family *waqf* implies that usufruct of the *waqf* property must be designated for the *wāqifs*' children and their offspring without their right to sell or dispose of the property. Private or philanthropic *waqf* is for a specific charitable purpose such as poor in a specific area, or buildings with its revenues to be used for *waqf*, masques, schools, etc. Accordingly, there are five broad categories of *waqf* beneficiaries, viz., general public, heirs, religious institutions, educational institutions, public health, and others (Foyasal Khan, 2010).

Waqf can be created anytime by owner of any asset(s), but in the case of will (*wasiyyah*), *waqf* cannot be of more than one-third of the *wāqif*'s wealth left for the inheritors. *Wasiyyah* is a gift of property or its benefit subject to the death of the person doing *Wasiyyah*.[8]

Kahf (1998) categorizes *waqf* on the basis of the output into two types: direct *waqf* and investment *waqf*. Here direct *waqf* means the donated assets that generate consumable services or are used directly by beneficiaries. Such a *waqf* could be a *waqf* in the former case, and in the case of one-time charity it might not be a *waqf*. Income or return on investment *waqf* has to be used by the intended beneficiaries as per the *waqf* deed.

To qualify as charitable institution, the ultimate purpose of the *waqf* must be of the nature of virtue and piety (Çizakça, 1998). It is the reason that *waqf* must be irrevocable, perpetual, and inalienable. According to Çizakça

(1998) and Abattouy and Al-Hassani (2013), the *awqāf* system has remarkable resilience, and many *awqāf* had survived even for more than a millennium and some considerably longer than half a millennium, and this was due to inalienability. The nature of the expected benefit or purpose of the *waqf* must be clearly stated in the *waqf* deed or document created by the donor. Further, law may explicitly provide a framework for cash and corporate *awqāf*, including their investment dimension and the list of beneficiaries.

To properly differentiate the public and the family *waqfs*, the jurists suggest that where more than 50% of the net available income of a *waqf* property is exclusively applied to any common religious and charitable purposes, such a *waqf* may be deemed to be a public *waqf*. Similarly, *waqfs* where more than 50% of the net available income is meant for the *wāqif*'s descendants, may be treated as family *waqf*. Ultimate objective of both public and family *waqfs* is virtuous, but the nature of beneficiaries is different, and this distinction has to be taken care of in the law. The law must provide for an explicit basis of distinction in the case of mixed *waqfs*. In any case, the *waqf* law must provide for proper management of even private *waqfs* with transparency and accountability to avoid misappropriation by some at the cost of the others.

Keeping in view some innovative forms of cash *waqf*, *waqf* can be created for movables, financial and intangible assets, e.g., cash, stocks, *ṣukūk* and other financial securities, transportation vehicles, rights on land and building, rights of leasing, and rights of intellectual property. Cash *waqf* deposits are being offered in countries like Indonesia and Malaysia. Affandi and Nufus (2010) have discussed the Indonesian Waqf Deposit (IWD) from the foundations of cash *waqf*. They also identified the amount of IWD's revenue, the amount of cash *waqf* allocation from IWD on productive sectors, and the amount of IWD's cash returns *waqf* fund. The categories and functions of *waqfs* of immovable properties and cash are shown in Figure in Figure 2.2.

2.6 Sustainability of *Waqfs*

Regardless of the category, a *waqf* has a characteristic of perpetuity, without which it cannot be considered a *waqf*. It requires that cash and liquid assets, fixed assets, and movables must be generating a flow of cash or returns that could be used for welfare of the beneficiaries. Sukmana (2020) defines the *waqf* as an endowment (donation) made by a Muslim under Islamic law to a fund manager (*mutawali/nazir*) who is responsible for generating profits that are subsequently used to support socioeconomic development. So, a *waqf* should be able to generate return over investments.

This is why the old literature of Islamic theorists suggests that *waqf* has to be an immovable asset. Cizaka (1998) defined the *waqf* with the same characteristics as a privately owned property ... endowed for a charitable purpose in perpetuity and the revenue generated is spent for that purpose.[9] So, an element of "investible asset that can generate some return", along

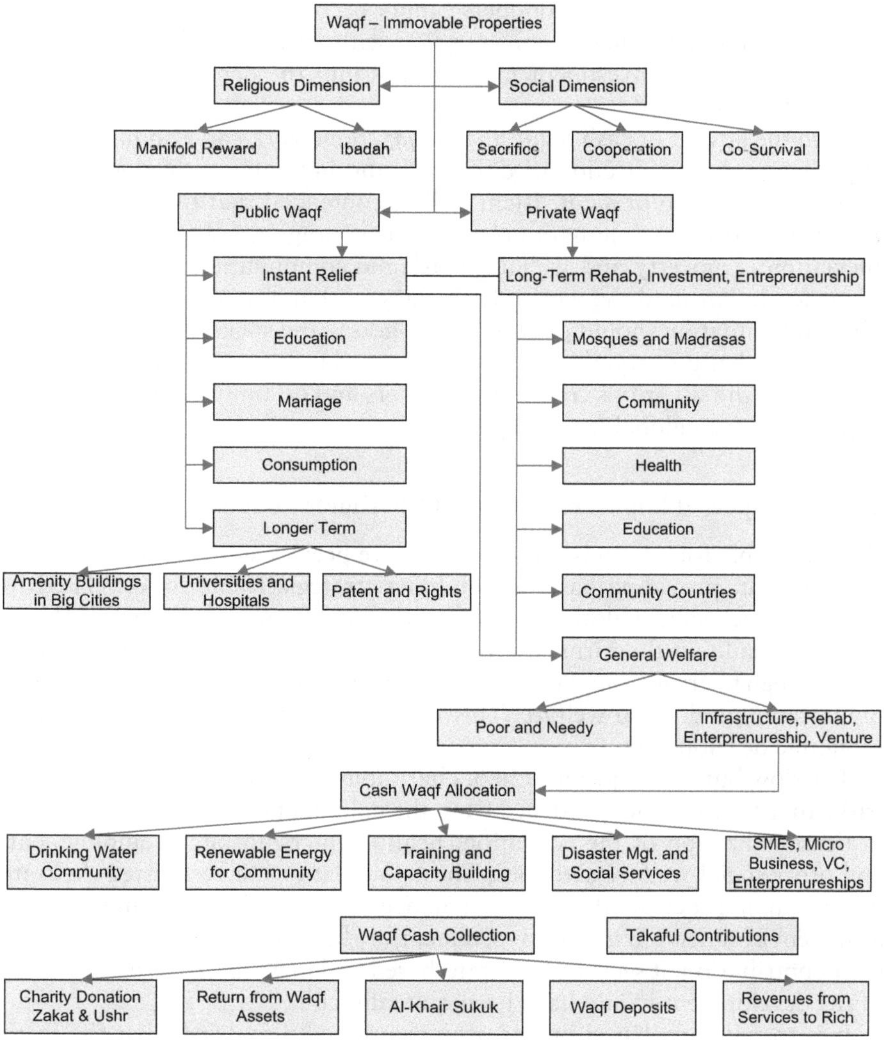

Figure 2.2 *Waqf* – Immovable Properties and Cash – Categories and Functions.
Source: Authors' own.

with the second element of perpetuity, is described by many of the authors as important characteristic of the *waqf*. M. A. Mannan socialized cash *waqf* in Bangladesh through Social Investment Bank Limited (SIBL). The SIBL issued Cash *Waqf* Certificate to collect funds from the rich, invested the funds in business and distributed the returns of the managed funds to the poor (Foyasal Khan, 2010).

While any act of charitable distribution or act of goodness could be a noble act, all the acts of the goodness cannot become a *waqf*. So, in that way, the direct charity leading to consumption without any possibility of generating cash through investment may not fall into the definition of *waqf*, as Kahf (1998) indicated.

With the advent of cash *waqf*, the *awqāf* framework can also be extended to global level for collection of donations and investments. It would be the internationalization of *waqf*. Islahi (1992) contended that the institution of *awqāf* needed to be internationalized by encouraging voluntary giving for alleviation of poverty and welfare of Islamic communities in OIC member countries and around the world. He suggested that a nongovernment world Muslim foundation should provide public goods and social services on larger scale to combat poverty, illiteracy, sickness, and lack of technical know-how. Combating the situations created by disasters and calamities could also be an objective of such global level *waqfs*.

2.7 The Expected Impact of *Waqf* and Charitable Foundations

The charitable foundations, historically, have been, a staircase for economic development, providing basis for building strategic frameworks related to economic inclusion. Giloth (2019) found that "foundations" help achieve concrete results in the form of economic development. Muslim rulers were wise enough to create foundations, across the Islamic history, for the purposes of education and social welfare. This way, they intended to ensure concrete economic development.

The slow but steady promotion of charitable foundations in Muslim countries, after they got independence from the colonial powers, is leading to the institutionalization of the education, health centers/hospitals, employment, and other social-welfare activities. These foundations have assisted the state in maintaining social and economic balance to some extent even in the capitalistic environment. Without involvement of the charitable foundations and their contribution, it seems that a state-based and mass-level extensive system of the development would have been quite difficult.

It is to reiterate, based on the aforementioned discussion, that the institution of *waqf*, particularly cash *waqf*, offers a community-based framework to build a sustainable bridge across the gaps created by operation of the forces of demand, supply, and competitiveness in market economy. So far, the philanthropists at individual level and the private and public sector organizations have not utilized the potential of the cash *waqf* concept which could be instrumental in taking the culture of formalized giving at micro level. The movement in many countries in the Middle East, Indonesia, and Malaysia during the last three decades is a step-forward in reviving the concept of spending for others through *waqf*. The effort by scholars and practitioners has revived *waqf* institutions by developing the financial products for the improvement of *waqf* properties.

This holistic framework comprising cooperation, brotherhood, care, and sacrifice for the psycho–physical enrichment and survival of those among the mankind who might remain behind due to market forces or any personal disability could lead to shared, broad-based, and sustainable socioeconomic growth in Muslim societies (Azad, 2018). Particularly, Islamic banks and other financial institution can take some *waqf*-related initiatives for promoting entrepreneurship in commodities and energy-producing sectors, thus alleviating poverty from society. Islamic banks and NGO/NPOs like that of *Akhuwat* in Pakistan may jointly create such *awqāf* and involve the well-off people in the society.

Promotion of fintech opens another avenue for enhancing the potential of formalized philanthropy through *waqf*. Financing to the technology-driven SMEs would accelerate economic value creation through investment in innovative businesses. Another development is creation of *awqāf* for "Intellectual Property". In Bangladesh, some *waqfs* of Intellectual Property have been created that consist of copyright of books. The beneficiaries of such *waqfs* who own printing presses and buildings are the children and families of the authors (Foyasal Khan, 2010). Capacity building through *waqf*-based learning centers could enhance intellectual capital through creativity, insights for innovation, know-how, and management skills. Promoting intellectual capital must lead to intellectual property rights (IPR) such as patents, copyrights, design rights, or trademarks to the natives for real and longer-term benefits for the people and economy of respective countries.

Regarding the current situation in many OIC member countries, of course, it is difficult to assess the potential of *awqāf* in alleviating poverty and playing a role in socioeconomic development. In Pakistan, for example, it seems to be nil because *awqāf* are presently serving some religious services to a group of society without any visible impact toward alleviating poverty. An effective application of this system with application of modern techniques of financing might be helpful in cutting government expenditure in all civic sectors.

2.8 *Waqf* and the UN's SDGs 2030

Abdullah (2018), like many other authors, finds that most of 17 developmental goals of the SDGs 2030 comfortably match with the long-term objectives of the Sharī'ah and so with those of the *awqāf*. He discusses some of the SDGs which are also congruent with the *maqāsid al-Sharī'ah*. He also finds that the *awqāf* system at global level may have sufficient financial capacity to help Muslim majority countries to realize some of the most relevant and urgent *maqāsid*-oriented SDGs in a timely manner. Abdullah also provides a framework for enabling the *awqāf* system to spearhead the initiative by Islamic charities in realizing the maqāsid-oriented SDGs in Muslim majority countries.

The SDGs pertain to all socioeconomic areas including health, gender, jobs, and poverty reduction, and are part of a comprehensive global agenda to end poverty in a single generation. Particularly, the redistributive and social equality elements of Islamic social finance, also including *waqf*, have an important role to play in realizing SDG1, "*End poverty in all its forms everywhere*", in the world (OECD, 2020). *Waqf* can also contribute to SDG4, "Quality Education", SDG6 "Clean Water and Sanitation", SDG7 "Affordable and Clean Energy", and SDG11 "Sustainable Cities and Communities". For that, the specific SDGs need to be indicated in the *waqf* deeds.

The twin goals of the World Bank Group to end poverty and build shared prosperity in a sustainable manner that also correspond to the SDGs are the top priority of any Islamic economy as well. Efforts for realizing the SDGs could also be helpful in promoting risk and reward sharing and entrepreneurship, financial and social inclusion, responsible governance systems and economic and environmental sustainability.

The OECD conducted a study in 2020 to identify the opportunities that Islamic finance presents for donors in Arab countries and anywhere in the Muslim society, as they look to deliver the SDGs. There are opportunities to accelerate the delivery of the SDGs through the development and use of several Islamic finance concepts and tools, particularly the social finance tools including *zakāh*, *waqf*, *ṣukūk*, and Islamic microfinancing.

There are different estimates of the *awqāf* assets worldwide. As per OECD (2020), DinarStandard considered *awqāf* assets to be $410 billion in 2016, while the Dubai government estimated that *awqāf* could amount up to $1 trillion. According to another estimate, assets might amount to $3 trillion, which, with an estimated return of 5% or $150 billion annually, could be used for socioeconomic goals. As reported by Shirazi et al. (2017), only a few developing countries have explored the untapped source of raising revenue through *waqf* and *zakāh* for social welfare and poverty alleviation.

Although there might be some issues from Islamic perspective in a few goals like those related to gender behavior, but the *awqāf* system and Islamic charities might not be facing any problem in education and empowerment of women while remaining within the basic norms of Sharī'ah.

2.9 *Waqf* Institution in Pakistan

While taking Pakistan as a case study for this book, four Waqf Ordinances were promulgated for the four provinces of Punjab, Sind, NWFP (presently KPK), and Baluchistan in 1979 during the period of General Muhammad Ziaul Haq (Abbasi, 2019). It was the time when many businesses and service sectors had been nationalized earlier by the civil government led by Zulfiqar Ali Bhutto. The main function of the Provincial *Awqāf* Departments was to take over the administration and control of the *waqf* properties to ensure, as claimed, better management of the properties, to improve the standard of religious services, to ensure that incomes are used for the original purposes and to enhance religious education.

The *Awqāf* Department of Punjab in Pakistan had around 37 famous shrines and 24 mosques under its management. Also, the government of Punjab had nationalized 276 shrines, 406 mosques, and 483 other properties as *awqāf*. It included 73,884 acres of land, 1,741 mosques, and 1,596 shops. It was also running one hospital and 14 dispensaries under its social-welfare program. In Sindh, the Awqāf Department controls around 189 shrines, mosques, and other attached properties. This department has 10,912 acres of land and 4,419 units including shops, houses, flats, and plots (Shirazi et al., 2015). In most cases, the Chief Administrator Auqaf took over the management and control of *waqf* property. In the KPK province, the *awqāf* department owns 65,108 kanals (8,138 acres) of lad and many shops. In Baluchistan, the number of *waqfs* is very small, and subsidy is provided by the government of Pakistan for running the administrative expenses.

Paradoxically, state regulation of *awqāf* did not lead to efficient use of *waqf* properties; it rather led to institutionalized corruption as is evident from a number of reported judgments in which officials of *awqāf* departments tried to grab *waqf* properties for their private use (for details about such inefficiency, see Abbasi 2019). The *waqf* land was illegally and dishonestly appropriated by the functionaries of the *awqāf* department for themselves to the detriment of the *waqf*. The land was divided into various plots, which were given on lease by the Chief Administrator for a period of 99 years at a nominal rent of Rs. 1 per *Marla* per month. (After litigations, the court declared the action of the Chief Administrator in granting lease to its employees to be without any lawful authority.)

2.10 Summary and Conclusion

The formal journey of *waqf* as giving for pleasing Allah (SWT), and longer-term benefit of the poor and the needy in a society started over 14 centuries ago from giving one's loved assets for manifold reward in the hereafter. Real estate was the form of *waqf* in early Islamic era, but later other movable, financial, and intangible assets were included, and the legal framework might allow and facilitate cash endowments. Later, *waqf* evolved as a financial intermediation system and a tool of financing during the second decade of the 21st century.

Historically, the system served the cause of society in all respect with morally accountable social ethos of Muslim society as the property donors, asset owners, and the managers felt spiritually and financially invested in uplifting the less fortunate. But then it deteriorated as the paradigm of life and approach of Muslims was changed due mainly to the direct involvement of colonial powers and the progression of interest-based system of investments and financing as normal practice of business even in Muslim societies (Khan, 2020).

Waqf can serve religious, educational, or charitable causes. It also benefits the community by financing housing sector, schools, and hospitals for serving the general public (OECD, 2020). One major milestone covered by the evolution was that of creating the cash *waqf* by anyone involving the common man. *Waqf* properties are inalienable as they have to remain *waqf* in perpetuity. Hence, the concept of cash *waqf*, investment of such funds and use of returns for welfare purposes resolved many problems enabling the institution to play multifaceted role in socioeconomic growth of economies and societies.

As indicated by Abbasi (2019), cash *waqf* led to further six schemes in public and private sectors, and at micro and macro levels. It turned the *waqf* into a kind of financial intermediation through which smaller amounts of charities could be channeled into many subsystems of socioeconomic welfare in education, healthcare, hospitality, and other infrastructural sectors.

As indicated by Timur Kuran, *waqf* at its height presented a "credible commitment device to give property owners economic security in return for social services" and was thus an integral tool for providing public goods through local trusts.

Awqāf can act as vehicles for both public and private giving if managed according to the Sharī'ah principles. As long as they are established with a view to delivering a social benefit to a community, the financial resources can come from government or private donors, business, and corporate entities. *Awqāf* can contribute to social infrastructure in developing economies over a long period of time, which could be used for humanitarian or development purposes.

Institution of *waqf* could comprise public, private, or corporate *waqfs*; direct and investment *waqfs*; and social *waqfs*. The private or family *waqf* is the one in which revenues of such *waqfs* are reserved for the benefit of the offspring of the founder. Corporate *awqāf* could be for welfare of stakeholders of any corporate entity that could be direct or indirect. Though to qualify as charitable institution, the ultimate purpose of the *waqf* must be of the nature of virtue and piety.

Cash *waqf* could be an alternative solution amid the inability of government in providing even minimum social safety requirements and welfare facilities for the public at large (Affandi and Nufus, 2010). According to Lahsasna (2010), cash *waqf* would promote entrepreneurship and equity-based financing of the SMEs. The mechanism of cash *waqf* could also provide interest-free loan (*qard hassan*) to the SMEs through a safety mechanism based on trusteeship model, profit equalization reserve, and surplus fund of the cash *waqf*.

The 21st-century innovations of securitization by way of *waqf/al-khair ṣukūk*, green finance, fintech, and crowdfunding has enabled the policymakers in Islamic societies to develop the system further to use the *waqf* institution for alleviation of hunger and poverty, promoting entrepreneurship and microfinance for shared and broad-based growth, and sustainable future for the mankind.

The well-off people in Islamic countries who give a sizable amount of charity, though unplanned, should create *awqāf* to address the specific needs of economy, while the middle-income population may donate to different cash *awqāf* that different institutions like banking and nonbanking companies and other entities in public or private sectors may create for socioeconomic purposes in the country. The state authorities need to facilitate giving formal charity, creation of cash *waqfs* by individuals, banking and nonbanking institutions, different chambers of commerce, business and industry for different welfare activities and socioeconomic development, and sustainable growth (Sukmana, 2020).

Notes

1 Maulana Maududi writes in "*Tafheem*" in this context, Their notion of "righteousness" consisted of outward, formal conformity to the code, and they evaluated all day-to-day actions, especially the trivial ones, in terms of conformity to that code. Narrow-mindedness, greed, covetousness, meanness, concealment of the Truth and readiness to barter with it lay beneath this veneer of formal piety. www.islamicstudies.info/tafheem.php?sura=3&verse=92&to=92.
2 According to Abdurrashid (2019), "The Prophet (PBUH) instructed the Second Caliph Umar (RAA) to sequester the principal and devote the proceeds for charitable causes, of his property". Here sequester means to isolate or restrict the property from being bought, sold, gifted, or inherited.
3 In the short run, political institutions might not be affected by the changes made in the economic and social institutions but in the long run many of the political factors are determined by the changes in economic and social institutions. So, in the long run, *waqf* should have an impact on the political institutions. In the "language/terminology of the institution", we can say that the political constraints can be altered by the changes in the socioeconomic institutions also including *waqf*.
4 Institutions that consist of both informal constraints and formal rules (constitutions, laws, and regulations) are devised to create order and reduce uncertainty (in exchange).
5 Homer, the poet, born in 8th century BC, is said to be the first one to identify this very law related characteristic of Prophets (May Allah Shower His Blessings Upon Them All).
6 The Endowment Charter (Waqfiyya) of Haseki Hürrem Sultan can be seen at https://islamicart.museumwnf.org/database_item.php?id=object;isl;tr;mus01;38;en
7 As per SBP's "Policy for Promotion of SME Finance" launched in 2017, six Regulations were issued for SMEs and SEs. But then in 2022, SBP provided separate definitions for the SMEs and the SEs (SBP, 2022). Small and medium enterprises up to 5 years old are considered start-up SEs and MEs. www.sbp.org.pk/publications/prudential/SME-PRs-Updated.pdf.
8 It is important to note that a will is valid irrespective of its being made in a state of health or during the last illness, and in both cases the rules applicable are the same according to all the schools of Islamic law. Of course, if one intends to create *waqf*, it must not have any link with the will. In the case of will, the endowment cannot be of more than one-third of the wealth left as two-thirds of inheritance has to be the right of the inheritors.
9 Murat Cizacka (1998) contends that waqf stands out as one of the major achievements of Islamic civilization.

3 Promoting Entrepreneurship through the System of *Awqāf*

3.1 Introduction

Entrepreneurship is the growth engine in any market economy and the best tool for broad-based and shared growth, leading to common welfare in any society (Durrani & Boocock, 2006). This particularly fits in the structure of an Islamic economy, the basic goal of which is a just and equitable distribution of wealth for common welfare in the economy. Entrepreneur takes the initiative to produce, creates job opportunities, and encourages social/development activities (Cravoy et al., 2009) resulting in the maximization of social benefits, as opposed to profit maximization in the capitalistic paradigm (Ahmed, 2007), and alleviation of poverty (Nixson & Cook, 2005).

As we discussed in the preceding chapter, originally *waqf* implied donating any land, building, or property for any religious purposes. Upon advice by the Prophet (PBUH), Umar (RA) retained the property as *waqf* (*sadaqah jāriyah*) with the condition that it would not be sold, gifted, or inherited, and to give its proceeds as *sadaqah* for the poor, kindred, wayfarers, and slaves. It was the beginning of social welfare to provide a sustainable source for the poor, needy, and the unemployed. Later, it became an institution for the general welfare of the public or any specific group of people with a focus on the poor and the needy, also involving commercial activities based on the resources of *waqf*.

It is important to observe that *waqf* as an institution for welfare did not emerge in response to socioeconomic issues created by the modern capitalistic paradigm. It had been there from the very beginning of Islam since the time of Prophet Muhammad (PBUH) until the last Ottoman Empire (Çizakça, 1998; Arshad & Haneef, 2016).

In the Islamic empire, guilds[1] rose from the 9th century in main Califate cities like Bagdad, Basra, Damascus, Cairo, Samarkand, etc. and developed strongly from the 11th century. As in Western Europe, the guilds had a complicated character and had religious, social, political, and economic functions (Gustafsson, 1987). They had an important role in providing a conducive atmosphere for the entrepreneurs and craftsmen. A unique function of the craft guilds was that they aimed at giving stable incomes to their members

DOI: 10.4324/9781003477549-3

and afforded equal opportunities to achieve a standard of living in accordance with their station. They also controlled the quality of the products with the aim of guaranteeing a stable market, turnover, and income to their members.

Waqf as a tool for general welfare played a crucial role in Ottoman areas, Mughal India, and the Malay region. Arab and Indian Muslim traders who settled in the Malay states also introduced a variety of public purpose and family *waqfs* (Alias, 2013). By dint of the juristic innovation of cash *waqf*, it involved providing job and business opportunities, rehabilitation from any calamity, education, and capacity building. Thus, cash *waqf* worked like a financial intermediary. If we add up all these functions, it will imply that *waqf* served as a tool for promoting entrepreneurship to provide business opportunities by financing or capacity building, and for providing socioeconomic infrastructure in Islamic societies.

There is a connection between the capitalistic paradigm and poverty. Elimination of poverty in Islamic countries is not possible without changing that paradigm to Islamically consistent human resource based societal development paradigm and process (Hasibuan, 2010). It would require entrepreneurship to be carried out at the micro level to produce goods and services for use by human beings, rather than serving merely as employees to get fixed wages or earning money from money on the supply side of finance. Such a system is human centered using values derived from religious teachings on sacrifice for others and cooperative risk and reward sharing.

The cash *waqfs* enabled the Ottomans to run the economy with a cooperative economic mindset and paradigm at a time when the concept of maximizing self-interest was the priority. It was based on the Islamic economy's contented, selfless, sharing, and participatory behavioral approach for mutual benefit and social uplift maximization (Bulut, 2021, p. 65). It also enabled fulfilling the needs of investors and entrepreneurs who wished to act in the framework of credit and partnership and sharing the concepts of economy in the areas of finance. The Europe-centered modern capitalism and mindset for maximization of self-interest at any cost penetrated the Asian, African, and American continents. However, it could not dominate the Ottoman Empire till its fall in the 1920s, and it was made possible by the institution of cash *waqf*.

Muslim societies, particularly the Ottomans, practiced the *awqāf* system for social and economic objectives since the 15th century. The objectives of *waqfs* were twofold: (1) financing and holding the purposes of the *waqf* as a social effect, and (2) extending loans for entrepreneurs as an economic effect (Bulut, 2020). Financial support for social inclusion as well as entrepreneurship was provided by the cash *waqfs*. In this respect, the Ottomans' experience of support for low-income groups in the society and enabling them to initiate any business or production activity through *waqf* and thus leading to socioeconomic development had been a golden experiment. The cash *waqfs* also offered loans to entrepreneurs in the market (Çizakça, 1995).

3.2 Entrepreneurship in Historical and Wider Perspective

Entrepreneurship reflects an instinctive part of human beings in the process of establishing a business or an enterprise. This instinct leads a person to be willing for initiating any economic activity or a business to generate an expected income at the cost of possibility of loss of his efforts and/or his physical assets in the process. The most crucial component in the process of entrepreneurship is the willingness to bear any risk involved in developing such an activity.

An entrepreneur is a person who establishes a business by bringing together labor, capital, and natural resources in order to make a profit, manages this business, and assumes the risk of loss of reward for work and capital. The act of establishment of businesses is as old as the civilization itself.

Only human beings can be entrepreneurs because it requires a decision whether to take the risk or face uncertainty involved in the activity. Those who are willing to take calculated business risks look forward to becoming entrepreneurs. Conversely, those who are not willing to take any risk in economic activity, choose to serve as labor against a fixed wage rate for specifically defined work.

In modern economics, it was after the Keynesian revolution that economic policy radically changed to focus on wage rate, labor market, and money market. This moved the concept of entrepreneurship to the "firm" "physical capital" and to financial and monetary capital that carried interest rates. It tended to reduce the demand for entrepreneurs for benefit of the owners of monetary and financial capital, thus increasing the share of monetary and financial sectors in national income and reducing that of the commodity-producing sectors (Ayub, 2022). Above all, the institution of interest did not allow financial resources to demand small entrepreneurs, particularly in developing countries.

Entrepreneurs could be primary or secondary. The primary entrepreneurs conceive and initiate the business, and are ready to bear the risk of loss, in case the eventuality arises. Their reward is post-determined, that is, what is left behind from value added after paying the wage/rent of the hired factors of production employed in the business (Ayub, 2022). They put their time, effort, and resources at stake in the business to bear the loss, if it arises. The secondary entrepreneurs offer only the usufruct of their resources (non-human capital), not on hire against fixed rent, but for a share in the profit (post-determined) and they also bear the risk of loss.

3.2.1 Determinants or Success Factors for Entrepreneurship

Before we discuss the role of *waqf* in promoting entrepreneurship, let's briefly see the determinants of entrepreneurship in any economy. The researchers have identified many personal and nonpersonal success factors for entrepreneurs. The personal factors include, *inter alia*, willingness to take rational and calculated business risk, knowledge and tech-based skills, hands-on training for experience, entrepreneurial creativity, honesty, patience, or willingness to sacrifice short-term gains to benefit in the long term, business networking, persistence, and last but not least, the leadership. These factors certainly have their impact of promoting entrepreneurship, but here we are primarily concerned with the nonpersonal factors including financial resources/financing and facilitations for capacity building that could be provided by cash *awqāf*. Availability of required infrastructure at affordable costs, taxation and trading policies, stable exchange rate system, and training and orientation opportunities for innovative businesses and techniques are some general factors that determine the level of entrepreneurship in any economy. Figure 3.1 gives a general idea of the determinants of entrepreneurship in an economy.

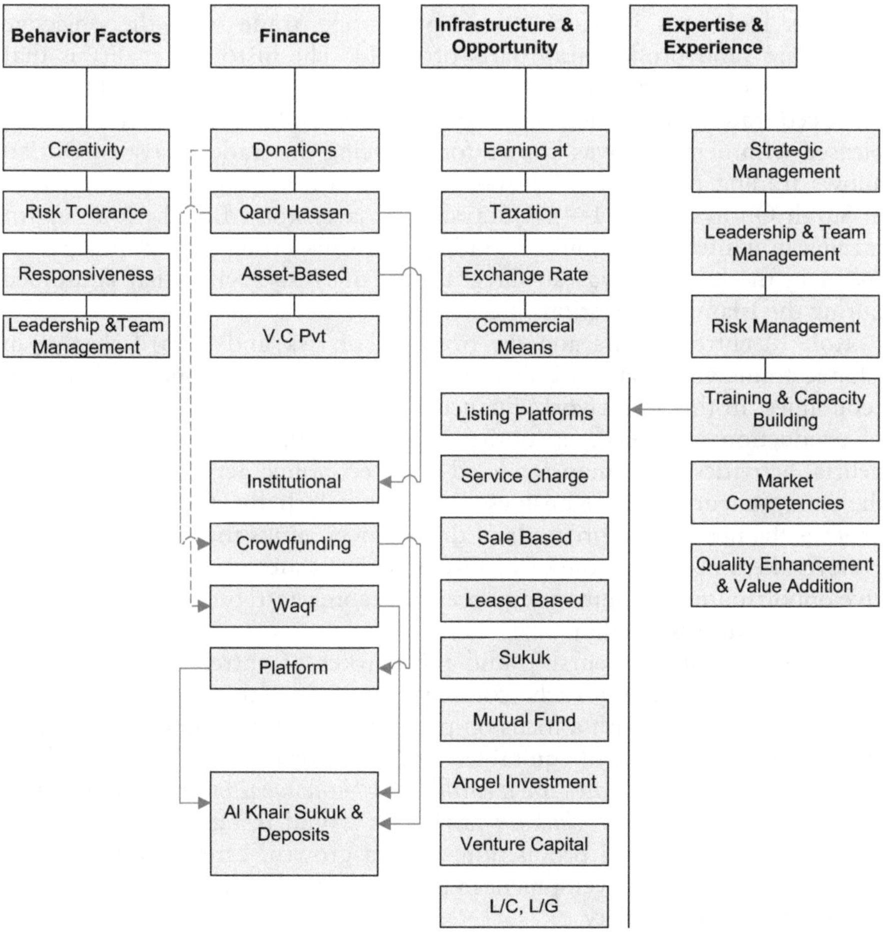

Figure 3.1 Success Factors for Entrepreneurship.

Source: Authors' own.

3.3 Role of Entrepreneurship in Socioeconomic Development

Balanced growth in a broader perspective is the key to any stable and growing economy. It is possible by promoting entrepreneurship to create wealth at micro and family levels. Corporate businesses are increasingly widening the gap between the rich and increasing poor in the national as well as global economies (Ayub, 2022).

Understanding entrepreneurs from the Islamic perspective, their market, and providing them the seed capital and working finance on fair and affordable terms and conditions has significance for growth and business opportunities particularly for Muslim countries. It could help their policymakers accelerate development and reduce the growing inequalities and distributive injustices that the capitalistic paradigm has created in all economies.

As the trade and business are included in the noble professions in Islam, Muslims had been instrumental in promoting trade with the objective of earning valid profits in all parts of world. The historical reality is that Arabs were entrepreneurs and traders, and the Prophet Muhammad (PBUH) practiced trade at young age. He married a woman (Khadijah, may Allah be pleased with her) who was known for financing the trade caravans. Qur'an allows trading profits (2:275) and mentions the trading custom of Arabs in Surah Quraysh (106:1–4). Quraysh were accustomed to the journey for trading in winter and summer.[2] Trading caravans brought them prosperity. As such, the business was an integral part of Arab society that continued during the Islamic civilization.

Role of entrepreneurs and the principle of risk and reward sharing in Islamic framework plays a crucial role in developing factors' markets and economies. In this framework, finance/liquid capital is a risk-bearing factor of production and hence encourages human beings to look for entrepreneurial activities more than for fixed-wage economic activity. Accordingly, the entrepreneurs take the business risk, particularly the risk of loss as their profit is the net of total proceeds of the business minus the expenses. Hence, policymakers in all economies of OIC member states must provide conducive opportunities for human resources to become entrepreneurs, rather than mere wage earners as labor.

Promoting entrepreneurship and the market of entrepreneurs must be the primary focus in any such economy that has capable human resources. A policy framework with a focus on promoting entrepreneurship in the perspective of the principle of equitable "*risk & reward sharing*" would help in understanding "*who creates the wealth*" and "*how wealth is to be distributed among the factors of production fairly*". It would result in increasing job opportunities, improved production, shared growth, care for the environment and sustainable development in the economy resulting in the welfare of all members of the society.

"*Beyond market*" institutions and tools of social finance, namely, *waqf*, *zakāh*, and *'ushr*, and supply of *qard al hasan* in special circumstances are the salient parts of Islamic economy that play their role along with the market economy based on efficiency, competitiveness, and motive of profit maximization. It would facilitate entrepreneurship in poor families and ensure the employment of all such persons who could do any value addition to the processes of production, distribution, and exchange of wealth, as per the market norms. Those who may not be in a position to add any value due to any inability would be sharing in the growth process by transferring payments through *waqf* and *zakāh*. The circle of community welfare is thus completed.

An overarching principle of any economy based on solid social norms is that while no one in a community should sleep hungry, the bare basic needs of all pertaining to food, abode, health, and education have to be fulfilled. The state as well as the rich and affluent are held responsible to ensure this, and it can be accomplished by promoting entrepreneurship, and/or by "beyond market" activities. The institution of *waqf* is one such tool for enabling fulfilment of the responsibility of community and the state.

In the developing/OIC member countries, access to finance is a challenge for micro business and the SMEs, and therefore for promoting entrepreneurship. As Muslims are becoming aware that Islam encompasses all aspects of life, including financial dealings, Islamic financial institutions, and Sharī'ah-compliant financing have evolved over last 50 years. But the role of social finance in development has not yet been explored. It is particularly the case of *waqf* that could take the form of a financial intermediary for financing the start-ups in industrial and technological sectors and the new businesses. Framework for financing entrepreneurs from *waqf* resources can be developed in the light of Ottomans' experience of financing the small businesses from *awqāf*. The objective of such a framework would be fulfilling the requirement of finance for *waqf*-based entrepreneurs in Muslim countries and societies.

The most common reason for lower levels of entrepreneurship in developing countries is the lack of finance. Commercial banks and other development finance institutions generally do not finance the start-ups, micro businesses, and the small enterprises due to lack of collateral with such groups. Here comes the role of *waqf*-based financial intermediaries for the purposes of business in general and for the social enterprises, in particular.

Waqf is the best tool for realizing the social as well as economic objectives of any growing economy. According to Lindawati (2019), eight characteristics differentiate social enterprises from general businesses: (a) social enterprises have a sustainable social mission in their production activities and services; (b) social enterprise businesses depend primarily on social funds or donations; (c) social enterprises are not-for-profit-oriented businesses; (d) social enterprises' employees, particularly the higher-level layer of management, are paid a minimum rate[3]; (e) social enterprises rely on stakeholders' voluntary actions; (f) social enterprises' business ideas are often initiated by the group members themselves; (g) the decision-making process in social enterprises is performed through a spirit of togetherness and participation by community members; and (h) social enterprises do not emphasize profit maximization but rather economic benefits for the community. It is established, therefore, that *waqf* being a social finance institution could be the most suitable tool for social-cum-economic development in any economy.

Waqf can be a good vehicle of entrepreneurship in pursuit of well-being. There is evidence that in addition to use of the *awqāf* system and the *waqf* funds for health and education fields, there are many instances of use of *waqf* funds to participate in establishment of cooperative housing, industrial companies, libraries, laboratories, and research centers. It thus has a direct effect on the promotion of economic growth and gross domestic product of the country (Ariff, 1991).

In many parts of the world, there is now a growing interest in *waqf* as a framework of business and entrepreneurship that essentially derives from the principles of wealth creation (Amuda, 2013). *Waqf* is well conceptualized in the context of a business model (Sanep and Nur-Diyana, 2011; Norinah et al., 2015), corporation (Muhammad, 2010), as well as social entrepreneurship (Salarzehi et al., 2010; Azliza et al., 2013). However, the workable models of *waqf*-based business entrepreneurship need to be further developed and practiced.

3.4 Entrepreneurship and *Waqf* Linkage

The historical roots of *waqf* and entrepreneurship need to be explored to create an effective linkage between the two and to derive a feasible model. *Waqf* system basically required endowments for the purpose of long-term welfare with a target group broader than that of *zakāh*, *'ushr*, or *sadaqāt* coming under any obligatory religious levy. From an economic perspective, *waqf* implies diverting resources and funds from current consumption to future welfare through productive and investment activities.

The immovable and real assets of high value are involved in the *awqāf* system with the characteristic of perpetuity. Therefore, the *waqf*-based welfare function may involve all social and economic activities that could play a role in poverty alleviation, empowerment of the poor and the weak, health, education, and civic facilities for the public, providing minimum level abode for all families, and financing the micro businesses and SMEs. It may lead ultimately to financial and social inclusion and shared, stable, and broad-based growth. All these functions would require organizing the system of *awqāf* on both sides of getting resources/funds in a variety of forms, and the use of such resources/funds for entrepreneurship.

Waqf provides flexibility in fund utilization as compared to *zakāh* which has to be given only to a specific group of beneficiaries (Qur'an 9:60). On the other hand, the institution of *waqf* can be used to provide a wide range of welfare services to Muslims as well as non-Muslims, and the beneficiaries could also be other living beings and the environment. For instance, animal protection programs and environmental preservation expenditures can be provided funds through *waqf*. Above all, *waqf* can transform capital into social and public infrastructure. It provides a permanent social safety net to the beneficiaries because of its perpetuity nature.

Resources available with the *awqāf* system would be augmented by the most effective way of using the immovable properties, investment of liquid assets of *awqāf*/ the cash *waqfs* created at micro and macro levels in the best possible Sharī'ah- compliant portfolios in terms of risk and reward. Other sources for sustainable *waqf* are voluntary contributions by the *waqf* borrowers as in the case of *Akhuwat*, contributions from the State institutions working for social welfare/poverty alleviation like *Ehsaas*/BISP (in Pakistan) and CSR funds of the corporate bodies, part of *zakāh* and *'ushr* funds that could be used for specific welfare functions, donations/charities by the banking and nonbanking finance institutions, unclaimed properties of the deceased persons in the society, the "wills/bequests" (*wisāya*) as per Islamic law[4] or any other social funds that the State may levy even on non-Muslim well- off persons in the society as part of their social solidarity services. Encouragements could also be announced for getting qualified donations (نذر)/dedicated amounts of funds for specific purposes of entrepreneurship by the unemployed and poor.

Islamic banks and nonbanking financial institutions (NBFIs) can play an effective role in promoting entrepreneurship in an Islamic economy. While banking institutions will be channeling resources for micro, SMEs, and small farmers and for projects financing to facilitate the entrepreneurs, the NBFIs including fund managers, crowdfunding platforms, venture capital (VC) and Startup Capital entities, *Mudarabah*, and leasing companies would facilitate the potential entrepreneurs to start their own production and business set-up at micro levels.

For the supply of sufficient funds for the projects, all NBFIs can also be enabled to provide facilities to get funds from the public on commercial as well as *waqf* basis and finance the micro-level entrepreneurs and specific small-scale projects. They will be serving as open-ended mutual funds funded by the general investors from the public. They may particularly finance the socioeconomic projects at micro and local levels. It would lead to an unprecedented model of financial inclusion and hence increase the growth in the economy. The entrepreneurs may get project financing either directly from the financier or by issuing any Sharī'ah-compliant certificates or *ṣukūk*.

3.4.1 Waqf *for Entrepreneurship in Historical Perspective*

In this subsection, we shall discuss the role that *waqf* played during the Ottomans' era and in other parts of the world in the past. *Waqf*, which was used for supporting the poor, and subsidizing the cost of living in many ways, was also a source of support for business initiatives. In Ottoman Empire only, there were already 2,840 *waqfs* in Istanbul and 485 in Aleppo by the 16th century. In the mid-18th century, revenues from *waqf* lands represented up to 30% of the imperial budget (Çizakça, 2000). Seventy-five percent of arable land in Türkiye were *waqf* lands (Singer, 2008) and a large portion of this consisted of Miri lands [lands that were given by the state for conditional public use (Çizakça, 2000).

Historical uses of *waqf* revenues, by the list of preferences, include (1) mosques, (2) education, (3) poor, needy, orphans, persons in prisons, and (4) health services. Mosques being the first use, is the most favorite and utilizes most of the revenues. Education came in the very beginning, as recorded by Kahf (n.d.), as a use of revenues where schools (*madrasa*) used to have a *waqf* property having regular revenues. As indicated by Kahf, Jerusalem had 64 schools at the beginning of the 20th century; all of them were supported by *waqf*-related agricultural and metropolitan properties in Palestine, Türkiye, and Syria. Of these schools 40 were made *awqāf* by the Ayubites and the Mamalik rulers and governors.

Schools might not be considered entrepreneurial ventures because the education was not private business; instead, it was voluntary and free education for everyone. But it comes under the social services. Social enterprises like support for orphans and the poor are also included among the social services that have an impact on business and economics as well. Health services can be considered an entrepreneurial activity. It is because the students (of religious education) used to learn *tibb* (medical education) for earnings. *Waqf* funds were used to provide free health services but there were formal private health services. Every *waqf* providing free health services must have hired the services of the *hakim* (doctor), thus providing a job to the medical graduates and creating the entrepreneur for medical professionals. So, organized medical facilities, most of the time in the urban centers, free for everyone but with paid work for medical professionals, can be considered an entrepreneurial activity.

Waqfs of the large agricultural lands in the Ottoman period were indeed dynamic and diverse entrepreneurs that generated income and vast surplus and brought the commodities to the market. It provided a stimulus for the development of the market economy. Besides, the urban *waqfs* at that time had their entrepreneurial departments out of which some manufacturing branches of *waqfs* were exclusive trader of their niche products. As such, *awqāf* helped develop and expand the internal market in the caliphate.

Waqfs could also be considered major credit institution for entrepreneurs at the Ottomans' time. It was the largest co-owner and administrator of urban property, besides conducting the operations of building and construction. So, its role was as a financier of urban producers. In the initial few centuries of the Ottoman caliphate, *waqf* remained an institution that commanded sufficient capital for investment with the entrepreneurs (Radushev et al., 2003). Besides generating collective capital, *waqf* had a role in the development of the private-sector development.

Then comes the role of cash *waqfs*, and incomes of the immovable *waqf* assets. All three main kinds of cash *waqfs* "neighborhood *avāriz* funds", "artisan guild funds", and "janissary funds" had enough probability to finance various kinds of entrepreneurs. There are instances when cash *waqfs* were also brought together in a fund pool.

Ottoman cash *waqfs* are perceived as an institution of capital distribution, as well as capital accumulation (Çizakça, 2000). The underlying result seems to be that capital accumulation was not as efficient as required to meet the financial requirements of the Ottoman caliphate. The strategy of capital pooling, among various funds, was adopted but the clientele was small businesses or consumers. Exception, at best, is an example from a European province of the caliphate, when cash *waqfs* of Bosnia financed merchants with major trade capital, as Faroqhi (2004, pp. 225–239) reported. Besides, Stefini (2014, pp. 12–14) observed substantial capital pooling by merchant partnerships from as many as 15 *waqfs*.

Most of cash *waqf* during the last century of Ottomans (1815–1915) were established in Anatolia. The late 19th century was characterized by the rise of small-scale cash *waqfs* across the Anatolian provinces. Anatolian cities had a greater number of cash *waqfs* with smaller amount of endowed capital whereas cash *waqfs* in Istanbul were greater in both number and capital. It seems that, as foreign banks started making their entry to the provinces, cash *waqfs* may have developed a comparative advantage on providing small-scale loans at local level. Studies on microfinance confirm that cash *waqfs* mostly provided credit to those who lived in close physical proximity to them.

Financing of merchants with "major trade capital" and "substantial capital pooling" by "merchant partnerships" from a large number of *waqfs* provides evidence that Ottoman cash *waqfs* were not mere source of redistribution of capital but functioned as an institution of capital accumulation, at least in some parts.[5] But the question remains here that why the Bursa cash *waqfs* avoided the financing of major trade capital, through substantial capital pooling for merchant partnerships, while the Bosnian ones were not. It refers to a focus on micro-level entrepreneurs against the capitalistic focus on corporate business emerging at that time.

Some more quasi-facts can also be deduced from the articles on Ottoman *waqfs* that should help understand the role of *waqfs* in facilitating entrepreneurs. Annual funds raised from the returns over the invested lands/investments received into the *waqfs* would have huge volume, and so it would have been a noncentralized development finance bank of the Ottoman Empire. Imagine the volume of return from three-quarters of all the arable land of *waqf* in Türkiye.[6] The sultans had got fiscal leverage and a system of successful collective operation (collection, recording, and distribution with prior plans and approvals) of funds. Indeed, each day should have added a permanent property/asset into the *waqfs* during the five centuries (15th through 19th). Besides, there was the capital accumulated by urban *waqfs*. This collective capital accumulated through *waqf* was not a tool for exploitation; instead, it was a tool for just redistribution.

Waqf was not mere revenue collection; instead, it was an interactive institution where everyone used to either donate, receive something or be part of management or at least get benefit of the facilities created by *waqf*. So, these were all the entrepreneurial skills for everyone, the ruler, the manager of *waqf*, and the users as well as donors.

Another aspect of Ottomans' *waqf* is centralization/nationalization of the *awqāf* system. It will be discussed in detail in chapter 6 on management and organization of the *waqf* system. It is crucial to indicate here that according to many authors, *awqāf* properties were a source of growth for private sector before the Ottomans resorted to centralism. Kahf (2012) contends in this context:

> Awqāf practically became part of the public sector, with all the known evils of waste of resources, lack of accountability, lack of motivation to improve performance and efficiency, slow and irresponsive decision making, favoritism, political interference in management and finally but not the least moral, financial, and economic corruption.

It implies the issues that authors like Kahf indicated in *awqāf* after being nationalized, such as inefficiency and morality.

Regarding the role of *waqf* in Muslim India, successive Muslim sultans in India had been very generous in funding *awqāf* from as early as the 13th century. With the arrival of Mughal Empire in the subcontinent, in the 16th century, the scale and magnitude of *awqāf* grew to unprecedented levels (Husain & Rashid, 1979; Habib, 1992; Abdullah, 2015). The *waqf* managed by the Mughal Empire benefitted mosques, and educational and religious institutions (Ansari, 1974). However, after the collapse of the Mughal Empire and the rise of British colonial rule in the Indian subcontinent, in the 18th century, this socioeconomic institution fell into disarray and lost its potential growth except in rare cases (Ahmed & Khan, 1998; Abdullah, 2015).

The Mughal rulers of Muslim India were capable of developing an organized and well-developed monitoring institution of *Sadru-us-sudoor* that supervised the *waqf* assets. But sufis were unable to utilize huge (regular, sometimes) donations for the betterment of the masses through investments into entrepreneurship. They could not take the steps that the Ottoman Turks took regarding *waqf*. Masses remained impoverished and subdued to the financial interest of Hindu *mahajin*, at first, and to the colonial wishes of the European anger, at last (Farooqi, 1986). Sufi shrines remained on the highest pedestal of the spiritual powers and enlightenment while the *madrasa* scholars never missed the highest grounds of Islamic law in personal lives and individual piety. However, these traits were not converted into the development of the collective lives of the Indian Muslims.

In most of the countries, under the European colonies or in the post-colonial regimes, *waqfs* were controlled by the government for two reasons: (a) to tame the spiritual leaders, and (b) to take control of the revenues and administer the huge number of employees attached to the *waqf* (Moumtaz, 2021; cf. Gennardi, 1921). Colonial powers were careful enough to initiate subsequent legislation, after the registration, to ensure that the state subjects should have a common reference point for obedience.

However, the real issue for either Ottomans or other Muslim countries was that neither the *waqf* funds nor the bank finance was utilized for a successful adoption of the industrial revolution through entrepreneurship. This caused very high levels of imports vis-à-vis exports and so led to the debt crisis.

In recent years, efforts have been initiated in many Islamic countries. In Pakistan, for example, steps have been taken to promote entrepreneurship through commercial as well as social channels. Within the social channels, the Ehsaas program that was developed by the government in 2019 by merging the BISP, zakāh, and 'ushr and some other poverty-alleviation schemes also considered the technical, financial, entrepreneurial, and outreach support that nongovernment stakeholders could provide to Ehsaas (Barber and Shahzad, 2022). As a mixed social and economic channel, *Akhuwat* with its headquarters at Lahore is running different programs for promoting micro business and entrepreneurs mainly in the urban areas of Punjab. However, these socioeconomic activities have no roots in the institution of *waqf* that have yet to be explored at conceptual level.

3.5 Possible Modes of Entrepreneurial Finance from the *Waqf* Funds

While the need for involving *waqf* in promoting entrepreneurship for balanced and broad-based growth in the economy has been established, the next area to be explored is the mechanism and process of involving *waqf* for financing the entrepreneurs from *waqf* funds.

Islamic banks may not be able to reciprocate adequate finances to meet the growing SMEs' demand in developing economies like that of Pakistan. So *waqf* funds may be required to step in to finance the entrepreneurs and micro/small businesses. The majority of Islamic banking products over the last five decades have also been developed to cater to certain types of financing where micro and SMEs are not part of the equation. Islamic banks, like conventional banks, are attuned to evaluate the repayment capacity of the borrowers through formal procedures, and the collateral that borrowers could offer.

Entrepreneurship-related uses of *waqf* funds would involve financing the entrepreneurs based on *qarḍ hassan* with or without service charge (to cover the actual cost of managing such financing and recovery operations), credit-based *murābaha*, *istisnā'a*, and *salam* sales for working capital finance, leasing (*ijārah*) and *sale & lease back*, project-based financing by way of *istisnā'a-ijarah*, diminishing *musharakah*, or any other hybrid financing structures developed in the light of Islamic principles of business and contracts. In the following, we briefly discuss the aforementioned options:

(a) ***Mushārakah-cum-Ijārah Product:*** The cash *awqāf* and the IBFIs that would create *waqfs* could join hands with professional construction, engineering, and manufacturing companies on *mushārakah* basis to produce such assets, energy-producing units, etc. on building and transferring on build, own and transfer basis. Such projects could be leased for medium and long terms. Upon completion of the assets, the same could be leased against rentals payable to the partners also including the *waqfs* based on their shares.

For providing infrastructure, project-specific partnerships of short duration can be created in which the assets and properties acquired could be held as community property until the end of the partnership period. The bank would be acting as one of the co-financiers and not distinct from other financiers. It could also be a long-term venture in which the bank might provide a portion of the equity of a newly established firm or buy into an existing corporation. The regulator(s) may determine the maximum amount of equity participation by the banks/NBFIs, and the minimum amount of participation by other partners in the ventures. The banks could be allowed to sell their shares whenever they deem it appropriate.

(b) ***Mushārakah-cum-Installments Sales Model:*** It could be the partnership of short- and medium-term duration in commercial, production, and services activities. The banks' share in the partnership could be sold on completion to the entrepreneur partner on installment basis with a profit margin for the financing partner(s).

(c) ***Istiṣnā'a-cum-Ijārah:*** An *istiṣnā'a-ijārah* mode incorporates an *istiṣnā'a* contract that applies to the construction phase of a project, and an *ijārah* contract for the operations phase. This structure is used commonly because the *istiṣnā'* matches the requirements of a procurement agreement, while the *ijārah* provides the mechanism for the repayment of the financing facility.

(d) ***Wakālah-cum-Ijārah Contract:*** The client is employed as bank's agent in accordance with the terms of an agency agreement for project financing. The client/agent would procure the design, engineering, construction, testing, commissioning, and delivery of the assets identified in the *wakālah* agreement for the financier who would bear the risk of all the aforementioned activities. After completion, the project can be leased to the client.

(e) ***Salam and Istiṣnā'a-Based Financing:*** *Salam* and *istiṣnā'a* have huge potential to empower men and women in the handicraft business to sell their innovative products by e-commerce through business partners who are trustworthy and wish to create wealth not only for themselves but also for the underprivileged men and women in the handicraft business. Financing based on these modes may enable the poor to become successful entrepreneurs and financially independent in a few years, provided the system is implemented by the regulators and managed with care and commitment.

Thus, the *waqf*-entrepreneurship linkage model could be as per Figure 3.2.

The linkage model conceives that income from the immovable properties of *awqāf* and returns on investment of cash *waqfs* will be pooled, first for the instant help of the needy, poor in routine, or any groups in problem due to calamities and disasters. Second, a major part of *waqf* resources will be used for promoting entrepreneurship because that would be helpful in business development, employment generation for poor families, promoting agro-based industries in all subsectors of farms, cattle, fish and

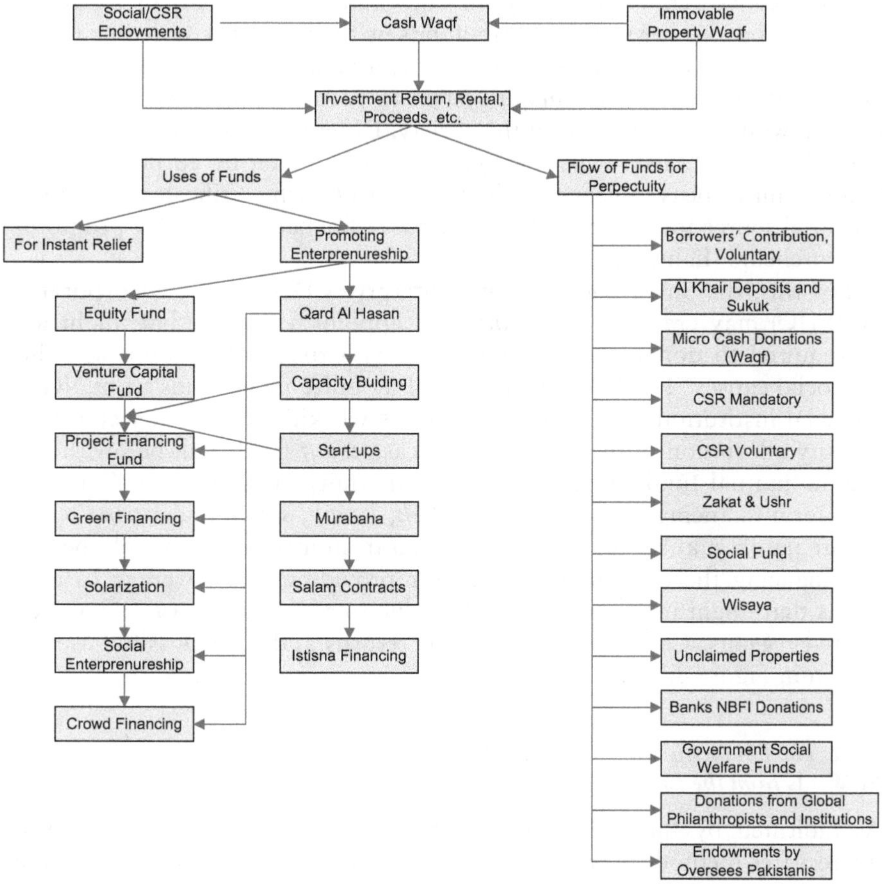

Figure 3.2 *Waqf*-Entrepreneurship Linkage Model.

Source: Authors' own.

poultry, exports enhancement, and import substitution, thus reducing the trade deficit.

Lahsasna (2010) has suggested a cash endowment (*waqf*) scheme for financing the micro-level entrepreneurs and other SMEs. The members of a business association would divert funds from consumption on *waqf* basis for investing in productive activities by the entrepreneurs. The donor himself could be one of the beneficiaries of the *waqf*. It will promote economic activities by providing the following: (i) liquidity to the business sector; (ii) financing the SME in the industry; (iii) circulating the fund in the market, and (iv) creating business and employment opportunities.

Flow of *waqf* funds must be maintained, to make the system sustainable, through micro-level *waqfs*, voluntary (as per Section 42 of the Companies Act, 2017 in Pakistan) and obligatory CSR funds (as in the case of oil and gas companies), endowments by the corporate sector, a part of *zakāh* and *'ushr* funds and other social security funds by the State. The state institutions may be required to give a part of the *zakāh* and *'ushr* and other schemes like poverty alleviation for the *awqāf* system to promote entrepreneurship even in the lowest-income groups in the society. Different *awqāf* and associations may also issue "*Cash Waqf Certificates*" to be taken by corporate bodies and philanthropists in general. The proceeds of such certificates would be a potential source for a sustainable *waqf-based* financial system for promoting entrepreneurs (Lahsasna, 2010).

For this, the Small and Medium Enterprises Development Corporation (SMEDC) may create a cash *waqf* and appoint a trustee that might also be required to donate matching amount as a token of virtuous spending for social causes. The SMEDC *waqf* will mobilize *waqf* funds from NGOs, financial institutions, and state institutions working for social welfare and poverty alleviation in the country. The cash *waqf* funds will be invested in Islamic mutual funds, stocks, time-bound equity, and other medium- and long-term financing based on *murābahah*, *Ijarah*, *salam* and *istiṣnā'a*, corporate ijarah ṣukūk, etc. Profits generated from investments would be used for financing the entrepreneurs and for providing risk coverage to those SMEs that might incur unbearable loss due to any calamity or any market-related reasons. Cash *waqf* funds, their returns and their possible uses are shown in Figure 3.3.

3.5.1 The Financing Contracts and Rates Charged by Waqfs *from the Entrepreneurs*

As indicated by Bulut (2016), the cash *waqfs* in the Ottoman era used interest-free methods in credit transactions. Islamic prohibitions set the limits by prohibiting interest, but it did not mean that the funds were necessarily return-free. There had been criticism about the financing methods applied in cash *waqfs* as contended by Gürsoy (2018) that cash *waqfs* were used to

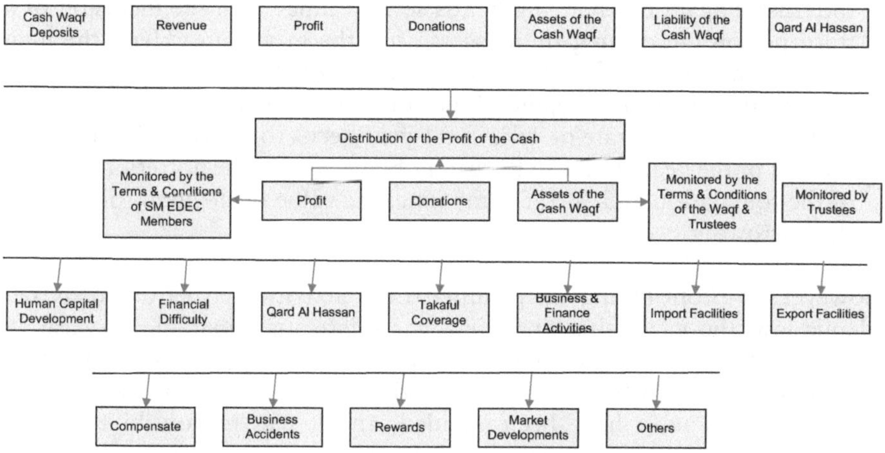

Figure 3.3 Possible Use of Cash *Waqf*'s Profits.

Source: Retrieved from Lahsasna (2010, p. 108).

advance credit against pre-fixed rates based on methods like the *ribā*. The rates charged were generally between 10% and 15%. According to Bulut (2016), as this rate remained stable for years, there was financial stability in the market, and entrepreneurs while making business decisions could foresee the finance rates. Further, as the rate charged on such trade-based financing was very close to the profit rates in the trade market, it also prevented capital accumulation in fewer hands. Bulut concluded that the financing rate in the cash *waqfs* was one of the factors that prevented the accumulation of capital in certain groups and persons in the Ottomans' period.

Cash *waqf* financing dealings followed two main borrowing procedures of Ottoman commercial transactions: "*Muamele-i Ser'iyye*" and "*Bey*" (Sic) (Gürsoy, 2018). But from late 19th century, the purchase of bonds was started as reported by Gürsoy (2018). *Muamele-i ser'iyye* was used as a *heelah* to avoid ribā agreement wherein money was advanced with an amount of profit, while there was another transaction of purchase and sale included within the process of lending, with a pre-approval of the Qādi (Gürsoy, 2015, p. 68). The "*bey*" as Özcan (2003, pp. 69–70) reports included "*bey'bi'l-vefa*" and "*bey'bi'l-istiglal*". *Bey'bi'l-vefa*, a type of sale agreement, where persons pledged their goods as security in order to get loans from the market. *Bey'bi'l-istiglal* means receiving the profit and revenue of a property. It is the type of sale in which an item was rented to the debtor for the purpose of benefiting from its income (Abdülaziz, 1992). About such tactical transactions as an effort to avoid *ribā* in letter, Gürsoy (2018) writes,

> The item sold by the trustee to the borrower on credit was returned to the trustee again by changing hands several times with the inclusion of a third person intervening the process after the procedure. Here, the item was sold not at its real value but at a price equal to the accretion of the borrowed money to be repaid. A person who borrowed from the trustee 1000 kurush at the rate of 15% for 1 year needs to repay 1150 kurush at the end of the year. The 150 kurush in between was the accretion revenue of the foundation and, at the same time, the value of the item sold during the borrowing.

However, as profit-taking on genuine trade activities is permitted as per Islamic law, the views that financing was interest is debatable. In case all requirements of valid trade as per Islamic law are fulfilled, the transaction and the profit would be valid. Use of juristic tricks to circumvent the prohibition of *ribā* must have been avoided, and it was responsibility of the Qādi. It is particularly important in the context of Ottomans' society that was sensitive in terms of avoiding *ribā* due to its prohibition, and that too regarding the conditions recorded in the "*waqf* deeds" (*waqfiyyahs*). If a person donates his property ever for the cause of Allah, he would not allow the *waqf* managers to engage in the interest-bearing transactions and even risk of interest (Bulut, 2016).

Of course, such practices have been classified as *hila* by many authors as viewed by many in the present-day Islamic banking operations. The Council of Islamic Ideology Pakistan in its Report (1980), Jeddah-based Islamic Fiqh Council, Bahrain-based AAOIFI, the most trusted institution in issuing Sharī'ah, ethics, and governance standards for the Islamic finance industry, and Sharī'ah councils in different parts of the world, Sharī'ah boards or supervisory committees of all IFIs across the world allow charging profit margin on trade-based modes of credit or forward sales, namely, *bai muajjal*, *murabaha*, *salam*, and *istisnā* wherein the ultimate price of the subject matter of the sale contract has to be agreed and fixed at the time of execution of the contract.

All categories of valid modes of business are crucial in economic activities in any economy (Ayub, 2022). Trade-based modes and contracts, as acceptable in the Islamic Sharīʿah, not only complement the sharing modes but also provide flexibility of choice to meet the needs of different sectors and economic agents in the society according to their risk profiles. *Murābahah* with lesser risk and better liquidity options has several advantages for financiers vis-à-vis other techniques, though may not be as fruitful in reducing income inequalities and generation of capital goods, as the leasing and participatory techniques. Yet, if applied properly they can be helpful in employment generation and alleviation of poverty.

Ijārah-related financing, which requires the financier to purchase and maintain the assets and afterward dispose of them according to Sharīʿah rules, requires the financing institutions to engage in activities beyond mere financial intermediation. Leasing can be very conducive to the formation of fixed assets and medium and long-term investments. This can help in capital formation in the economy and the institutions including cash *awqāf* may resort to this mode for financing of the development activities.

Salam can also be used for financing by any *awqāf*. It has a vast potential in financing productive activities in SME and micro-business sectors, particularly agriculture, agro-based industries, and the rural economy. It also provides incentives to enhance production. Since the seller in *Salam* gets the price in advance, he will spare no effort in producing, at least the quantity needed for settlement of the amount of funds taken by him. *Salam* can also lead to creating a stable commodities market, especially the seasonal commodities and therefore to the stability of their prices. Further, it would enable the savers to direct their savings to investment outlets without waiting, for instance, until the harvesting time of agricultural products, or the time when they need industrial goods and without being forced to spend their savings on consumption.

Accordingly, in case the "Deed" of any cash *waqf* or any landed property, small or large, *waqf* provides for financing the SMEs and entrepreneurs from the *waqf* funds on any interest-free basis, financing could be provided by way of any modes provided the transactions do not involve interest, uncertainty regarding the subject matter and its delivery, and/or the price (*gharar*) and gambling.

Waqf-based project financing and fund management can also play a crucial role in promoting entrepreneurship in the country (Ayub, 2018). *Waqf* funds, *zakāh* and *'ushr* funds, and *hajj* funds can provide finance for various social, economic, and religious activities. Such funds would be invested in various socioeconomic projects like energy supply in a locality, capacity building and training centers, agro-based small- and medium-level units, and any diversified pool of properties. The "Fund of Islamic Funds" would serve as a multimanager and might be operated jointly by the regulator's representatives and the private-sector investors to help any fund at the time of dire need for liquidity. In many cases the properties of *awqāf* can be securitized through the issuance of *ṣukūk* on the usufruct of *waqf* properties. The proceeds could be used to expand operations and build new social projects.

3.6 Summary and Conclusion

The institution of *waqf* achieved its apex during the Ottoman period in terms of numbers, assets, and the services it rendered to the citizens ranging from municipal services to religion, education, health, culture, and business. As a multipurpose tool for social and economic development, it played a role throughout Islamic history, of course with some gaps due to colonialism and the commercial mindset emerging from the western capitalistic paradigm. Prophet Muhammad (PBUH) dedicated his *awqāf* for all welfare-oriented purposes including, inter alia, the poor and needy, disaster relief, the travelers, the migrants, etc. (Cajee, 2022). While educational institutions, hospitals, and travelers' inns were included in the *waqf* beneficiaries list soon after the Islamic state expanded in AD 8th and 9th century, the Ottomans started financing the traders, craftsmen businesses, and farmers from the *awqāf* funds.

Cash *waqfs* served the role of financier, granting loans to people in need of them (Çizakça, 2000). The returns obtained by the cash *waqfs* were also channeled to the public purposes determined by the *waqf* founder ranging from education to food support for the poor, etc. (Çizakça, 2006). The *waqf*-based structure of Islamic social finance has a broader scope for spending the funds donated with virtuous objectives for better socioeconomic impact in terms of shared growth and welfare of the community.

The banking and nonbanking financial institutions operating under the capitalistic framework are not inclined to finance the entrepreneurial start-ups that could activate poor and developing economies for realizing the objectives of sustainable growth and shared prosperity. The re-emerging institution of *waqf* can fill the gap as an institution for social and entrepreneurial finance by generating and providing perpetual social finance. Flexibility in the rules of *waqf* enables it to serve beneficiaries directly or through financial institutions and to provide a wide range of social services.

Balance growth in a broader perspective is the key to sustainability. It is possible by promoting entrepreneurship for creating wealth at micro and family's level. For commercial reasons, microfinance programs in general usually miss the poor and hence are ineffective in reducing poverty or facilitating growth (Saad & Anuar, 2009). "Beyond market" institutions and tools, namely, *waqf*, *zakāh*, and *'ushr*, and supply of *qard al hasan* will be facilitating the entrepreneurship in poor families. It will ensure employment of all such persons who could make any value addition to the processes of production, distribution, and exchange of wealth as per market norms. Those who may not be in position to add any value due to any inability would be sharing in the growth through transfer payments.

Lack of finance and avenues for capacity building for the younger population are the major causes of low levels of entrepreneurship in developing economies, of course, with some other infrastructure and policy-related factors (Haneef et al., 2014). The improved capacity building and health infrastructure developed with funds from the cash *awqāf* can enhance the income-earning potential of *waqf* beneficiaries. Developing cash *waqf* financing model would improve the financial services for micro- and medium-level entrepreneurs. Based on such financial infrastructure, the micro-level businesses and production activities would overcome their financial challenges and obligation in business and commerce (Lahsasna, 2010).

As most of the Muslim-majority countries are developing with huge debts and debt-servicing obligations resulting in fiscal deficits, they generally lack capacity for development spending and financing the micro-business and production sectors (Shaikh et al., 2017). Any growth-oriented finance programs for micro business and entrepreneurship in commodity-producing sectors also need to provide training, capacity building, and micro takaful facilities (Obaidullah & Khan, 2008). In the economies like that of Pakistan, developing the *waqf*-based financing framework could be helpful as a complementary alternative to governments, banks, and financial institutions which might not be in a position to finance the start-ups and the entrepreneurs because of lack of funds and collateral or commercial nonviability.

Cash *waqf* funds would be invested in diversified portfolios with proper risk-mitigation measures and the return thus generated would play a crucial role in augmenting the incomes from immovable properties of *awqāf*. The funds thus collected could be used for financing the entrepreneurs on the basis of all valid modes like *qard*, in which case the loanees may like to donate as cash *waqf* at their discretion, as in case of 'Akhuwat' , trade and leased based contracts and partnership-based modes, and hybrid structures while ensuring that every financial contract has proper linkage with the real sector activity or business based on Islamic law of contracts. Bahrain-based AAOIFI has provided the best benchmarks for Sharī'ah-compliant and feasible contract structures in the form of Sharī'ah standards, the governance standards, and the ethics standards.

The *awqāf* would also establish capacity building, training in emerging technologies, and orientation and awareness centers. Such capacity building centers may also enable the senior/experienced professionals such as software engineers, engineers in other technologies, and doctors to offer services through the *awqāf* network for growth, and welfare of the entrepreneurs and their families. It has been empirically proved that such professionals are eager to donate both time and money with welfare objectives (Shaikh et al., 2017).

Unlike *zakāh* money, *waqf* funds have a flexible option for investments and using for either public or the deserving. So, *waqf* can provide a better usage for the best allocation of resources. Use of *waqf* or other social funds for business entrepreneurial financing has not been a priority in Islamic society. Of course, there is a possibility that cash *waqfs*, based on returns from investment of *waqf* funds and the immovable *waqf* assets, are used for permanent source of earnings for the poor, and the potential entrepreneurs. *Waqf* funds may provide a large spectrum of opportunities for developmental activities. Such activities may include farming, production of goods and services, trade of goods for public use and facilitating the government services or subsidizing the public goods, and many more.

Notes

1 Guilds (*naqabat*), by definition, were organizations intended to provide a support network and protect the common interests of their members, craftsmen, traders, or members of a certain profession generally. These were the pre-capitalist industrial organization in Western Europe from the 12th century. These continued up to the middle of the 19th century when the craft guilds were abolished with the introduction

of free trade (Gustafsson, 1987). So, Ottoman craftsmen's organizations – guilds were the organizations for providing a support network.

2 In summer, they traveled northward to Syria and Palestine, for they are cool lands, and in winter southward to Yaman, etc. for they are warm.

3 In the capitalistic structure, the difference between the salaries of the top management and the employees in lower and even middle cadres is untenably high. It is the case even in present-day Islamic banks and financial institutions resulting in unfair treatment and injustice with the latter (employees) (see Ayub, 2019).

4 According to Islamic law of transfer of property to others, one can write a *wasiyah*/ "will" to give, during life, a part of wealth to anyone and for any purpose, with a condition that transfer will be effective after the testator's death. Only up to one-third of one's property, not beyond that, could be given so that the rights of the legal heirs are not adversely affected. *Wasiyah* can be made only for the benefit of nonheirs.

5 Here three interesting phrases are used by the author. The words used, "major trade capital", if depict the reality, suggest that entrepreneurial activity was a main objective of these *waqfs*. Second phrase is "substantial capital pooling" that shows that there was not a small *waqf* effort by trading entrepreneurs. Third phrase is "merchant partnerships" which indicates that these were ribā-free arrangements.

6 Most of the *waqf* land was being managed through Timār. Timār was a land tenure system for the conquered lands that were distributed among soldiers against their free service in sultan's army.

4 *Waqf* for Accelerating Socioeconomic Development

4.1 Introduction

In Islamic history, *waqf* has been working as the most effective institution for broad-based socioeconomic activities with mutual efforts in an organized way. It facilitated for (re)distribution of resources for social as well as economic objectives, with other tools like *zakāh*, *sadaqat*, and *infāq fi Sabeel Allah* (IFS) (Tohirin, 2010). In the present-day Islamic world, *waqf* must be revived and used as a tool for economic and community-based services.

Economists may suggest this institution to the policymaking departments in Islamic countries' economies to complement the "market" and the State's efforts for growth and prosperity with social progress. It will help in the accomplishment of the responsibility of the state and make the economy efficient and socially inclusive.

The State must provide the means of sustenance, that is, food, clothing, housing, and such other basic facilities so that everyone may maintain a family in a befitting way. These are fundamental rights and everybody, irrespective of race, religion, caste, and class, is entitled to them. The State, the society, and the individuals are responsible for ensuring that no one sleeps hungry or is shelterless. The Prophet's saying, "*Each one of you is a shepherd, and all of you are responsible for your flocks*" (Bukhari, 893). It explains responsibility at different levels. The Prophet (PBUH) encouraged the provision of security for the widows, orphans, and the poor as he highlighted in one of his sayings:

> The one who looks after and works for a widow and for a poor person (dependent), is like a warrior fighting for the cause of Allah, or like a person who fasts during the day and prays throughout the night.

Historically, *waqf* played a role in developing various aspects of society and the economy (Zuki, 2012). The *waqf* went beyond meeting the immediate needs of the poor to provide means for long-term amelioration and welfare. Çizakça (1998) indicated that from the Atlantic to the Pacific, all over the vast Islamic world, the *awqāf* system financed and maintained, for

DOI: 10.4324/9781003477549-4

centuries, magnificent works of architecture as well as a myriad of services vitally important for society.

Waqf also played a role in realizing *maqāsid* al *sharī'ah* and safeguarding the Islamic beliefs, values, and culture in the colonized areas of the world. Bosnia, once the land of *waqf*, was a great example of this system in Eastern Europe during the Ottoman Caliphate's rule (1463–1878). There, it helped the Muslims against the constant threat to socioeconomic, political, and cultural problems and eased many of their worries by granting them greater recognition and protection as opposed to their marginalization by the Roman and Byzantium empires (Omercic, 2018).

According to Kahf (2003), *waqf* emanates from principles of the sharī'ah and Muslim culture. It involves immovable properties like land and buildings, and liquid *waqf*, shares and stocks for public utilities, social work, agricultural machinery, livestock, etc. (Omercic, 2018). Although *waqfs* have served predominantly for specific religious purposes it has also been used in education, health, infrastructure, etc. (Çizakça, 2000; Sadeq, 2002; Kahf, 2003). *Masjid* which is *waqf* for Allah (SWT) has been serving as a "Community Development Centre" throughout Islamic history (Spahić, 2014).

While conventional economics results in "survival of the fittest" (Pirson & Lawrence, 2010), broad-based welfare-oriented development is ultimately good for human society and requires the concept of "Mutual survival" of mankind. This objective can better be served by promoting the culture of doing charity by developing the system of *waqf*.

4.2 The Concept and Facets of Socioeconomic Development

Development can be defined as a process of self-reliant growth, achieved through the participation of the people acting in their own interests as they see them, and under their own control (South Commission, 1990). It implies that the participation of the people for their own interests as they consider, and under their control is the crucial element in the process and objective of development.

Human beings by nature are social beings and the opportunity of living in society does bring several benefits and creates some responsibilities (Hasan, 2007). The development in an Islamic country would require that the growth process must involve the ethical and social norms of Islam that conform to the norms prescribed by the divine authority as per the natural requirements of human society. Therefore, the social sector entailing religious (belief system), social, and cultural aspects is part and parcel of an Islamic society. The objectives of such a process would be to eliminate extreme poverty, provide productive employment, and satisfy the basic needs of all through the efficient functioning of market forces, and by transfer of resources based on beyond market institutions (Choudhury, 2009; Ayub, 2022). It is the broader concept of welfare, which was accepted even by the father of modern economics, Adam Smith. Smith [1976 (1837), p. 46] made several points to establish an important link between the philosophical and economic aspects of his study of man in the society, while constituting a reminder that welfare should not be considered solely in economic terms.

Traditionally, socioeconomic development refers to the development in economic and social indicators in an economy leading to the welfare of the society. It refers to the transformation of the society in an economy about social and economic dimensions. The significance of socioeconomic development is explained by Stemplowski (1987, p. 5). A sufficiently high growth in GDP, PCI, and other measure of economic growth would be supplemented by equity and income-distribution aspects and improvements in the social indicators. It involves a higher level of efficiency, well-being, human development with humane consideration, and social policy with justice adjusted with the economic policies.

Social development is the ultimate objective of economic development to bring about sustained improvement in the well-being of individuals, families, community, and society at large. Socioeconomic development embraces changes taking place in the social sphere, mostly of an economic nature (Chojnacki, 2010). It involves a sustained increase in the economic standard of living of the masses, normally accomplished by improvement in living standards in relative terms while keeping in view the social and cultural norms of any society.

Two basic types or models of the development process can be distinguished: (1) spontaneous processes, and (2) target-oriented processes governed by the activity and behavior of people and designed to achieve certain specified final states that can be the goals of any development-related activity.

Islam provides the second model of socioeconomic development involving economic as well as philosophical aspects. It not only harnesses the instinct of self-interest in line with the market forces that operate with a right and nature-oriented discipline but also makes others' interests competitive to self-interest by putting a divine reward of spending for others more than 700 times the worldly reward (Qur'ãn 2:261). Based on this paradigm, the inner and behavioral part (values system) must be integrated into the outer life socioeconomic matters. Accordingly, economic thought and practices must be restructured based on values that are the same in all religions. Thus, a broader-level composition of an Islamic economy can be depicted in Figure 4.1.

For a balanced society characterized by common welfare, Islamic law provides a framework that creates a desirable balance through efficient market forces and the best allocation of resources. The state is required to take remedial measures in case justice is not available to any group or individuals in society. The tools include both obligatory and optional activities involving the transfer of resources for creating balance in the society for peaceful co-survival. Such optional actions are charities beyond *zakāh* and *'ushr*, relieving hardships of others, and cooperation for risk and reward

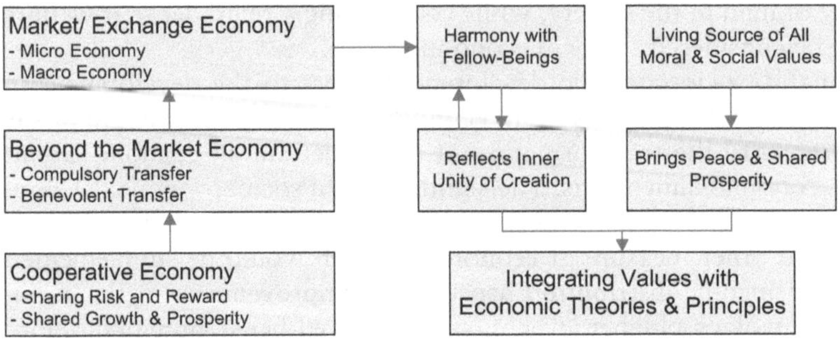

Figure 4.1 Broader-Level Composition of an Islamic Economy.

Source: Ayub (2022, p. 277).

sharing at the community level. The voluntary institution of *waqf* provided an effective tool for the Ottomans to face the challenge of the rising capitalistic paradigm of concentration of wealth in the era of colonization. *Waqf* was basic to the redistribution policy.

Waqf is a specialized institution for "socioeconomic development" (an umbrella phrase for broad-based welfare of society), achieved through the provision of health, education, and shelter besides widening the choices for economic opportunities. Community development is the better word that should be used to reflect the changes that the *waqf* organizations can initiate for social inclusion. In this study, therefore, we will elaborate upon socioeconomic development mainly in the context of community development.

In line with features of an Islamic economy, as depicted earlier, socioeconomic development leading to balanced and shared growth can be depicted in Figure 4.2.

Waqf played a role in the development of agriculture and rural economy, industry and urban economy, and business. The institution was developed systematically to take care of social, economic, financial, and commercial needs and even relationships between different stakeholders in the economy including artisans, entrepreneurs, investors, employees, and even the associations of artisans and traders called "guilds". Guilds were part of traditional Ottoman economic organizations at the time when capitalism was taking its roots in Europe. In the 17th century, there were several hundred guilds in Istanbul. During this period, the urban community was literate and innovative and could help keep a balance between the growth of emerging industries and the system of corporations. Guilds organized the craftsmen by registration, training, and providing credit. They were part of an effective model for the development of the economy as an Islamic alternative to capitalism.

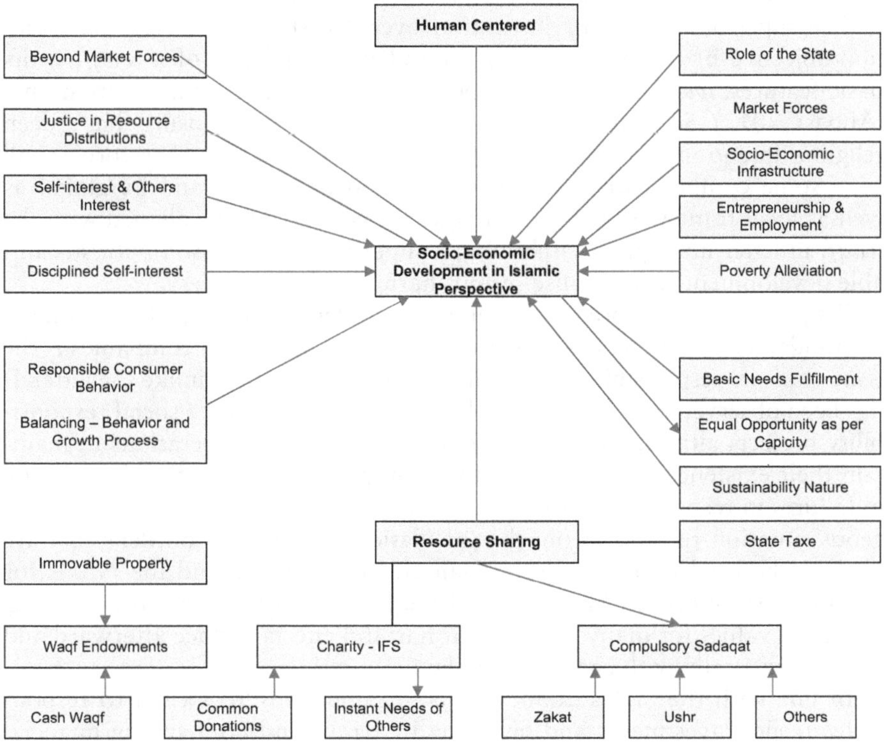

Figure 4.2 Socioeconomic Development in Islamic Perspective.

Source: Authors' own.

4.2.1 Waqf *Foundations versus Companies: Role in Development*

Modern companies/corporations represent the main pillar of present-day capitalistic economies to maximize the shareholders' value. The *waqf*-based structure, on the other hand, coupled with the Islamic perspective of remuneration of various factors of production, tends to maintain a balance in the distribution of resources among all members of the economy (Ayub, 2022, pp. 143–166, Chap. 6). *Waqf* and trust (as used in present-day economic framework) both are aimed at socioeconomic development. As indicated in Chapter 2, the term "trust" is borrowed from the Islamic term "*waqf*" (Wynen, 1949). The added feature of "*waqf*" of course is its religious ground in the light of which believers are incentivized to spend in the cause of Allah (SWT) with a sentiment of sacrifice for others' benefits. Contrary to the present-day companies, the most significant element underlying the establishment of *waqf*-based foundations, movable or immovable, is the idea of social responsibility, cooperation, and common welfare for self-purification.

The superiority of *waqf* institution over "trust" stems from the intention/objective of the donating person and the perpetuity of a *waqf*. In its basic features, *waqf* is irrevocable, perpetual, inalienable, and unconditional (Abbasi, 2012). So, it requires an environment that must ensure that a deep religious intention stays within the framework of the *waqf*. Therefore, it will have some conflict with the secular tradition of "trust" and its global as well as local frameworks. Such frameworks will have to be aligned with the *waqf*, in letter and spirit. Otherwise, a superficial comparison with sustainable development would cause serious harm to Islamic society.

Waqf foundations pool the resources, as modern companies do. But one of the fundamental differences between *waqf* foundations and companies is the issue of social responsibility that is inbuilt into the former, unlike the latter. It has been observed that present-day businesses underestimate social responsibility projects although they perform compact financial operations to maintain their existence. However, the focus on profit maximization is resulting in failures in respect of the social and sustainability factors. The disadvantageous situation resulting from the calculation of the extra burdens that are likely to be bred by the projects financed by the banks and the NBFIs for earnings maximization has estranged the businesses from social and environmental values for many years. Their harmful effects surface afterward and rise incrementally with each passing day.

In line with the SDGs 2030, efforts are underway to switch to responsible/greener investments and financing by banks and nonbanking financial institutions (NBFIs) and funds. However, little success is visible, and it has been noticed that the bigger banks and NBFIs of developed and industrialized countries are bigger offenders of the green financing protocols. A recent study concludes that[1]

> The findings have been calculated by looking at the overall carbon footprint of the UK's major banks, including investment in fossil fuels, and the proportion of their overall net assets represented by each £1,000 saved by an individual in the bank.

Accordingly, only a system with an inbuilt discipline like Islam's social finance system could help avoid social and environmental hazards.

By virtue of the endowments made on a *waqf* basis, the support offered to the poor, widows, and orphans, the sick and disabled, those who are about to start a business or get married and other needy people reflects the major function of the Islamic social system. The foundations during the Ottoman era that served just like the social security institutions or pension funds in our day also provided for the repair and maintenance of architectural works of art and infrastructural investments. As a notable indicator of the care for the environment, the underground and overland natural sources in the Ottoman state functioned as foundation enterprises (Gürsoy, 2018).

4.2.2 *Awqāf-Related Business Associations and Economic Development*

Micro businesses, cottage industries, and small business associations may serve as an effective link among the state institutions dealing with welfare aspects, the entrepreneurs and business community getting funds from *awqāf*, employees, and the donors/holders of *waqf* certificates/*al-khair ṣukūk*. This process would be like that of Ottoman guilds and similar associations that maintained an effective linkage among the various stakeholders. There were hundreds of thousands of artisans with skills, expertise, and experience in all spheres of life. Their scientific education, innovation, and industrialization of their innovative products could have led to the indigenous industrial revolution.

But there was no conscious effort to support the innovative options of the guilds. It was also due to ignoring the power of the collective capital accumulation by *awqāf* and the financial support for the innovators at the community level. It had a cost that the industry in the infancy stages was not adopted at a collective level by the *waqfs* and the guilds. Instead, it turned into a capitalistic move. One such example was contracting the construction of the railways to European firms. This is how the centuries-old institution of guilds was not utilized for development.

Many studies have argued that cash *waqf* can pool more resources and ensure wider participation of individual donors (Sadeq, 2002; Sheikh et al., 2017). The idea of perpetual corporate entities that are based on share capital/equity has already been accepted by the Sharīʿah scholars.

4.3 Islamic Perspective of Market Economy and *Waqf*

An Islamic economy is also a market-based economy added, of course, by value proposition and inbuilt disciplines for exchange and nonexchange dealings. The paradigm and the approach are different from that of capitalistic liberalism. It tends to make human beings responsible for using carefully the resources created by nature, and in dealing with others. In other words, it deals with (i) the market or the exchange economy at micro and macro levels, (ii) beyond market economy – also termed as the third-sector economy which comprises the benevolent transfer of resources, value-based social enterprises, social cum microfinance systems, social business, care for others, etc. (Molla & Alam, 2013). Specifically, it involves compulsory as well as benevolent transfers to the poor and the persons of lesser means; and (iii) the cooperative economy where people share the risks and the fortunes for attaining shared prosperity. According to Qur'ān (2:177), the real virtue, in addition to a firm belief in Allah (SWT), is spending on the near kinsmen, the orphans, the indigent, the wayfarers, and the needy, and in freeing the slaves and keeping up the prayer, and paying the *zakāh* . It highlights the virtuous and cooperative behavior that Islam cherishes and requires for human society.

The State must protect the life, property, respect, and other civil rights of all citizens. The state has also to play an enabling role in providing infrastructure and a peaceful atmosphere necessary for efficient working of the markets. A *hadith* beautifully defines the fundamental rights of everyone in a society, "The Son of Adam has no better right than that he would have a house wherein he may live, a piece of clothing whereby he may hide his nakedness and a piece of bread and some water" (Tirmidhi, 2341, 4/150). The rulers have to be mindful to fulfill this responsibility as they are accountable to Allah (SWT) for this. In a famous saying, the pious Caliph Umar (RA) said, "*If a sheep dies on the bank of the Euphrates, Almighty Allah will ask me about it on the Day of Judgment*" (cf. Ayub, 2022, p. 275).

Society as a whole or the Muslim community is also responsible for ensuring that all people of a community can fulfill their basic needs. According to a hadīth (Hanbal, 2001, Vol 8, p. 481), if a person in a community remains hungry overnight, the whole community is removed from the protection of Allah. It may imply that if a community is not able to provide necessary food to all its members, a hungry person who commits the crime of theft for food will not be punished by the amputation of hand.

4.3.1 Consumer and Firm Behavior and the Role of Waqf

The behavior of individuals and firms is crucial in enabling society for realization of the objective of socioeconomic development. Self-interest at the micro level is associated to the community's interest in such a way that individuals abstain from devouring the others' rights, while they are eager to help others in an orderly and formal manner. It would result in an exchange system based on independent market forces and sharing of resources for the community's welfare at a larger level.

Negation of extravagance and consumption beyond required limits would help in sharing resources for the welfare of all in society. Maximizing wealth in self-interest without caring for the just rules of exchange, and then giving charity in an unsystematic way may not be leading to development with social inclusion. It highlights the role of *waqf*, particularly the cash *waqf*. The act of creating *waqfs* gets strength from belief in Allah and the Day of Judgment (*ākhirah*). As per a *hadith* reported in Sahih Muslim, "*When a man dies, all his acts come to an end, except three: ongoing charity, beneficial knowledge by which people benefit, or a righteous child who prays for him*". It provides sufficient incentive to rich Muslims to donate their assets to the beneficiaries or the Ummah for their well-being.

Rationality in the Islamic perspective is the use of common sense in the perspective of normative values. Hence, rationality reflects an attitude of responsibility in behavior while remaining within the limits set by the Sharīʿah and fulfilling the needs of the fellow being. This has to be done to please Allah SWT and for self-betterment in this life and the hereafter. Height of righteousness can be attained only by serving human beings and spending good/loved things for benefit of others (Qur'an 3:92).

There are specific rules for exchanging common goods and that of money. The most important rules in this context are: (i) one cannot get the right of others in any exploitative/illegal way; (ii) there must be complete disclosure and transparency in exchange matters; (iii) money is only a medium of exchange, not a tradable commodity like other goods; and (iv) short selling is banned except with the conditions applicable for *salam* and *istisnā'a* sales.

Mutual care by the members of a Muslim society became the basis of the Islamic legal maxim "*al-dharar-o-yuzal*" (damage/harm/calamity should be removed/eliminated). Due to its broader coverage, Islamic socioeconomic system is unique as developed by the Prophet (PBUH) and the Companions (RA) who were also the merchants, under divine guidance (*wahi*). Under this system, income/profit can be earned as much as possible, but through legitimate means, keeping in view ethical values with complete disclosure and free consent of the other party to the contract.

Box 4.1 The Basic Principles of *Infāq fi sabil Allah*

(i) Seeking countenance of Allah with high standard of intentions and not to expect any favor from anyone in return;
(ii) Spending for increase in self-purification, not to showoff;
(iii) Patience and self-contentment expected of the givers and takers – *deserve before you desire*;
(iv) Must be practiced at home first;
(iv) To be paid when others' need is seen, on time when due;
(v) Proactive behavior – finding out the needy and making the best possible use of spending for others;
(vi) Purposive spending – to accomplish good causes, e. g. poverty alleviation, treatment of the sick, provisioning of civic facilities to the deserving class, etc.;
(vii) Inclusiveness – spending for anyone from the needy like relatives, orphans, poor, the wayfarers to get reward from Allah (Qur'an 2:215);
(ix) Altruism in charity – considering that being in a position of giving in charity is a gift of God and spending for self-purification; and
(x) Secrecy in charity, the best option of spending; could be open to encourage others (Qur'an 2:270, 4:114).

(Hasan, 2007)

While extravagance and conspicuous consumption are discouraged and, in some cases forbidden (Qur'ãn 7:31), spending generously for the benefit of others and the society is emphasized and highly appreciated. A Muslim is not expected to go on increasing its consumption without any limit just because of an increase in income. "*He is not a believer whose stomach is filled while the neighbor to his side goes hungry*", warned Prophet Muhammad (PBUH) (Albani, *Sahih al Jamie*, 5382).

Infāq fi sabilillah (IFS – virtuous spending in the way of Allah SWT) is a unique tool for Islamic system, which is not available in the conventional framework, due to the reward of such spending in the hereafter. A minimum of such spending or donation is obligatory and is called *zakāh* and *'ushr*. *Infāq* (of wealth for the benefit of others) is part of the voluntary economic sector. It leads to socioeconomic justice, equality of opportunities to all, and an exploitation-free distribution system. This way, the Islamic economy integrates values with economic theories and principles and creates harmony within fellow beings. The inner unity in society brings peace and prosperity at all levels. The resultant "social inclusion" leads to general welfare in the cooperative framework.

The basic principles of IFS as indicated in Box 4.1 are fully met in making endowments or creating *awqāf*.

The discussion in the aforementioned paragraphs implies that well-to-do people in an Islamic society are responsible for ensuring that all in one's neighborhood are fed. An Islamic economy is to ensure sufficient food for all by prohibiting overeating and lavish style of consumption. It is regarded as extravagance. The Prophet (PBUH) said,

> The Son of Adam will not fill a pot worse for himself than his stomach. It is enough for one to eat a few bites that strengthen his spine. If he likes to have more, then let him fill a third with food, a third with drink and leave a third for his breathing.
>
> (Ibne Ma'jah, 3349)

Accordingly, avoidance of wastage of resources by conspicuous/lavish consumption, motivation to spend for the needy, disclosure and transparency, and creating market efficiency are the distinctive features of economic policy in the Islamic framework. It creates an enabling role for charity giving for the welfare of the society as shown in Figure 4.3.

4.3.2 Potential for Charity Making and Donations for Common Welfare

Islam requires efficiency in creating wealth and justice in distribution. While efficiency is required for maximization of economic prosperity, equity, equal opportunities, and fair treatment to and care for all are key to social harmony. Beyond market economy has to play a role in creating balance in the society, while the State has to play an enabling role in this regard.

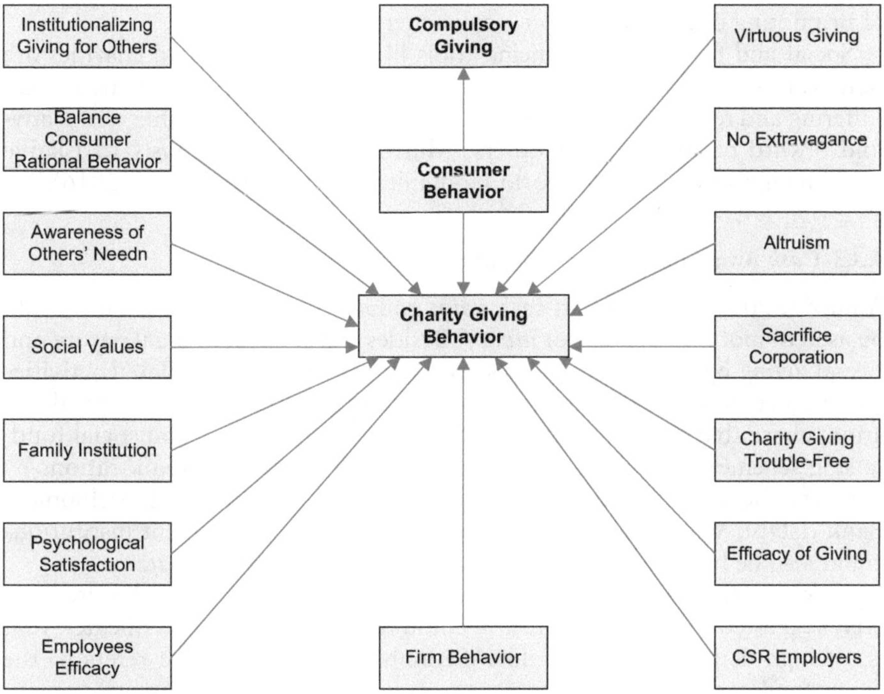

Figure 4.3 Socializing Charity Giving in an Islamic Society.

Source: Authors' own.

But the economic development neither takes place on its own nor is it imminent. It requires certain careful, planned, and financed actions. In this perspective, if the belief and norms of the society are not taken care of, the results could go wrong due to the social disruption. The social disruption can be intensified if the concepts, approaches, methodologies, and finances are borrowed from such foreign and value-free sources that may create extremely poor majority with a few ultrarich and cause socioeconomic disruption in the economy and society. So, *waqf*, based on the Islamic approaches and methodologies, having funding from the well-off citizens in the society and managed efficiently, may avoid any economic and social disruptions.

It would need an institutional framework for systematic transfer of resources from the rich to the poor. The objective of such transfer of resources to the poor can be their permanent rehabilitation, enabling them to do any business in micro/SME framework, and not making them parasites and economically inefficient.

This tends to promote a wider distribution of food, as individuals are encouraged to eat what is required. This is the most salient feature of Islam's "beyond market economy" concept, in contrast to the capitalistic approach of promoting overconsumption – consumerism.

Social and faith-based financing tools like *zakāh*, *waqf*, and charities are significant sources of financing that can be better leveraged to alleviate human suffering and reduce vulnerability. As a part of faith in the hereafter and manyfold reward of spending for others, Muslims donate generously to Islamic social finance mechanisms (World Humanitarian Summit – WHS, 2016).

4.3.3 Cash Awqāf *for Common Welfare*

Ahmed (2007) indicated that cash *waqf* and *waqf ṣukūk* or certificates could be used to mobilize capital for *awqāf*. Besides charity of perpetual nature and casual giving by the public, other sources of fund for *awqāf*-related activities and projects could be the government institutions dealing with poverty alleviation, charitable entities, NGOs working for social welfare, and social fundraising schemes by various groups in the society. CSR-related allocations by banks/financial institutions and other corporations, Islamic Development Bank (IsDB), World Bank, and other international development institutions could also be helpful in supply of necessary funds for the *awqāf*.

Sadeq (2002), while proposing an integrated approach to alleviate poverty, suggested that *waqf* institution could issue two types of certificates, that is, of high denomination and low/medium denomination. He refers to the macro and micro instruments to raise funds for growth and development. The institutions and individuals would be buying these certificates according to their saving capacities. By this, the *waqf* institution can pool cash funds and finance-development projects on sustainable basis. *Takaful* reserves and profit-equalizing reserves can be introduced as a safeguard for the beneficiaries in the case of loan defaults caused by any unforeseen events.

4.4 *Waqf* for Socioeconomic Development in Islamic Cooperative Perspective

Islamic economy seeks to ensure equitable distribution of wealth through its social support system (Hasan, 2007). The four areas of support and cooperation are: (i) *takaful* within the family – provision of maintenance including food, health, clothing, housing, education, marriage support for close relatives, and inheritance and bequests; (ii) *takaful* within the community through *zakāh*; (iii) cooperation among small groups and associations of neighbors and local residents; and (iv) voluntary charities and endowments/ *waqf*.

Waqf served as a tool for general welfare throughout Islamic history. The Ottomans' experience of support for low-income groups and enabling them to initiate any business or production activity through *waqfs* had been a golden experiment. Cash *waqf* also facilitated in providing job and business opportunities, rehabilitation from any calamity, education, and capacity building. It would imply fulfilling the basic needs of all enabling them to add value one way or the other to the community cause.

Poverty is the most serious social problem and *waqf* can play effective role in reducing poverty. Tariq Khan (2015) has indicated seven problems of poverty that could be meted by the *waqf* system. These include (i) hunger – malnutrition (shortage of food leading to ill health); (ii) ill health – inadequate levels of health, lack of medical facilities, medicine, and nonhygienic life; (iii) lack of education and educational opportunities; (iv) lack of shelter, clothing, and empowerment; (v) lack of economic opportunity, economic resources, and lack of income; (vi) lack of water (for drinking, sanitation, and irrigation), public utilities, social welfare, and deficient social relations, poor social, and cultural life.

During the last couple of decades, *waqf* also turned out to be a contributory tool for bridging infrastructural deficit. With this feature, *waqf* can be used for promoting entrepreneurship to provide business opportunities for employment generation, import substitution, enhancing export potential, and thus realizing the objective of financial and social inclusion. Application of *waqf* in social and economic sectors like health, education, civic facilitation for urban population, financing the rural economy and commodity-producing sectors at micro, small, and medium levels could revolutionize the economy of the OIC member states. In the following, we discuss all these aspects in detail.

4.4.1 Economic Role of Awqāf

Development is based on an inquiry about political economy, "*whether the goals of the economic system should be focused upon the exchange value (profit centered production-oriented market based capitalistic system) or upon the use value (impact on people and prosperity for all)?*" If capitalistic system is preferred, then the market decides whom to benefit and whom to exclude. Here, development targets, like the framework of *waqf* and even the SDGs, would be subordinated to the market.

However, the state institutions have to ensure the development for all and not to leave all the decisions on the impulses of the market. A group, in the market, might be getting an increasing share in the wealth and created resources due to any fair or unfair means, while the others might be increasingly devoid of even the basic needs for life. So, the conflict is basic that requires an ongoing review of the results of the market forces while deciding to ensure the aims and objectives of the welfare state and change the implementing strategy as and when needed. It would need efficient function of beyond market or the third sector of economy for transfer of resources to achieve the objective of fair, just, and equitable distribution, and shared growth. The focus of the strategy would be creating a balance between efficiency and social justice while ensuring that economic values are not superimposed on the social values.

It implies that for effective role of any system like that of *waqf*, the present paradigm of maximization of self-interest at any cost will have to be replaced with society's norms and value system. Socioeconomic emergence marks a real turning point, passing from a poor economy to a better with a balance of efficient, equitable, and sustainable growth. Rostow's five stages (1960) for moving from a traditional society to maturity and the age of mass consumption may explain it with the added element of community's role for social cohesion through the beyond market norms and institutions. A voluntary sector of *waqf* is basic in this perspective, to the redistribution policy.

Waqf solves the problem of the undersupply of public goods (and services). Cizkca (1998) reports that the essential services such as health, education, municipal services, etc. were provided through *waqf* at no cost to the government. As such, *awqāf* can significantly contribute toward reduction in government expenditure, and so toward reduction of budget deficit. It lowers the need for government borrowing thus curbing the crowding-out effect and may lead to a reduction in money market rates consequently reining a basic impediment for private investment and growth, Çizakça adds. Thus, the *waqf* system can significantly contribute toward that ultimate goal of every modern economy.

Çizakça (1998) also contends that *awqāf* system can provide basis for gradual elimination of *ribā* and such enabling role of *waqf* should be given serious consideration in countries like Pakistan that have to transform their economies to Islamic principles as per their Constitutional requirements and the Shariah court's judgment (Federal Shariat Court, 2022). Islamic banks, having higher levels of interaction with the real market with the Islamic financial products will have better probability to survive during all good/bad times. Islamic financial products have better appeal for the market being Islamic and then having favorable terms for the producers. So, *ribā* would be eliminated over the time from the market or will become a useless instrument, having no real impact on the financial markets.

4.4.2 Waqf *and Community Development*

Waqf is a crucial tool for ensuring social justice system of Islam (Samiul, 2007). It is comparable to the state's welfare departments, or even more, sustainable, durable, and beneficial for the community, if looked at from the angles of institutionalization, because *awqāf* institutions continue from one government to the other, without any unwarranted interference by political governments.

Community development and SMEs' development are the two main approaches adopted for the socioeconomic development. This approach of socioeconomic development is close to that of the community development that is "*pursuit of solidarity and agency by adhering to the principles of self-help, felt needs, and participation*" as indicated by Bhattacharyya (2004).

The *waqf*-provided finances are injected, by default, to (1) the most deserving people for instant needs, education, and health, and (2) small farms and entrepreneurs that ensure uninterrupted production of goods and services at reasonable rates for the urban population and thus reducing the inflation. The support through financing (and skills) through *waqf* projects is durable and sustainable. It is provided for the poor and the skilled (or for those ready to improve skills) who utilize funds for permanent employment (self-employment) and production. It may lead to the resolution of issues including (i) employment of masses to the most appropriate levels, (ii) best use of the available financial resources that remain underutilized in most of the developing countries due to the lack of trust (among the banks and the entrepreneurs) and due to the lack of implementation of finance related legal frameworks and injustices prevailing at the ground levels, and, last but not least, (iii) production of necessary goods and services at the most affordable prices. It serves the purpose of community development at grassroots level.

Production and enhancing the level of supply (of goods and services) can ease down the inflation pressures. Small farmers and firms financed by *awqāf*, unlike the big corporate entities, can undertake immediate productive activities utilizing local solutions to produce the required goods providing employment at community level. This can lead to reducing the impacts of recessions and inflation for the common people.

Awqāf Properties Investment Fund (APIF) managed by the Jeddah based IsDB on *mudarabah* basis is an investment platform with social impact. Usually, the *awqāf* ministries, directorates, and institutions, Islamic banks and financial institutions, donor institutions, and individual investors provide subscription capital to the APIF. This funding is helping women and young people in Bangladesh with training to develop skills, and a small grant to help them set up their businesses. The training provides knowledge of the business, and reduces the negative impact of discrimination, and human rights (Awqāf Properties Investment Fund, 2022).

In the following, we discuss the role of *waqf* in community development in specific sectors like education and health.

Waqf's *Role in Enhancing Education in Muslim Societies*

Ghani et al. (2019) indicate that educational institutions established under the concept of *waqf* include mosques, schools, and universities.[2] Since the beginning of Islam, in the early 7th century, education has been financed by voluntary contributions and *waqf*. Through *waqfs*, all students, be a poor or a rich, had opportunities available for self-development and knowledge. Government financing of education also used to take the form of constructing a school and assigning certain property as *waqf* that provided regular revenues to cover the operating expenses of the school.

Awqāf of the Ayubites (1171–1249) and the Mamalik (1249–1517) in Palestine, Syria, Lebanon, and Egypt are good examples. Islamic cities like

Cairo, Baghdad, al-Quds, and Nishapur were relics of *waqf*-financed education. The 9th-century University of al-Qarawiyyin in Fez is the oldest existing university in Morocco. Excellence was exercised by many Islamic institutions like al-Azhar University (Mujani, Abdullah, & Bakar, 2012) and public institutions of Malaysian higher learning (Mujani, Muttaqin, & Khalid, 2014), to name a few.

Waqf financing of education usually covered libraries, books, salaries of teachers and other staff, and stipends to students. Financing was not restricted to religious studies; it covered all branches of knowledge including science, philosophy, and translation of books from other languages. In addition to freedom of education, this approach of financing helped creating a learned class not derived from the rich and ruling classes. At times, the majority of Muslim scholars used to be coming from the poor segments of the society and very often they strongly opposed the policies of the rulers (Kahf, 1992).

Caliph al-Ma'mun made a vital change in the institutionalization of the *waqf* by giving an important concept of "*agency endowment*". Al-Mamun argued that the continuity of educational/scientific activity was not dependent on philanthropic rulers only, but also required public support (Ashrohah, 2012). Agency endowment meant the establishment of independent *waqf* organizations with the financial support from rulers as well as from public philanthropic donations. It resulted in establishing scientific and cultural institutions that can be termed as permanent endowments, or the independent *awqāf* that were neither under the state nor under the clergy. These served as purpose-guided (educational and scientific studies) *waqfs*, supported by the state, *'ulema* and the public. Many of these took the form of family *waqf*. The advent of the independent "agency *waqf*" and the "family *waqf*" was a key aspect of institutionalization of *waqf*, which took the form of "trust" in the western civilization. The socioeconomic value of this change in the nature of the *waqf* has yet to be understood, in full.

The educational institutions and systems of pondok in Malaysia in 15th century and *madāris* in Pakistan and India by Muslim rulers since the beginning of the 8th century after the conquest of Muhamad Bin Qasim and Arab countries point toward the inevitability of the *waqf* for the Muslim society.

Malaysia had *waqf* practices among the earlier Muslims when pondok and madrasah (religious schools) were founded on *waqf* land. Examples include Madrasah Hamidiah (now Maahad Mahmud) in Kedah, Madrasah al-Sultan Zainal Abidin (now a university) in Terengganu and Kolej Islam Malaya (now Kolej Islam Klang and Kolej Islam Sultan Alam Shah) in Selangor (Khoo, 1980; Mohd Syakir et al., 2015 as reported in Mujani et al., 2017). The nationalization of these *waqf* institutions by the government caused a disruption into the tradition of *waqf*.

Currently a variety of *waqf*-related activities for promoting education are undertaken in various parts of the world. The sources for *waqf*-funded education in Malaysia, Indonesia, Türkiye, and the United Kingdom comprise cash *waqf*, business activities by *awqāf*/trusts, and allocations by government and respective alumni. Pitchay et al. (2018) and Mahamood & Rahman (2015) indicate that *waqf* funds are alternative sources of funding for universities which could reduce the burden of the government in supporting the university's expenses. This type of *waqf* is important in providing the financial assistance to the community and also strengthening the academic quality of the students. In Malaysia, the instruments of cash *waqf* are used to solicit donation from public raised either through salary deduction via electronic means or by setting up special fund for education purposes such as research, development, providing education facilities that benefit the students, and so on.

In Bangladesh, the "IsDB-Bhaban" building is a *waqf* property of the Islamic Development Bank and Bangladesh Islamic Solidarity Education Waqf (IsDB-BISEW) estimated to be worth $50 million. The complex has been rented out allowing the *waqf* to earn stable financial income. For the year 2018–19, the gross income of the complex was approximately $4.56 million. It has enabled IsDB-BISEW to have a sinking fund of $10.68 million. The *waqf* allocates about $1.23 million each year for educational and human resource development purposes and to support the programs including (i) the IT Scholarship Program, (ii) the Vocational Training Program, (iii) the Madrasah Program, (iv) Scholarships for 4-Year Diplomas in Engineering Program, and (v) the Orphanage Program. These programs have served over 42.5 thousand beneficiaries, creating over 6.5 thousand job placements. The IT scholarship program is to transform unemployed non-IT university graduates into a productive workforce. The Vocational Training Program aims to help high school dropouts and boost their abilities to create jobs in the fields of electricity, mechanics, and welding and fabrication. It is also to create opportunities for Vocational Program graduates of the Madrasah Program to complete 4-year Engineering Diplomas in government polytechnic institutes by providing necessary expenses. *Waqf* also helps in several running courses for orphans of the Khaiyarbhanga Orphanage in Madaripur.

In Iran, Pakistan, India, Khurasan, Transoxania, and Afghanistan, madrasahs were also endowed with permanent sources of income, such as land, or rent-bearing urban property, set aside in perpetuity. These *waqfs* paid the salaries of the faculty and stipends for students. In Bangladesh, more than 8,000 educational institutions have been established on the basis of *waqf* as reported by Salarzehi et al. (2010).

b) Awqāf *for Health Facilities*

Other users of *waqf* revenues include health services which cover construction of hospitals and spending on physicians, apprentices, patients and medicines, and medical pharmaceutical research. Hospitals and medicines had been the most famous subsectors of *awqāf* (Ahmed, 2007). *Awqāf* for health services covered the expenses on patients as well as the provision of physicians and training, besides construction of hospitals. In addition to construction of male and female bathrooms in hospitals, *waqf* provided food and special clothes to the patients. In *awqāf* created by women, health services received the lion's share and many hospitals had been established offering medical education and free treatment to poor patients (Tariq Khan, 2015).

In 88 *hijrah*, the Caliph Walid ibn Abd al-Malik was the first who built a hospital (*bimāristan*) and appointed doctors and paid them to care for the sick and for quarantine of the lepers. The revenue of *waqf* was used for the maintenance and running costs of the hospital, and sometimes even small stipends to the patients upon discharge. Such hospitals in the 3rd Islamic century were spread all over the Islamic world and were a source of happiness for the Muslim community because the patients received treatment, care, food, and clothing. Additionally, many hospitals performed the function of a medical education center along with treating the patients.

Mannan (2005) and Hasan (2006) indicated that an important beneficiary of Muslim *awqāf* had been the health and hygiene sector. In Egypt, Ibn Tulun built the first hospital in 261 H, and endowed it with several *waqfs* to provide for its expenses. According to Abattouy and Al-Hassani (2013), in every town of reputation in Islamic world, particularly Cairo, Baghdad, Makkah, Madina, Aleppo, Tunis, Ray, Granada, and Marrakech, there had been at least one *waqf* hospital.

Al-Nuri Hospital was built on *waqf* land in Damascus in AD 1145. It remained in operation for seven centuries and was one of the first hospitals to adopt medical records. Doctors were paid from the endowed funds and the *waqfs* covered all expenses on food, lodging, medicine, and treatment of the patients. In the early 20th century, *awqāf* healthcare centers and hospitals were established in Türkiye. Shishli Children Hospital was founded in 1898 in Istanbul out of the *waqf* fund.

In Spain, hospital facilities were available for both Muslims and non-Muslims alike. The well-known Qalāwūn Complex built by Sultan Al-Nasir Muhammad Ibn Qalawun in AD 1284–85 in Cairo included a hospital, a school, and a mausoleum. It was once the most impressive hospital of its time and functioned throughout the late Ottoman period, till 1910. In the Complex, medicines were prepared in addition to the research and *teaching* facilities. The hospital provided medicine, food, clothing, and shelter to the sick and poor. Pharmaceutical drugs were also produced for medical treatment.

4.4.3 Waqf, Maqāsid al Sharī'ah, *and the SDGs*

Well-being of community is one of the higher purposes (*maqāsid*) of sharī'ah (Khan et al., 2019). *Waqf* as an optional and perpetual charity in the form of endowments of tangible and liquid assets plays a crucial role for alleviating poverty and realizing the higher purposes of Sharī'ah by extending welfare and benefit (*maslahah*) to mankind and preventing it from harms and hardships (*mafsadah*). Accordingly, researchers suggest that there is a deep and strong interrelationship between *waqf* and *maqāsid al sharī'ah* for preservation of humans.

Waqf resources are used for spreading the message of Islam, creating awareness among the people about the injunctions of Qur'an and Sunnah, and for understanding the righteousness, piety, and contentedness. It provides sustenance to the poor, orphans, needy, sick, and unemployed, thus helps in building the social bridges in the society for coherence. *Waqf* also helps in keeping the Islamic traditions and culture alive as the tradition of teaching Islamic *fiqh* and memorizing Holy Qur'an, management of *masājid*. Last, but not least, it helps in promoting entrepreneurship, developing agriculture and micro business, strengthening industry, thus realizing the economic objectives.

The SDGs (2030)/the targets in areas of poverty reduction, health, education, job opportunities and empowerment of women, and sustainability of climate are part of a comprehensive global agenda to end poverty in a single generation, and sustainability of human beings. Since 2015, the IDB and UNDP have been working for realization of the SDGs through a memorandum of understanding. According to the IDB-WB Report (2016) the World Bank Group aims to achieve a more equitable distribution of growth benefits by focusing on the advancement of the poor and vulnerable segments of the society. It relies on policies such as (i) raising growth potential, (ii) financial and social inclusion, (iii) fiscal sustainability, (iv) environmental sustainability, and (v) institutional and governance reforms.

All aforementioned policy-related functions require funding which is becoming increasingly scarce in developing countries due mainly to the increasing debt-servicing requirements. *Waqf* could be the best option for Islamic countries facing debt stress provided a proper framework is made available in making formalized charity easy and its effective use in all socio-economic areas in the economy.

Globally, the development of educational institutions such as Harvard, Oxford, and Cambridge has been through the concept of *waqf*-like endowments. "The Sutton Trust Report (2003)" states: "the way forward is through endowment". *Waqf* fund injection can reduce the government expenditure for specific purposes, especially education. The study also observed that *waqf* fund successfully upgraded the education system in these countries and provided opportunity for the poor and needy.

Abdullah (2018) finds that most of 17 developmental goals of the SDGs comfortably match with the higher purposes of Sharī'ah and so with those of the *awqāf*. There might be some cultural issues in respect of some goals but the goals that are crucial in welfare of a Muslim society certainly include: no poverty, zero hunger, good health and well-being, education for all, clean water and sanitation, affordable and clean energy, decent work environment and economic growth, industry, innovation and infrastructure, sustainable cities and communities, responsible consumption and production, climate, life on land, life below water, and partnership to achieve the goals. Islamic countries and societies are required to realize the SDGs in line with their own ethics, culture, and civilization.

Sekolah pondok – Islamic boarding schools – are one good example of *waqf*-based education that began in 1450 in Malacca state of Malaysia. It spread to Kelantan, Terengganu, and Kedah in the 19th century and attained popularity in the early 20th century with trained religious teachers, strong religious beliefs among the Malays, and adequate facilities. However, by 1918, sekolah pondok began to wane due to the colonial mindset with English and Malay schools. In spite of the pressures and challenges, it was not completely eliminated. Among madrasah cum pondok models that are built on the *waqf* land and financed by *waqf* funds include Madrasah Hamidiah, in Kedah, Madrasah Sultan Zainal Abidin in Terengganu and Kolej Islam Malaya in Selangor (Khoo, 1980).

Some government bodies also contribute for *waqf* funds in Malaysia generally to the *awqāf* established by the Universities. University Sains Islam Malaysia (USIM) is managing AL-Abrar USIM Waqf Funds. Under this fund, establishing medical clinics by USIM is a priority which aims to facilitate needy people to get health service. It also gets funds from the Islamic Religious Council of Negeri Sembilan (MAINS) that provided a grant of MYR 2 million. The grant consisted of MYR 1 million as *waqf* endowment and the leftover 1 million as interest-free loan (*qardhul hasan*) to be returned without any cost.

In Indonesia, *waqf funds* finance some higher education institutions such as in Pondok Modern Gontor Darussalam (PMGD) and Islamic University of Indonesia (UII). PMGD is developing more than 20 branches with 21,892 students. Subsequently, alumni of PMGD are widespread around the world. PDMG has 31 kinds of SMEs which consist of material shop for the construction, restaurant, pharmacy shop, stationary shop, and mineral factory. This business uses Mudārabah contract.

In Türkiye, there are no private universities. Whosoever wants to establish university, it must be a nonprofit organization, it cannot be business for profiteering. In 2016, there were around 200 universities; 75 of them were owned by *awqāf* while the rest were in the public sector. Ilim Yayma Foundation is one famous *waqf* in Türkiye. It established Istanbul Sabahattin Zaim University in 2010. This institution is one of the success examples of the *waqf*-based universities in Türkiye. In many cases, the endowment funds by the business community also finances public sector universities based on the principles of *waqf*. There are several requirements from the government for establishing any university.

4.5 Need for *Waqf*-Based Socioeconomic System in Economies Like That of Pakistan

Pakistan is currently facing a serious socioeconomic problem emanating mainly from the huge budgetary and trade deficits, heavy and increasing debt servicing, and unstable exchange rate. The unrestricted market-based trade, bank-friendly monetary and other economic policies have resulted in widening the gap between the rich and the poor. There had been some poverty-alleviation programs but with limited impact. There was some revival in 1980 after reversing the nationalization, as was witnessed in the form of economic growth, increased remittances, improving macrocconomic situation, and decreasing poverty. The *zakāh* and *'ushr* system introduced in early 1980 also played some role as *masjid*-based *zakāh* committees were involved for better utilization of funds for instant use and rehabilitation. But subsequently the system lost its effectiveness due to sectarian differences and politics involved in *zakāh* committees.

The poverty rates increased in 1990s, as the economic situation worsened with high unemployment and external debt plaguing the economy. This period saw limited developments in new antipoverty programs like the launching of the Bait-ul-Mal and Social Action Program (SAP).

The Benazir Income Support Program (BISP) launched in 2008 expanded the coverage of antipoverty schemes. BISP was the largest social safety network in Pakistan with nearly 5.7 million families benefitting by the unconditional cash transfers. The BISP was expanded over time to include conditional cash transfers in the *Waseela-e-Taleem* initiative and livelihood generation. When *Ehsaas* program was launched in 2019, by the new government, BISP became one of the implementing agencies of *Ehsaas*. *Ehsaas*, headed by Dr. Sania Nishtar, worked to integrate more than 134 fragmented and poorly implemented social protection programs under one new program.

Ehsaas comprised 16 programs for 16 disadvantaged groups, 292 initiatives in their support, and 6 quantifiable goals. There were several agencies implementing *Ehsaas'* initiatives. *Ehsaas* has crucially moved beyond the singular cash-transfer model that BISP offered – in line with the global move toward integrated poverty reduction schemes. Instead, in forming a comprehensive approach to antipoverty, BISP-Ehsaas program is moving toward developing the capacity and human capital of beneficiaries, as well as the Government of Pakistan's capabilities to deliver on innovative and comprehensive programs with limited resources (Barber & Shahzad, 2022). However, the available resources are deficient in fulfilling the need for an efficient socioeconomic development process.

The institution of *waqf* and its model for rendering services to the community can be replicated easily, provided a proper and suitable framework is developed and applied in the country. It would also be helpful in realizing all such SDGs 2030 that pertain to economic development and social inclusion in Muslim societies. Accordingly, there is a need to assess the compatibility and usefulness of the *waqf vis-à-vis* the *maqāsid al sharī'ah* and the current focus on UNDP's development agenda like SDGs 2030.

4.6 Summary and Conclusion

Any system, institution, or discipline must involve the effective utilization of society's resources for the well-being of mankind (Smith, 1976). An economic system based on ethics, values, and beliefs provides the best structure for realizing socioeconomic objectives of any society. Every stakeholder in such a system is morally anchored for a common cause that is better served based on the values like excellence, fairness, trust, equity, and cooperation and sacrifice for others (Hassan & Shahid, 2010). The growth and prosperity achieved through the market-based efficient allocation of resources alone is insufficient to attain a balanced and harmonized social environment and broad-based welfare (Alam et al., 2018).

An effective tool for such kind of system is *waqf* that has historically proved its usefulness. It played a significant role in welfare activities by rendering socioeconomic services in the areas of education, healthcare, civic facilities in urban areas, environmental, and other community-based programs. It provided all the essential services to the public at no cost to the state (Çizakça, 1998). As such, *waqf* also played a role in realizing the *maqāsid al Sharī'ah* (Alam et al., 2018).

Waqf creates a permanent, cumulative, and continuously increasing capital base that sustains growth, as well as expands the scope of benevolent activities in addition to compulsory *zakāh* and normal charities. This tool of benevolence benefits all areas of social welfare and economic activities and such sectors that are considered a part of the domain and responsibility of governments (e.g., health, education, and defense) (Kahf, 2012).

Proper education for all is an established tool for social as well as economic growth, and historically *waqf* has played impressive role in this regard. Throughout Islamic empire, it financed educational projects and covered books, libraries, salaries for teachers, and stipends for the students. The support for education facilitated the creation of an educated class beyond the rich and ruling class of society. It implied that offering *waqf*-financed education provided the poor an equal opportunity with the rich in acquiring education. It also contributed to the dynamics of leadership change and wealth circulation in Muslim society, circulated power and wealth, and eliminated the opportunity of creating an aristocratic class that monopolized wealth and political power (Kahf, 2012b).

Fair play, justice, economic equity, and social harmony have to be the basic objectives of economic policy in Islamic framework. All this requires a well-defined enabling role of the State in functioning of the market and beyond market sectors, also including *awqāf*, for socioeconomic justice. A well-functioning *awqāf* system may lead to reduction in government expenditure with associated benefits.

However, the role of the State must not go beyond providing an effective legal, organizational, and regulatory role for ensuring transparency in fulfilling fiduciary and religious duties by *mutawallies*. Nationalization of *awqāf*, and interference in administrative matters of *waqf* properties or use of *waqf* funds caused serious harms to the noble cause of welfare of mankind through *waqf*.

The operational framework of *waqf* may be developed while taking care of all issues pertaining to (i) the *waqf* deed containing different provisions or conditions, (ii) the *wāqif* (the founder of *waqf*), (iii) purpose of *waqf*, (iv) beneficiaries of the *waqf*, and (v) instructions regarding appointment of the trustee (*mutawalli*). The conditions of *waqf* as indicated in the *deed* are crucial and have to be employed as long as they are not against any Sharī'ah injunctions. Legal maxim, "شرط الواقف كنص الشارع" – implying that the condition of the founder of *waqf* has an equal obligation to be fulfilled like the text of the sharī'ah, is crucial in this context and does not allow the State or the management to use the *waqf* funds in any other avenue. Hence the framework must involve such guideline for the potential *waqf* founders.

The institution of *waqf* must be revived in all Islamic societies for rendering socioeconomic services. This role covers much more than the current role of *awqāf* properties dedicated for *masājid*, shrines, and other ritualistic causes as in the case of Pakistan. It would include all nonprofit or for-profit non-governmental sectors entailing social and related economic activities that could lead to welfare of any segments of the society. Islamic banks and financial institutions can use *waqf* to provide social finance for fulfilling their CSR-related and allied obligations toward the society. It suits them better for rendering social obligations by banks against the huge business they are getting from the society, than in the case of typical CSR activities that might be undertaken presently. If handled properly and intellectually, *waqf* could be helpful in realizing all such objectives of *Sharī'ah* that pertain to any facets of socioeconomic aspects of society.

Notes

1 https://pressreleases.responsesource.com/news/103288/britain-s-worst-banks-for-carbon-emissions-revealed/ [13 October 2022]

2 It is important to note that mosque is also categorized as an educational institution.

5 *Waqf*-Based Financial Intermediation, Fintech, and Crowdfunding for Realizing the Potential of Islamic Social Finance

5.1 Introduction

Financial intermediation in human societies is as necessary as blood circulation in human bodies. Modern-day financial institutions are formal intermediaries between those who might have money more than their instant needs and those who might need money for consumption and business purposes. The intermediary services must be as equitable and efficient as the heart is required to efficiently supply blood to all organs required for a healthy human body as a whole. The financial institutions, currently under operation, created problems of inequity leading to rampant poverty in both developed and underdeveloped countries and concentration of wealth in increasingly fewer hands.

The increasing share of the financial sector at the cost of the real economy, and the resulting inequitable income distribution and excessive consumption habits have resulted in catastrophic socioeconomic, financial, and environmental impacts. Despite huge financial gains and increases in production, hunger, poverty, financial and social exclusion, and environmental crisis are the critical challenges faced by human societies. The system based on profit maximization at any cost is leading to injustice, inequity, and an increasing escalation of the environmental crisis.

It requires easy, affordable, and sufficient access to finance by the production and business units in the real economy that could be translated into equitable sharing of resources for fulfilling the basic needs of all in the society without the choice of exploitative production and excessive consumption by the rich. *Waqf* is a discretional part of faith-based philanthropy that makes the rich spend for others and provides financial institutions with an impressive tool to align themselves with the sustainable development paradigm. By involving the community at the micro level through *waqf* creation and management, Islamic banks (IBs) can provide affordable finance and address the issue of inequity and injustice being meted out currently.

Islamic finance was institutionalized in the second half of the 20th century in OIC member countries to resolve the problem of increasingly inequitable income distribution due to exploitation tools of *ribā* and *gharar*. The UNDP,

DOI: 10.4324/9781003477549-5

World Bank, and other forums also initiated efforts for poverty alleviation and the latest move in this context is the adoption of SDGs 2030 agenda as we indicated in the earlier chapters. But both the initiatives failed, so far, in creating a dent in poverty as can be seen in the "World Inequality Report, 2022"[1] and similar other evidence coming over the last few years.

5.2 Financial Intermediation for Social Inclusion

Financial intermediation for social inclusion is much more than bringing all persons in a society under a formal banking network. It necessarily involves providing micro credit and finance to those who do not have access to formal institutions. It would mean "*full and fair access to collective resources and activities; the maintenance of social relationships with the family, friends and acquaintances, and the developing of the sense of group belongingness*" (Aparicio, 2013). The goal would be balanced growth benefiting all groups in the society with efficient and just working of market and "beyond market" sectors in the economy. Scarcity amid abundance as of now is one major factor that needs to be taken care of through any value-based, just, equitable, and benevolent financial system.

Regarding the failure of conventional microfinance schemes during the early years of the 21st century, Stewart et al. (2010) found that some people were made poorer by some microfinance programs, particularly micro-credit clients. Sinclair (2012) indicated the need for reconstructing the microfinance system in suitable ways to avoid failures. Therefore, ultimate objective of financial intermediation must be social inclusion in addition to financial inclusion.

The best tool for intermediation leading to common welfare could be the social cum business finance based on *waqf*, benevolence, and the principles of risk and reward sharing on an equitable basis. The risk-sharing system needs to be re-emphasized both by the public and the private, banking and nonbanking financial institutions as well as at the State's level. Murat Çizakça (2014) presented case studies of the 13th-century Venice, the 19th-century Germany, and the 20th-century United States to show the histrionic achievements of risk sharing in the West.

5.2.1 Cash Waqf *Enhancing the Potential of* Waqf *as a Financial Intermediary*

Cash *waqf*, as a financial intermediary, has great potential and benefits to society and can effectively meet different needs. Çizakça (2004a) defined Cash *Waqf* as "charitable endowments established with cash capital". Çizakça (2004b) also defined it as a "Trust Fund established with money to support services to mankind in the name of God". Kahf and Mohomed (2017) defined Cash *Waqf* as "a perpetual or temporary holding of endowed cash to produce repeated benefits or usufructs for an objective of general or private righteousness according to the founder's stipulated conditions".

This broad definition encompasses both forms of cash *waqf*, which is using cash as lending *waqf* to provide interest-free loans and investing cash and assigning its net return to the *waqf* beneficiaries. Kahf (2014) deliberated that the principal of cash-lending *waqf* is used for easing the liquidity problems of beneficiaries, whereas, in cash-investment *waqf*, only the income is used for philanthropic, religious, or private beneficiaries as assigned by the *waqf* founders.

Kahf (2014) affirms that cash-investment *waqf* dates back as early as the 1st century of Hijrah. He added that there was enough evidence that cash *waqf* existed throughout Muslim history, particularly in areas where the Maliki or Hanafi schools were prevalent. He provided evidence from Imam Bukhari, Imam Malik, and Ibn Nujaym.

Cash *waqfs* also operated since the early times of the Ottomans who used the *waqf*'s basic principle of perpetuity as the main tool for collective, and not individual capital accumulation which otherwise was not a function of the medieval Arabs. Therefore, Turks resorted to the most basic conversion toward the permanence of the *waqf* as financial intermediary. The utilization of the collected capital in the form of cash *waqf* could be termed a "public development bank" – a bank that has a successful experience of working for over four centuries. Cash *waqfs* maintained their importance with the economic modernization and globalization of the 19th century and operated at the periphery of the financial sector that was dominated by foreign capital. In all these aspects, cash *waqfs* had a competitive edge over local branches of major foreign and domestic banks.

Çizakça (2004b) found that about 20% of the Bursa cash endowments had survived for more than a century according to Bursa Cash Waqf Census Registers. There were 2,517 *waqfs* established in Istanbul during the period 1456–1551 out of which 46% (1,161) were cash *waqfs*, while in Bursa, there were 761 cash *waqfs* during the 18th century. In the year 1954, extant Ottoman cash *waqfs*' capital was pooled to create a modern bank, the Bank of Awqāf (Vakiflar Bankasi) in Türkiye (Çizakça, 2004a).

Collation of *waqf* properties and funds could be useful in providing large funding and building capital assets that produce an ever-increasing flow of revenues/usufructs to serve the diversified objectives and social welfare activities (Alam et al., 2018). In that sense, *waqf* can be considered an early version of present-day corporations (Kahf, 2003). As the cash *waqfs* do not pay any interest or payment to the capital owner, the cost of capital for a cash *waqf* is zero, which leads to the transfer of profits through social and pious purposes (Çizakça, 2000).

According to Çizakça (2004), cash *waqfs* had an important role in the economy for capital distribution among small consumers and entrepreneurs. The credit and deposit volumes of *awqāf* were limited to endowed cash and its returns. Bulut (2021) also considered the cash *waqf* as a redistributor of capital in a society instead of considering them as capital-accumulation institutions. Some statistical data has shown that the borrowers of cash *waqfs* were small consumers instead of entrepreneurs and investors (Çizakça, 2000: 35). Thus, cash *waqfs* not only met the basic social and pious investments but also met capital needs of small farmers and consumers.

Mohsin (2013) discussed the Sharī'ah aspects of cash *waqf* and its role in different countries focusing on six cash *waqf* schemes (*waqf* shares scheme, deposits cash *waqf* scheme, compulsory cash *waqf* scheme, corporate *waqf* scheme, deposit product *waqf* scheme, and cooperative *waqf* scheme). Mohsin (2013) affirmed that in the 21st century, cash *waqf* schemes are being practiced in several countries.

Ramli and Jalil (2013) analyzed the structure of the corporate *waqf* model applied in "*Wakaf* Selangor Muamalat" established in 2012, a collaboration between a state-owned *waqf* management institution and an Islamic commercial bank (BMMB). Aziz and Yusof (2014) evidenced that students in Malaysia need *waqf* bank to get Islamic finance for their education cost. At least four universities in Malaysia have their *waqf* endowments. One of the universities has constructed rentable buildings. Based on the survey conducted by Aziz, et al. (2014), it is evidenced that students in Malaysia need *waqf* bank to get Islamic finance for their education cost. Every year, IIUM succeeds to help 4,000 students to have scholarships funded from *waqf* funds.

Islam (2015) worked on Social Investment Bank Ltd which was the first in Bangladesh to introduce Cash *Waqf* Certificates (CWC) in 1995 and used the cash *waqf* for micro, small, and medium enterprise financing in terms of fund mobilization from the individuals, organizations, SME members, and government, and its investment.

5.2.2 Sustainability of Cash Waqf

The sustainability of the collected funds is an important requirement for *waqfs*. Arshad and Haneef (2015) contended that in the management of liquid *waqf*, it is important to preserve the original value of funds and to develop the value over time. Shulthoni et al. (2018) offered three approaches for that: (1) the venture philanthropy of the *waqf* model, (2) the value-based capital model of *waqf*, and (3) the social enterprise *waqf* fund model. Various models have been developed by Mahamood (2006), Mohammad (2006), Jalil and Ramli (2010), Alias (2012), and Zakaria, Samad, and Shafii (2013).

Shulthoni et al. (2018) suggest the venture philanthropy *waqf* model (VPWM) where *wāqif* endows a fund to the *nāẓir* who would invest in the highly prospective social impact enterprises. The main goal of VPWM is to maximize the social benefit rather than to concentrate on financial return maximization as accomplished in traditional venture capitals. The second model is Value-Based Capital Model of *Waqf*. The focus here is to preserve the value of the dedication rather than the physical object of the subject matter.

The third model is Social Enterprise *Waqf* Fund model. Here welfare is the ultimate priority and so it is the most suitable model for cash *waqf* management. Administrators have to innovate new practices to produce additional and various sources of revenue. In this model, *wāqif* (founder) contributes to the social enterprise through *waqf* handing over to the *nāẓir*. *Nāẓir* manages and invests *waqf* fund. The investment returns can be distributed to *nāẓir* not more than 10% of the return, while 90% of it should be circulated to the beneficiaries.

5.2.3 Institutions for Financial Intermediation

Islamic finance institutions, both banking and nonbanking financial institutions, briefly termed as IBFIs, can play an effective role in promoting financial as well as social intermediation. The institution of *waqf*, both fixed assets, and liquid assets like cash- and ṣukūk-based *waqf* donations would be providing funds for carrying out socioeconomic operations at different levels. The tools of *waqf* for financial intermediation include cash *waqf*, takaful, *al khair ṣukūk*, *al khair* bank accounts (ABAs), *waqf* for financing government debt, *qard hassan*, and financing infrastructure projects.

The banking institutions will be channeling resources for micro enterprises, SMEs, small farmers, and for project financing to facilitate the micro-level production sectors, SMEs, and entrepreneurs. The NBFIs, Fund Managers, crowdfunding platforms, Venture Capital, Startup Capital entities, Mudārabah, and leasing companies would facilitate the potential entrepreneurs to start their own production and business concerns at micro levels while keeping in view the protocols for green finance and ESG.

Crowdfunding is a well-suited technique to raise *waqf* funds and other philanthropic donations from a large audience, where everyone provides a small amount of the funding requested. It takes place through social networks, especially the internet. The entrepreneur gives the objectives, the business plan, and the potential business activities. It is the main innovation of community funding for other forms of finance, as the entrepreneur might not need an intermediary like banks, and get resources directly from the investors (OECD, 2015, p. 53). Crowdfunding may take the form of donations, *qarḍ hassan*, reward or sponsorship, a variety of credits, private equity, and time-bound equity instruments like ṣukūk, etc.

Waqf-based intermediation is also possible through *takaful*. *Waqf* and *takaful* are used in combination to provide Sharī'ah alternative to insurance. *Takaful*, starting in 1979 in Sudan, has been adopted the world over, with its global market reaching $73 billion by the end of 2021 (Rifinitiv, IFDR, 2022[2]). *Waqf* emerged as a part and parcel of *takaful* system, particularly in the case of *wakālah* model. *Takaful*-based risk cover on a mutual basis can be provided to all on an equitable basis by employing *waqf* where every member contributes toward the *waqf* funds and receives the mutual indemnity against the agreed-upon contribution to the *waqf* pool. In fact, mutual insurance, where participants themselves are the owners, is nearest to the Islamic concept of mutual loss mitigation or *takaful.*

Waqf and *takaful* have many conceptual and practical similarities. Nasir et al. (2021) clarify that takaful originates from the philosophy of brotherhood, mutual contribution, assistance, and cohesive utilization of donations by members. If the concept of *waqf* is used by *takaful* entities based on *Musharaka al- ta`awuniyyah* model (Ayub, 2017), it could help realize the objectives of social welfare and equitable risk and reward sharing by the members.

It is the primary responsibility of the state institutions and government representatives to provide a platform where takaful is overseen by a joint forum of *waqf* and takaful, though banking and finance industry can also be part of the initiative. In this way, the orientation of the *takaful* industry would change from the corporate culture as at present to the cooperative one and thus would be able to provide durable and long-lasting socioeconomic solutions.

For re-*takaful*, the best option is that all *takaful* companies in the country create a joint risk pool that would serve as a buffer for bearing the losses possible to risk pools of the individual companies. Alternatively, such a re-takaful entity can be created at the OIC level. Besides, there can be numerous re-takaful private bodies wherein *takaful-waqf* funds can enjoy the liberty of pooling their funds within the country and abroad and link themselves with the chain of some other large Islamic financial institution that can have the financial ability to provide re-takaful.

A mutual and community-based *takāful* system based on *mushārakah al-ta'āwuniyah* (mutual cooperation, protection, and responsibility) is a special feature of Islamic culture that can be traced back to some pre-Islam historical systems including, inter alia, *al-nahd*. The cooperative entities serving as the "*Mutuals*" would aim at community well-being at grassroots levels. Various community organizations, charities, *waqf* funds, and individuals would become members to pay donations/contributions to a common pool managed by the representative of the respective community. Such "*mutuals*" may also serve the function of Fund Managers for the investment of the pool or its members' savings and funds. They may also give *qarḍ h*asan, or even grants for consumption by the poorest, or for small businesses by those who have the potential to be entrepreneurs. This mutual system could also be used as a vehicle for savings/investments and house construction/motor vehicle/education/marriage, etc. IFIs may also become members of such organizations as part of their community services programs that could be funded from bank equity, current accounts balances, or even the *awqāf* for help to the indigent and the poorest. Community *takāful* in the proposed structure could become an institution for social and financial inclusion of those who either abstain from banking and insurance due to Sharī'ah prohibitions or are not in a position to approach conventional institutions due to some deficiencies.

5.2.4 Waqf *and Recent Finance-Related Moves for Welfare*

During the last decade, a few moves have been initiated at the global level to enhance the welfare of the common man, the most pertinent of which is setting the SDGs 2030 by the UNDP. In this perspective, the *waqf* entities in the world offer opportunities for Islamic finance institutions to move to social finance and create *waqf*-based banks for broad-based growth development and social inclusion at the global level. As reported by Omercic Jasmin (2018, pp. 155–158), the BIH [Bosnia and Herzegovina] Waqf Directorate had great opportunities to create a *waqf* community bank with the help of the Bosnian Muslims living in Germany and elsewhere.

The UN Secretary-General advocated, in the World Humanitarian Summit (WHS) held in Dubai on January 17, 2016, for recognition and use of Islamic financial solutions. The session was convened to secure collective commitments toward the development of platforms for Islamic social financing mechanisms, leading to the mobilization of additional financial resources for humanitarian assistance. The WHS also called for supporting innovations for mobilizing finance such as the issuance of social impact or humanitarian ṣukūk (HS) programs, and enabling funding from nontraditional sources directly to frontline responders. Cash *waqf* is the most crucial innovation in this context to be explored actively.

Many wealthy persons in Islamic societies may be eager to help the indigent and spend their wealth on social welfare. There must be specific institutions to formalize such welfare moves and organizations. This can be accomplished with the revival of the institution of "Cash *Waqf*". It implies that the cash capital donated perpetually by the philanthropists might be invested on the basis of risk and reward sharing (Çizakça, 2000). It may need forming community associations at city, town, and even village levels to create such cordial relationships among members of the society that they help one another in all times of sorrow and happiness. Such associations may also establish *awqāf* and charities, and launch various schemes for providing finance for micro businesses to the members and for mitigating losses to the community. It will also help in realizing the SDGs.

5.3 Cash *Waqf* and Modern Banking

The cash *waqfs* that started to be involved in the Ottoman financial system by the end of the 15th century continued their existence for about 450 years. Perpetuity of the cash *waqfs* was ensured by an active cash management strategy where the potential decrease in the fund was prevented.

The competitors of cash *waqfs*, domestic banks, appeared as late as 1909 that reached the rural market and financed large landowners and the urban merchants but not small producers, as Hüseyin and Akar (2019) documented. On the other hand, cash *waqfs* were meant for the public in the neighborhoods and were determined to provide financing for masses, farmers, and artisans at the founder's declared low rates. Karagedikli and Tunçer (2018) suggest that cash *waqf* was an appropriate option for local borrowers due to providing (trade-based) credit at lower transaction costs.

The cash *waqf* open-fund pool is for benevolent purposes and an IB, as the fund manager, is not expected to charge a management fee, particularly when (i) CWF is partially funded by temporary *waqf* deposits and external donors. This is because the CWF benefits the IB in terms of image and market reputation and charging a management fee for managing the CWF for its customers may have a moral issue of customers' exploitation especially if the funds come from CSR, and (ii) the financing is restricted to the IB's customers only. If the bank does not restrict the scheme to its customers only, it may then charge actual management expenses.

The funds for cash *waqfs* may also come from CSR contributions of IBs individually for internal CWF, and collectively for different cash *waqf* foundations. Some donors may give funds as *waqf* permanently, but some may choose to give temporary cash *waqf* funds subject to redemption on demand or after a given period. The open fund structure can accommodate temporary *waqf* funds. Kahf (2014) discussed this issue saying that people might be willing to help with their available financial resources for a given time, but they would like to retrieve their principal later. He added that this becomes like loans as defined in Sharī'ah "an act of charity in which the lender sacrifices the benefit of using cash during the period of the loan".

Investment of cash *waqf* is different from other property *waqfs* owing to the nature of the endowment. The Awqāf Properties Investment Fund (APIF) of the Islamic Development Bank (IsDB) defines the investment as "development and growth of *waqf* properties, whether assets, rents or surpluses through Sharī'ah permissible means of investment". The *nāzir* is not restricted to any specific form of investment – can change investment from one asset to another. The OIC's Islamic Fiqh Academy resolved in 2004 (Resolution No. 140-15/6) that if cash *waqf* funds are invested in any assets, it is as if the *nāzir* bought with its real estate or manufactured with it an item, and those objects and assets do not become the *waqf* assets in place of the cash; they may be sold for continued investments and the *waqf* remains the original amount of cash.

Risk-management measures by *awqāf* administrators include avoiding high-risk investments, diversifying portfolio, relying on economic feasibility studies, making efforts to achieve social return without sacrificing profit for the benefit of original beneficiaries and abiding by the endower(s) conditions for *nazir's* use of endowment properties.

5.3.1 The Source and Uses of Funds in Waqf-*Based Banking*

Various kinds of donations, deposits, and returns on the earning assets of *waqfs* are the sources of any *waqf-based* banking channel. The experts have suggested a variety of instruments like Cash *Waqf* Certificates (CWS) and

ABAs. For getting a donation in the form of cash *waqf*, a "Form" has been developed in Türkiye, which takes care of all aspects of donations made for any specific purpose or the beneficiary. This form is copied here as Cash *Waqf* Donation Form (Figure 5.1).

As can be seen, the cash *waqf* form is comprehensive in terms of the intention of the person who donates with demographics and the currency of donation, the area(s) where the amount is to be spent or given as finance with the mode of finance and the rate (*murābahah*, leasing, etc.), the profit sharing ratio, the purpose (education with level and nature), religious service (with the specification of service), fight against poverty and others (restorations, infrastructure, social policy, or without any constraint). Such a form will have to be finalized and conveyed by the central banks to the banks.

While "*cash waqf certificates*" would reflect perpetual donations for welfare purposes, time bound *al khair* deposits could either reflect *waqf* forever,

Cash Waqf Fund Donation Form

DONOR INFORMATION

T.R. Identification number:
Name - Last name:
Date of birth:
Place of Birth:

Photo
(Not required)

WAQF INFORMATION
Donated amount:
Donated currency: ☐ TL ☐ USD ☐ EURO ☐ GBP

Operation method (%):

Murabahah	Mudarabah	Musharakah	Ijara	No constraints
Percentage:	Percentage:	Percentage:	Percentage:	Percentage:

Borrowers (%):

Individuals	Private sector	Public sector	No constraints
Percentage:	Percentage:	Percentage:	Percentage:

Purpose (%):

Education	Religious services	Fight against poverty	Other services
Bursary:	Mosque/masjid:	Food:	Restoration:
School:	Qur'an course:	Good:	Infrastructure:
University	Dormitory:	Soup kitchen:	Social policies:
Library:	No constraints:	Refugees:	No constraints:
Laboratory:		No constraints:	
Dormitory:			
No constraints:			

Information:
1. The credentials of the person who donated the money should be written donor information area. This section may be filled in person or may be filled in by proxy.
2. The donated amount, in cash, refers to the capital for the waqf. If there is no legal and compulsory stoppage, this money is considered as the capital of the waqf.
3. The waqf accepts donations in four currencies. However, other currencies other than the Turkish Lira are converted into Turkish Lira unless the donators request otherwise.
4. Donated money is evaluated by four basic Islamic/interest-free financial methods.
   Murabahah: The cost of goods is notified to the customer and the profit is added and sold.
   Mudarabah: Express labor-capital partnership.
   Musharakah: It is similar to Mudarabah, where both parties participate in the capital.
   Ijara: Leasing.
5. The percentages in operation method are for understanding the method by which the money is operated. For foundations that want to protect their capital, a certain rate can be selected as mandatory in the murabaha or ijara methods.
6. Borrowers refer to the persons and institutions that can borrow from the foundation. Percentages represent the amount of money to be used from the capital.
7. Four purposes is determined under the purpose area. For example, bursary under the title of education refers to scholarships to be given directly to students. The other titles refer to both construction and needs-based assistance. The titles under the religious services are intended for construction and needs. The titles under the fight against poverty refer to direct assistance. Other services refers the restoration, infrastructure and social policies that the waqf management finds appropriate for assistance.
8. With the realization of the donation, the control of the money goes to the waqf management.
9. The waqf management has to manage the money under the conditions determined by the founder.

Figure 5.1 Cash *Waqf* Fund Donation Form.

or a qarḍ hassan for the purpose of onward financing. As a large number of current accounts holders are currently keeping huge sums in the banks without getting any return, it is amply possible that many well-off persons will keep term-based *al khair* deposits with advice to the banks that the same would be the part of the *waqf* pool created by the bank and used for *qarḍ hassan* for micro businesses, micro farms, and small entrepreneurs. This, however, will require a brisk regulatory step to be taken by the central banks to initiate awareness campaign for the public and to oblige the banks to divert a part, may be up to 50% of their current accounts' balances for the *waqf* pools, if the account holders may so desire.

The idea of the "*open cash waqf*" fund is to enable the *waqf* to receive contributions at any time in contrast to a closed fund. Islamic financial institutions may come up with innovative ideas to encourage their customers to make *waqf* contributions to this fund that is for a benevolent cause whether by cash contributions or other means. For example, Al Rajhi Bank has an innovative Islamic credit card – the Ehsan card that enables cardholders to make a charitable donation to the Orphan Care Organization via points accumulated through purchases that are converted into cash equivalent.

Lahsasna (2010), quoting from Mannan (1998), has mentioned cash *waqf* deposits and CWCs for promoting finance for SMEs and the micro businesses (Figure 5.2). CWCs can be taken in the name of other beloved family members to strengthen family integration among rich families. Mannan suggested the following objective of CWCs:

- to equip banks and other *waqf* management institutions with CWC,
- to help collect social savings through such certificates,
- to help transform the collected social savings to social capital, as well as to help develop the social capital market,
- to increase social investment,
- to encourage rich communities' awareness on their responsibility for social development in their environment, and
- to stimulate integration between social security and social welfare.

Waqf-related fintechs are all about the cash *waqf*. In most of Islamic countries, so far, the cash *waqf* is not a popular mode of donation. However, it is a growing area under the fintech, as the fintech itself is growing. In fact, the fourth industrial revolution is shaping the economy through innovations by enabling easy access to internet services for all in various fields of needs and activities including digital financial services. Islamic financial service providers are also using digital platforms. *Waqf* foundations, being among the financial service providers, have to rise to the occasion to realize the potential.

The profits from the cash *waqfs* will be used as per the policy given in the *waqf* deed and shared with the contributors. A specific policy for spending

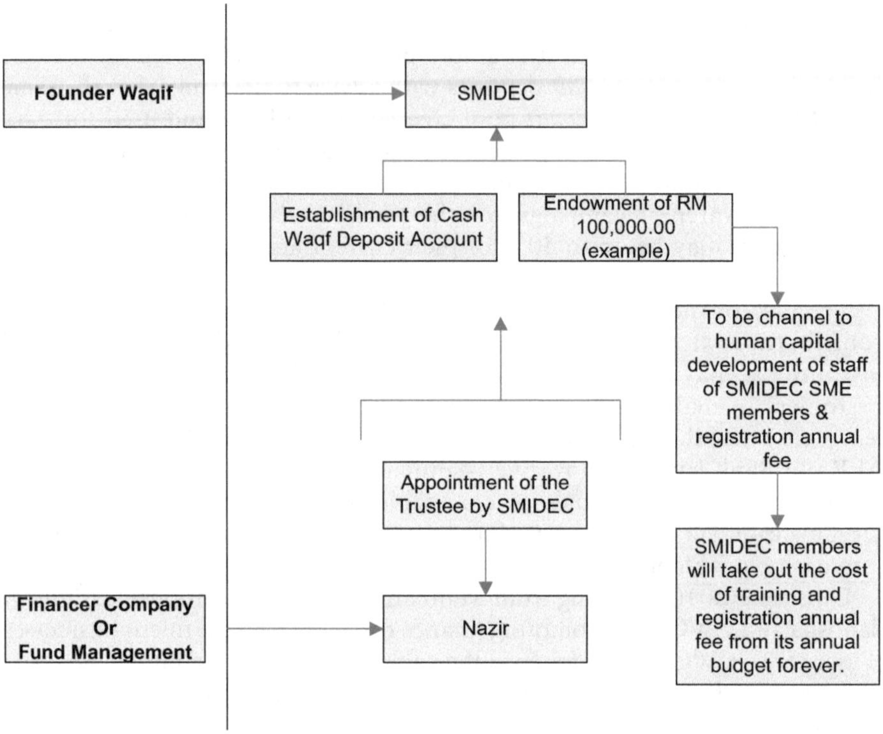

Figure 5.2 Cash *Waqf* Deposit Account by SME Development Corporation (SMEDC).
Source: Lahsasna (2010).

waqf funds in the form of an agreement will provide guidance in all related matters. Such a policy for the operation of the cash *waqf* scheme as provided by the social investment bank in Dhaka (IABC, 2013) is given hereunder:

(a) *Waqfs* are made in perpetuity and the account is opened in the title given by the *wāqif*. The amount in cash *waqf* of the account is a perpetual deposit.
(b) *Wāqif* has the opportunity to create multiple cash *waqfs* at a time. The deposits can start with any amount.
(c) *Wāqifs* have the right to give standing instruction to the institution for regular realization of cash *waqf* at a rate specified by him/her from any other account maintained with the institution.
(d) *Wāqif* has the liberty to choose the purpose(s) to be served either from the list provided and identified by the institution, covering (a) family empowerment credits, (b) human resource development, (c) health and

sanitation, and social utility services or any other purpose(s) permitted by Sharī'ah.
(e) *Wāqif* can also instruct the institution to spend the entire profit amount for the purpose specified by him/her.
(f) Cash *waqf* amount earns profit [to be used for the above purposes] at the highest rate offered by the institution from time to time. Cash *waqf* amounts remain intact and only the profit amount is spent for the purpose(s) specified by the *wāqif*.
(g) Unspent profit amounts are automatically added to the *waqf* amount and earn profit to grow over time.

Sarker (2019) analyzed the role of Cash Waqf Deposits (CWD) in the banking sector of Bangladesh that are playing a beneficial role in the socioeconomic development of the country. CWD started with BDT 250 million in 2010 and increased to BDT 1056 million in 2016. It reflects the growing participation of the people in the socioeconomic activities of the country. If proper policies are formulated and the prime stakeholders like the *waqf* administration of the Government, the National Board of Revenue, and Bangladesh Bank create the overall environment-incentivized marketplace, the socioeconomic infrastructure of the country would grow further for socioeconomic development.

The operation of cash *waqfs* to be created and managed by the banks and other financial institutions is depicted in Figure 5.3.

The use of *waqf* funds and investments is the main and most critical dimension of the *waqf*. Among them, financing of the old *waqf* properties is also crucial and requires a careful strategy for the advancement of the *waqf*-based financial intermediation on a sustainable basis. If planned and executed with caution, the development of old *waqf* properties as in countries like Pakistan can lead to the way to salvation in many backward communities.

5.3.2 Ottoman Cash Waqf-*Based Microfinance*

As indicated earlier, cash *waqfs* remained involved in the Ottoman financial system for about 450 years. Perpetuity of the cash *waqfs* was ensured by an active cash management strategy where the possible decrease in the fund was prevented. The strategy was to use *awqāf's* own cash assets instead of borrowing from (money) markets at low rates and offering credit at higher rates, thus avoiding the financial leverage.

The Ottoman foundation system involved three types of pooled *waqf* funds: *artisan funds*, *avāriz funds*, and *Janissary squad funds* aimed at sustaining the socioeconomic needs of society. These were available in every neighborhood: rural and urban. Fund trustees were elected from among the notable members along with the decision of a predecessor.

Agriculture Bank (*Ziraat Bankasi*) of Ottomans had a good chance to reach the farmers, though with the Western and non-Islamic financial practices.

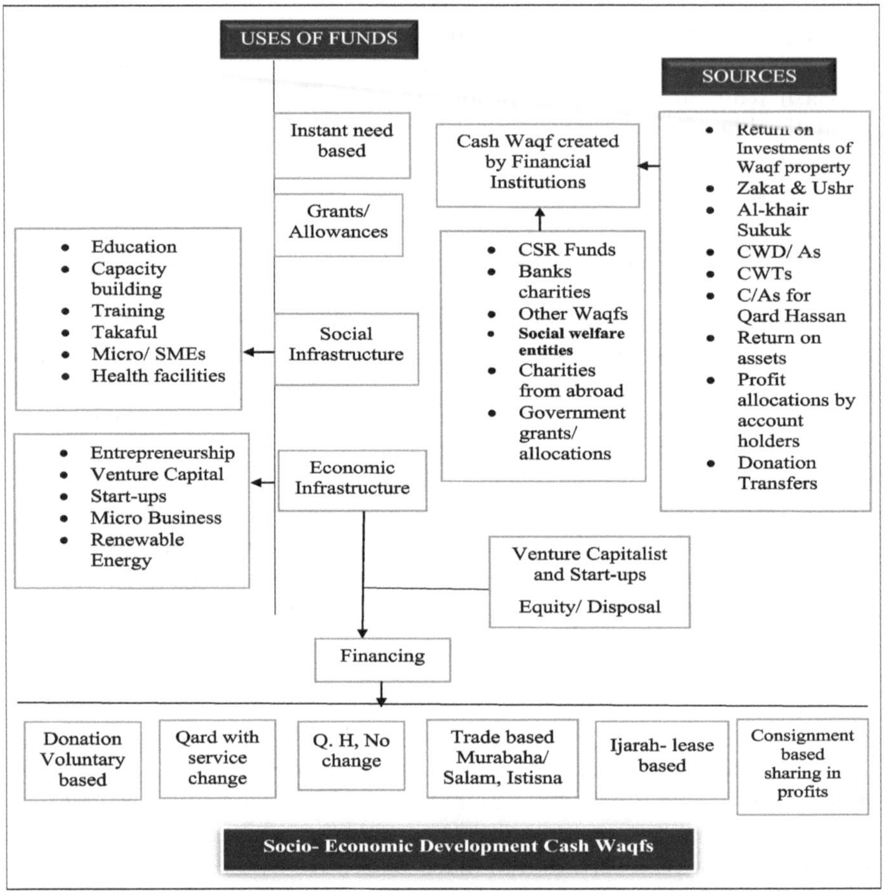

Figure 5.3 Operations of Cash *Waqf* by Banks and Financial Institutions.

Source: Authors' own.

However, its credit did not reach the small producers and cultivators as the local moneylenders used to borrow from the bank to lend to the peasants with higher interest rates. As against the cash *waqfs*, it had higher collateral requirements. Of course, it could have been used as a supervisory bank for cash *waqfs* to avoid the aforementioned problems.

The experts suggest precautions for making investments of *awqāf* properties. These include avoiding high-risk investments, diversifying the portfolio, relying on economic feasibility studies, making efforts to achieve social return without sacrificing profit for the benefit of original beneficiaries, and abiding by the endower(s) conditions for *Nazir's* use of endowment properties.

IsDB has played an important role in revitalizing the *awqāf* properties. One such model is developed by the APIF which drives a shift away from short-term fixes for hard development issues toward long-term, intergenerational solutions. IsDB's Awqaf Properties Investment Fund (2019) defines the investment as "development and growth of waqf properties, whether assets, rents or surpluses through Sharī'ah permissible means of investment".

Pakistan shares a legacy of Mughal dynasty where shrines and *Sufi* tradition had a very influential role in the education and awareness of the masses. Sufi shrines cover a vast majority of the *waqf* properties from where the society used to receive the lesson for tolerance and self-purification. There is a need to involve the *Sufi* traditional leaders in the development of the *waqf* properties on modern lines. *Waqf* properties have to be managed and developed on modern lines so that they should provide enough returns which could be used for social purposes.

5.3.3 Al Khair Ṣukūk

For moving to social finance, IBs would have to take the lead in issuing *Al Khair Ṣukūk* to be issued to those who wish to become a part of the social welfare scheme. The proceeds would be used to provide financing based on *qarḍ hassan*, trading- or leasing-based contract to microbusinesses, small entrepreneurs, and farmers, as per the *ṣukūk* deeds.

Waqf ṣukūk could be issued by IBs to provide a sustainable source of funds for continuing *qarḍ hassan* projects by them. Khan (2016) has suggested philanthropic *ṣukūk* to provide people of small means with opportunities to have acts of perpetual charity to their credit for reward from Allah (SWT). After a *waqf* fund is established by any bank, it may be issuing perpetual and redeemable charitable *ṣukūk* so that it could serve as a hub for social inclusion in an area/society.

Waqf ṣukūk that would not bear any profit or return on investments for the holders may be registered with the stock exchanges. Thus, if any of the affluent persons wish to give their excess funds forever or for any given time, *ṣukūk* could be issued to them, and if holders of time-bound *ṣukūk* wish to withdraw from the scheme, they could do so by exchanging the ṣukūk in the exchange at par to others, intending to participate in the social welfare scheme (Khan, M. Fahim, 2016). The banks would be able to issue such *ṣukūk* through a special-purpose vehicle (SPV) created for this purpose. Such *ṣukūk* would not bear any profit or return on investments for the holders.

Al-Khair Ṣukūk and Social Impact *Ṣukūk* certificates can be issued by *waqf* and other nonprofit institutions and philanthropists for social welfare projects. In this social finance network, IBs need to involve the donor and *waqf* institutions.

The *waqfs* once created by the IBFIs could be replenished by: (i) bank's shareholders allocating a certain percentage of the bank's profits for this purpose; (ii) account holders contributing, at their discretion, by direct donation or by a percentage of profits earned from their deposit/investment accounts regularly; and (iii) the government and international donor agencies may donate to the *waqf* as part of their poverty alleviation initiatives.

Though cash *waqf* collection increased six times in Malaysia from RM 0.39 million in 2010 to RM 2.8 million in 2019, it makes only RM 0.28 per Muslim in the country, which is quite modest (Ismail, 2021). It shows that the government of Malaysia needs to invest into fintech for *waqf*. Some studies, such as Pitchay et al. (2014) suggest that the cash *waqf* contributions could reach RM 4 billion. Regarding the use of funds so collected, Pitchay et al. (2014) suggested the priority-wise list as first being education, second being health, third being masjid/madrasah, and fourth being social care/welfare.

Projects-based Islamic microfinancing with *waqf* and charity funds and investments by the affluent in society could be helpful in building a caring society to live in peace with shared prosperity. It is through mutual help, cooperation, sharing of wealth with the poor through *zakāh*, *waqf*, and charity, close monitoring, and follow-up that poverty can be eliminated to achieve a just society that makes the Islamic system unique and universal.

5.3.4 The Idea of a Separate Waqf-*Based Capital Market*

Once the *waqf* capital becomes sustainable, then the entrepreneurs facilitated on the basis of *waqf* may have their own capital/stock exchange. It is because of the commitments and the peculiar characteristics that the *waqf*-based system and *waqf-supported* entrepreneurs do require different laws and different dimensions.

Based on the concept of collective capital accumulation under *waqf*, and mutual cash endowment schemes in different subsectors as we discussed in the earlier section, a separate capital market can be developed for entrepreneurs associated with *waqfs*. Assets of *waqf* are perpetual; they don't diminish over time, if not get doubled or redoubled, as they make returns. Careful use of the returns at the individual *waqf* level as well as at the collective level under the guidance of the central *awqāf* administration makes *waqf*-based *sukuk* sustainable for long time. It may become a self-sustained and progressive system for realizing the objective of socioeconomic growth. If buildings/assets of *waqf* are rented, then their secondary markets can also exist. As there could be a rent agreement with a definite clause of increase in the rent by a fixed percentage, the return can be securitized to serve as short-term assets eligible for investments by private investors as well as the banks. For banks, such *ṣukūk* or *waqf* certificates could also be eligible for their statutory liquidity reserves (SLR) requirements. Such a stock exchange could serve as the Islamic alternative to the interest-based and *gharar*-led exploitative tools and instruments.

Ṣukūk are priced using profit-sharing modes or some variations of it and are not based on paying a pre-agreed fixed interest irrespective of the outcome of the use of funds. Accordingly, an equity-based behavior is encouraged, namely, that the investors and the fund users, through SPV, agree to share in the risk of the investments (hence a profit share) while the latter has to give ownership of part of the assets to the investor. It restricts unlimited borrowing by businesses. As contended by Safari (2013), "*Ṣukūk* are somewhat like socially responsible investment firms that put people and planet before profits". Mutual funds that subscribe to socially responsible investments also put people and the planet before profit as their motto (Safari, 2013).

5.4 *Waqf*-Based Development and Public Sector Financing

Waqf can provide effective solutions to the financing of large-scale infrastructural projects in various sectors like water and sanitation projects, sustainable and affordable energy, transport, roads, and shelters for the extremely poor. Investment into infrastructure is needed to support the expansionary macroeconomic projects to create jobs, raise incomes, and generate demand. Hence, a developmental plan is needed that might lead to social inclusion.

Re-distributive mechanisms of Islamic economics and finance ensure that the benefits of production do not miss out on the poorest ones, yet the levels of production are kept in focus. Islamic finance could be helpful in keeping the economy away from greed, unearned income, speculation, and gambling. There are quite rational approaches under the Islamic framework that ensure the appropriate allocation of the available resources, among them, is the *waqf* financing for financial intermediation.

Waqf and other charities historically played a vital role in alleviating poverty and led to wider social and financial inclusion. *Waqf* funds can be used for the provision of social infrastructure such as education, hospitals as well as economic infrastructure such as roads and bridges (Sadeq, 2002). It has been argued that the entire health, education, and welfare budget during the Osman caliphate based in Istanbul came from charity foundations (Çizakça, 2004).

While some OIC member countries have developed policies for the revival/development of *waqf* properties, other countries like Pakistan need to devise laws of *awqāf*, also allowing the cash *waqf* to help recover, preserve, and develop the *awqāf* system.

5.4.1 Easing the Issue of the Budgetary Deficit through Waqf

Regarding public finance, Pakistan has been taken as a case study. The ironic condition of Pakistan's economy is that with the low level of economic output, its debt to GDP stood at 83.50% on June 30, 2021 while domestic debt was 55.1% of GDP.[3] The government takes measures to counter the rising debt levels by selling out public assets or increasing [mostly the indirect] taxes that further harm the production capacity and export competitiveness of the commodity-producing sectors. *Waqf* can be used as an alternative Sharī'ah compliant Islamic solution.

The development projects also involve education, health, and civic facilities sectors that, in turn, play a crucial role in strengthening the development base of the economy. Other relevant development projects may be that of renewable energy (solar, wind, and hydel) and infrastructure for micro farms, business, and value-adding production units aimed at import substitution and export enhancing. As we discussed in the chapter on promoting entrepreneurship through *awqāf*, any *waqf*-based projects and schemes could reduce the public sector expenditure for building the overall infrastructure in the economy.

For development-oriented projects involving the social infrastructure, *waqf ṣukūk* can be issued involving the affluent/philanthropists in the society. The government would declare the infrastructure assets like schools and hospitals as *waqf*, so such projects and their management departments can be dealt with as *waqf* for public welfare, with funds donated for continued reward in the *hereafter*. Such welfare-oriented projects will have funding ease by the UN, World Bank, IsDB, other global infrastructure institutions, and philanthropist entities abroad.

Çizakça (1998) believes that "*the waqf system can significantly contribute towards the ultimate goal of every modern economist; massive reduction in government expenditure which leads to a reduction in the budget deficit, which lowers the need for government borrowing*" (p. 44). *Waqf ṣukūk* can be initiated for social-sector development projects. *Waqf* can also assist modern governments in eradicating interest (*ribā*) as well as promoting better distribution of income. This can be achieved by instructing Islamic banking institutions to combine cash *waqf* with *mudārabah* firms or "joint-stock company shares" (Çizakça, 1998). The government may also ask all banking companies in the country to create huge collective *waqf* for public welfare projects based on the returns that the banks get from investment of current accounts balances with them on which they pay no return to the depositors.

During the Ottoman caliphate, the *waqfs* used to send their surplus amounts every year to the central government. Such a scheme can also be adopted with some of the *waqfs*, in particular, with the public *waqf* foundations that are established in public-private partnerships. For the integrity of the system, there should be a state-led independent commission that should work out the assessment of the emergency and the transfer of the funds from the *waqfs* to the public sector projects and government.

5.4.2 Waqf-*Based Islamic Fund Management*

Islamic fund management plays a significant role in mobilizing savings to promote economic growth while ensuring Sharīʿah compliance (Al Rahahleh and Bhatti, 2022). Islamic funds address many issues faced by an individual investor seeking Sharīʿah-compliant investment avenues, including selecting investments with the lowest cost, analyzing financial ratios of investee companies, and Sharīʿah governance in the form of investment reviews and audits. There could be a regulation that all cash endowments given under the *waqf* system might be invested in listed Islamic funds. Return on such investments could be used for any socioeconomics objectives also including entrepreneurship for providing business opportunities and enhancing production capacity in the economy.

Waqf can be used to strengthen business support to the institutions to lower the cost of supply of goods and services to the poor and to support and build infrastructure institutions. Types of funds regarding the investment portfolios and the managers that best suit projects financing are private and corporate equity funds, wealth funds, commodity funds, venture capital funds, pension funds, index funds, fund of funds, real estate investment trusts (REITs), and other funds suiting various investors based on their risk and profit payments requirements. Islamic funds would invest only in Sharīʿah-compliant stocks, portfolios, or projects, based on the approved Sharīʿah screening process and compliance criteria. In this regard, the Guiding Principles on Governance for Islamic Collective Investment Schemes (ICIS) issued by the Islamic Financial Services Board (IFSB-6) must be implemented.

5.5 *Waqf* and Fintech

Fintech is an effective way of enhancing financial inclusion. *Waqf*-related fintech is a process of using technological advancement to enable *waqf*-related Sharī'ah-based financial services in collecting funds, investing, receiving back returns, and spending for public welfare. As those who generally donate cash as *waqf* are literate and mostly aware of tech-based banking and finance, *waqf* fintech can be useful for the provisioning of public goods and social services and realizing socioeconomic objectives. Adoption of fintech in Islamic social finance (*waqf* and *zakāt*) can increase financial inclusion as it necessitates the opening of bank accounts to access the funds. Most beneficiaries usually conduct one transaction per period to withdraw the entire funds which are then spent to meet their daily needs. Islamic finance can be utilized to make these beneficiaries of donations self-sustaining, and eventually, contribute toward lifting others out of poverty.

Social funding can be collected and channeled through digital bank accounts which may also be supported by blockchain technology thus reducing the incidence of fraud, while ensuring the financial inclusion. Fintech can provide integrated solutions to the entire *waqf-zakāh* value chain encompassing the collection, distribution, and intermediation of funds to the improved identification of beneficiaries. Technology can also facilitate bringing more donors to the network.

Ismail (2013) finds that cash *waqf* is also useful for public goods such as education, health, social care, and commercial activates. Ismail (2021) also indicates that contributors of cash *waqf* are literate urban Muslims that have a higher ranking for education and health. Such a priority ranking points toward the requirement of urban civic facilities through *waqf* in the most modern Muslim societies show that Islam is still relevant. So, the use of recent technologies for the provision of basic civic facilities would enhance the relevance of Islamic culture, Islamic organizations, and Islamic institutions.

Waqf fintech has been suggested for small farms in agriculture, where banks generally do not provide finances. PT Patel Agriculture (Indonesia) offers fintech-based contracts in *murābahah*, *mudarabah*, and *salam* to finance agri-projects (Bilal et al., 2021). Ali et al. (2019) have recorded all the apps of fintech in Islamic countries, among them are apps for crowdfunding for social finance that include Beehive, Ethics Crowd, Kapital Boost, and Narwi.

Tajudin et al. (2020) conducted a case study that helps prove a specific conclusion that, using *waqf*, fintech can help alleviate the poverty of the underprivileged Muslims. Citing some studies, Al-Shater (2022) suggested that the specific way of crowdfunding, used to establish *waqf* endowments, can still be used through fintech. Zain et al. (2019) recommended crowdfunding for the *waqf* model. Crowdfunding is found by an effective tool for solving the problem of idle *waqf* properties according to an applied study of Azganin (2019). Hapsari et al. (2022) suggest that it can be a source of sustainable funding for *waqf*, where fintech companies can provide a valuable platform. They also found that education on *waqf* is the most critical component in raising public awareness about crowdfunding for *waqf* and should be promoted among beneficiaries such as schools, mosques, government offices, and social groups.

With a customer base of nearly two billion people, projected to reach around three billion people by 2060, the *waqf*-based Islamic fintech sector has the potential to take the global finance industry beyond the time-honored bottom line of profit. It offers ethical and sustainable alternatives in terms of investment methodology and products. The fact of the matter is that Islamic finance provides sustainable models along with higher Sharī'ah objectives coupled with financial digitalization and e-commerce thus giving a perfect foundation for a societal build-up enough to cater to the development of a nation.

Some of the successful Islamic fintech entities include Kuala Lumpur-based philanthropic fundraising giant "Global Sadaqah", UK-based Qardus, Islamic Finance Guru, Path Solutions (serving over 150 Islamic institutions across 40 countries), US-based Wahed, P2P financier Amartha Mikro Fintek & Bank Sumut, UK-based peer-to-peer property investment platform "Yielders", BNPL platform "PayHalal", Sydney-based MRHB DeFi Network and coinMENA for the MENA region.

Fintech-based *waqf*, like fintech itself, would need an Efficient Account Information Service (AIS) and a Payment Initiation Service (PIS) that could be provided through the "Regulatory Sandbox" as a tool for financial innovations, and a part of the comprehensive and effective regulation. Leaving fintech without regulation or a robust legal framework will render the whole innovation susceptible to abuse, misuse, and devastating manipulations.

While cash *waqf* in Indonesia has been legalized by the law, fintech apps are permitted as long as they are not in breach of the law. A wave of fintech-based *waqf* started in 2018 under the (informal) umbrella of government *waqf*-governing agencies. The Itqan mobile company collects funds through crowdfunding and then, with the help of some financial intermediary platform, provides the collected donations as capital to small firms, again through mobile apps, on large scale, the return of which is then spent for social welfare projects (Nurhayati, 2021).

For the current applications of fintech in the Islamic capital market, there has been a significant increase in the adoption of technology and innovative solutions in leading jurisdictions offering Islamic financial services. For instance, in Malaysia, the Investment Account Platform (IAP) was introduced as a cross-border multicurrency platform for facilitating regional and global financing opportunities for emerging business ventures. The IAP is based on a consortium of several IBs that help as financial intermediaries to channel the funds to deserving business ventures. Malaysian fintech dialogue, a year-wise dialogue platform, that works under Malaysia Digital Economy Corporation, a government body to regulate the fintech, is to build an inclusive fintech ecosystem that should include *zakāh*, *waqf*, and sadaqah space.

5.5.1 Fintech Sector in Pakistan

The authors of this study conducted various interviews and arranged focal group meetings. For Pakistan, some research participants suggested that *waqf* should be allowed to be set up through the Roshan Digital Account. State Bank as well as the SECP, as per their due diligence policy, may facilitate in establishing such *waqfs*. A retired SBP officer indicated that the Roshan Digital account's concept paper was started in 2016. In such accounts, charities are authorized to get donations provided they are registered with the Economic Affairs Division of the Government as approved charities. So, it was recommended that *waqfs* should be authorized to get such donations. Roshan Digital Account which is approved for Pakistan is very convenient for getting donations from abroad through digital accounts.

The fintech ecosystem is subject to several hindrances comprising threats to data security and intellectual property, trouble attracting the right talent and customer base, and an uncertain regulatory environment discouraging entrepreneurs from venturing into the fintech environment. Besides, overall low economic performance is also responsible for little progress in the development of fintech. The problem of low financial access, only 7% of the adult population, has long plagued the Pakistani economy (World Bank, 2017). Pakistan occupies a low rank in financial inclusion when compared to regional and global standards (Nenova & Ahmad, 2009). High intermediation costs with high interest rate spreads, financial illiteracy, high collateral requirements, and prohibitive lending rates have put finance out of the reach of small and medium enterprises.

Of course, Pakistan is an attractive market for fintech growth, owing to being fifth largest youth population, disruptive internet, smartphone penetration, consumer preference for mobile phones and social media, booming online commerce facilitating digital payments, and an overall financial system having absorption capacity for innovation. Rizvi and Naqvi (2018) found that the verification of 132 million biometrically certified SIMs paved the way for digital wallets and payments through mobile phones. Among nonbank players, Easypaisa, by Telenor Pakistan is a prominent mobile phone app with more than 70,000 agents in the country. Karandaaz Pakistan, a nonprofit organization, is also providing them grants to fintech start-ups in Pakistan for access to financial services, payments, e-commerce, and interoperability.

Meezan Bank, the premier IB in Pakistan, has launched a digital supply chain financing platform (*Wisaaq*) in partnership with Haball, an Islamic B2B fintech that digitizes business payments to enable a cashless and digital supply chain. Wissaq connects distributors, banks, and the corporate on a single platform and enables clients to benefit from improved cash flow efficiencies. It provides an investment solution for nonresident Pakistanis. Wisaaq will be available through the exchange's Karachi Internet Trading System (KiTS) and will facilitate any digital account client of an IB focused on investing in Sharī'ah compliant securities, through the services of over 100 securities brokers and trading right entitlement certificate (TREC) holders that use KiTS as an order management system. All such systems can help promote the institution of *waqf* with sustainable sources of funds and efficient use of funds for all social and economic sectors of the economy. SBP has also developed a mobile application for Asaan Mobile Account (AMA) to facilitate mobile banking interoperability.

A digital asset management regulation was issued on August 1, 2022 by the SECP outlining the role of digital asset-management companies (AMCs) as licensed nonbanking finance companies (NBFC). In this concept, the regulator intends to lower the barrier to entry. [Details about fintech-related financial regulations can be seen in research by Rizvi and Naqvi (2018)].

5.6 Summary and Conclusion

Welfare-oriented financial intermediation which should potentially be the objective of every economy must lead to full and fair access by all to resources while helping those who might remain behind due to any inability or functioning of the market forces. Financial intermediation for social inclusion is much more than merely bringing all under a formal banking network. Academic studies conclude that tools of Islamic social finance such as *zakāh*, *sadaqah*, *waqf*, Islamic microfinance, and cooperative *takaful* models lead to financial as well as social inclusion and help reduce income inequality. Such intermediation services could be provided through cash *awqāf*.

A good tool for social and financial inclusion is the cash *waqf* (Ismail, 2009). Cash *waqfs* relieved the budget of the Ottoman Empire by doing such investments in education, health, and infrastructure which were financed by governments in the economic structure of other parts of the world. Thus, the capital need of the empire was reduced, and the money demand of the government decreased which caused lower interest rates in the entire economy (Çizakça, 2000).

In the present world with innovative concepts of fintech and crowdfunding already well established, *waqf* can play a more effective role in enhancing financial and social inclusion by collecting donations at the micro level and investing the return from the fixed properties *awqāf* for socioeconomic purposes. The role of the regulator is crucial because it has to implement and monitor the *waqf*-related community laws, fintech rules, as well as financial laws and regulations.

Running expenses for managing the affairs by the trustees of public and financial intermediary *waqfs* will have to be limited to a certain extent, say 10% of the income in the case of general *waqfs* and 5% in the case of financial intermediary *awqāf*. The cash donation forms to be used by the banking and nonbanking institutions will have to be approved by the regulators and the central Sharī'ah committee.

The *waqf* base intermediation system could also be used as a vehicle for savings/investments and providing relief packages to the poor and middle classes for education, house construction, motor vehicles, etc. IBs and financial institutions may also become members of such organizations as part of their community services programs that could be funded from banks equity, current accounts balances, or *awqāf* funds for help to the indigent and the poorest. Community *takāful* in the proposed structure could become an institution for social and financial inclusion of those who either abstain from banking and insurance due to Sharī'ah prohibitions or are not in a position to approach conventional institutions due to some deficiencies.

The social welfare and development concepts, principles, and theories in the Islamic perspective will also apply to the *waqf*. So, the *waqf-related* intermediary services would require experts to work out the practical options at each phase of the work.

Islamic finance, as inclusive finance, may also promote, under *waqf*, modern methods of green financing through the issuance of green *ṣukūk*, as in Malaysia and Indonesia, which can be attributed as one step ahead toward clubbing belief and sustainability.

Islamic finance, digital economy, and *waqf* could be termed as the Key Economic Growth Activities (KEGA) for the OIC member countries. They must build an inclusive fintech ecosystem comprising IBs, AMCs, fund managers, Islamic fintech start-ups, corporates, NGOs, *waqf* and *zakāh* platforms, and practitioners in the areas of *waqf*, *zakāh*, and charities. Globally, a total of 138 companies were offering Islamic fintech services as identified by the

IFN Islamic Fintech Landscape across 11 verticals as of the end of December 2019 (Aziz, 2021).

Leaving fintech without a robust legal framework will render the whole innovation susceptible to abuse, misuse, and devastating manipulations. Therefore, regulatory technology or RegTech may have to step up its proactive regulations to regulate fintech applications. A RegTech framework has been experienced in Malaysia with the enactment of the Capital Markets and Services (Prescriptions of Securities) (Digital Currency and Digital Token) Order 2019. Malaysia is also said to have the most sophisticated Islamic fintech regulatory framework (Aziz, 2021).

Pakistan and many other OIC member countries are lagging behind some other Islamic countries in promoting the use of fintech for enhancing financial and social inclusion. They must build an inclusive fintech ecosystem comprising IBs, AMCs, fund managers, Islamic fintech start-ups, corporates, NGOs, *waqf* and *zakāh* platforms, and practitioners in the areas of *waqf*, *zakāh*, and charities. Beyond RegTech, there is a need for a regulatory sandbox for the application of fintech in financial services.

Notes

1 Prepared and coordinated by Lucas Chancel (Lead author), Thomas Piketty, Emmanuel Saez and Gabriel Zucman, UNDP as Scientific partner (World Inequality Lab, 2021).
2 The report accessed from: www.refinitiv.com/en/islamic-finance
3 www.finance.gov.pk/rebuttals_details1.html#:~:text=However%2C%20the%20positive%20development%20is,GDP%20from%2056%25%20last%20year. Accessed on Aug 22, 2022.

6 Management and Governance of *Awqāf* as Social Finance Institutions

6.1 Introduction

The success of the financial management strategies of *awqāf* depends a great deal upon long-term planning by the founders to maintain the sustainability of their foundations, the activation of control mechanisms by means of coordinating the incomes and expenses of foundations and the diversification of economic instruments under the market conditions (Gürsoy, 2018).

Three traditional principles of *waqf* are perpetuity (assets/purpose), inalienability, and irreversibility. However, contemporary scholars take a lenient view and accept temporary *awqāf* as well as reversibility under certain conditions for ensuring sustainability. The *Waqf* Core Principles (WCP) as indicated by a Working Group on Waqf (IWG-2018) acknowledges that there are different schools of thought related to the law and the implementation of *awqāf*. Cash *waqf* becomes important in this context and it has taken the form of a financial intermediary connecting philanthropists with a variety of beneficiaries. The WCPs have been structured around certain basic building blocks focusing on "benevolence" and "mutual benefit" from cash and tangible assets *awqāf* while also seeking to harmonize alternative viewpoints (IWG-2018, p. 12).[1]

As *waqf* and charitable organizations share similar characteristics (Sadeq, 2002), so the conception of governance, the hallmark of public sector governance overlaps with that of nonprofit institutions like that of *waqf*. However, there is certainly a difference between governance in corporate culture and the *waqf* and other social institutions' governance. While the conventional corporate culture focuses on efficiency for earnings maximization, *waqf* involves accountability to God, human beings, society, and the environment as part of the belief system. This aspect makes much difference between the management of the corporate entities and that of the *waqf* institutions that might be working at the micro or corporate level.

There are recent empirical studies that assess various aspects of management around all the aforementioned concepts. Accountability is a rather more effective feature of governance of institutions that manage people's money for people's benefit, and common welfare in the economy. It requires a deep

DOI: 10.4324/9781003477549-6

understanding of the working for the sake of meeting the expectations of the endowers, beneficiaries, and other stakeholders in using the *waqf* resources to achieve the desired pious ends. Hence, the management of such belief-based institutions has to be based on principles different from that of the management and governance of conventional corporate business entities. It requires different factors and processes for meeting the expectations of stakeholders by using the donated funds optimally and efficiently.

6.2 Framework of *Waqf* Management and Governance

Ensuring good governance is the hallmark of the *awqāf* system. The overall structure of management and governance of the institution of *waqf* has a wider spectrum than that of management in general or corporate governance. There are recent empirical studies that assess various aspects of management around all the aforementioned concepts. Accountability is a rather more effective feature of governance of institutions that manage people's money for people's benefit, and common welfare in the economy. It requires a deep understanding of the working for the sake of meeting the expectations of stakeholders in using the *waqf* resources to achieve the desired pious ends.

Standards of governance pertain to independence, fairness, and accountability. Accountability in *waqf* management measures responsibility, transparency, disclosure, participation, self-regulation, and adherence to the founder's objectives/donors' rights [governance, privacy, and others]. Such a standard of governance helps in maintaining the integrity of the system and acceptability among the masses.

Sundqvist et al. (2014) indicate four close corporate concepts of management namely efficiency, effectiveness, quality, and governance. They define efficiency as "meeting all internal requirements for cost, margins and asset utilization" while effectiveness is meant for "satisfying all requirements of the customer". In the case of *waqf*, accountability to Allah (SWT), fellow human beings, and society is equally important. It can be depicted as in Figure 6.1.

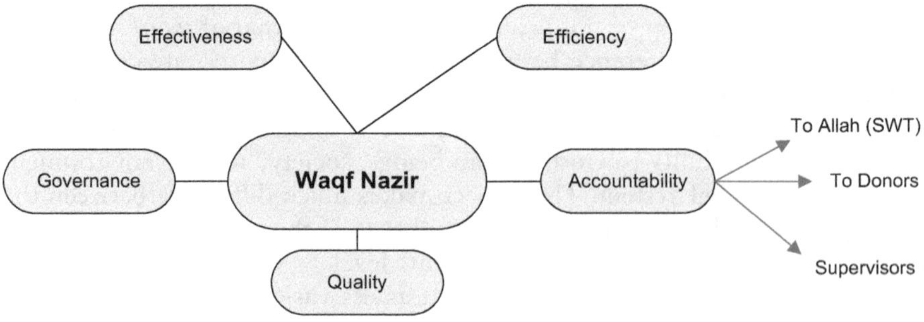

Figure 6.1 Five Factors of *Waqf* Management.
Source: Authors' own.

The major reason behind this is the difference in the objectives – public welfare and thanksgiving to Allah SWT and getting His favor in the former, and profit/earnings maximization in self-interest in the latter case. This wider spectrum of *waqf* management and governance is depicted in Figure 6.2.

The aforementioned structure implies that the mutawalli (*nāzir*) is expected to manage all affairs under the guidance of the *waqf* board with the help of professionals like accountants, auditors, and supervisors/regulators. The process covers all stages starting from the creation of *waqf*, getting donations, and providing instant and long-term solutions to the needy with proper disclosure and accounting processes. It requires that we discuss the formation of the *awqāf*, related parts of the AAOIFI's Standard on *waqf*, duties of *nāzir* and related matters, accountability as a special feature of *waqf* institutions, and the WCPs as suggested by IWG on *waqf* (2018).

Nāzir is the main role player for *waqf* and is considered a change maker as his dynamic leadership paves the road to the institutional evolution of *awqāf*. Historic records suggest that *nāzir* used to have some flexibility that helped initiate institutional changes, such as the pooling of cash *waqf* assets, that too working under an environment of strict Sharī'ah law. However, the flexibility has to be carefully watched for proper risk management, particularly in respect of cash *waqfs* and the use of *waqf* funds for financing entrepreneurs and other socioeconomic projects.

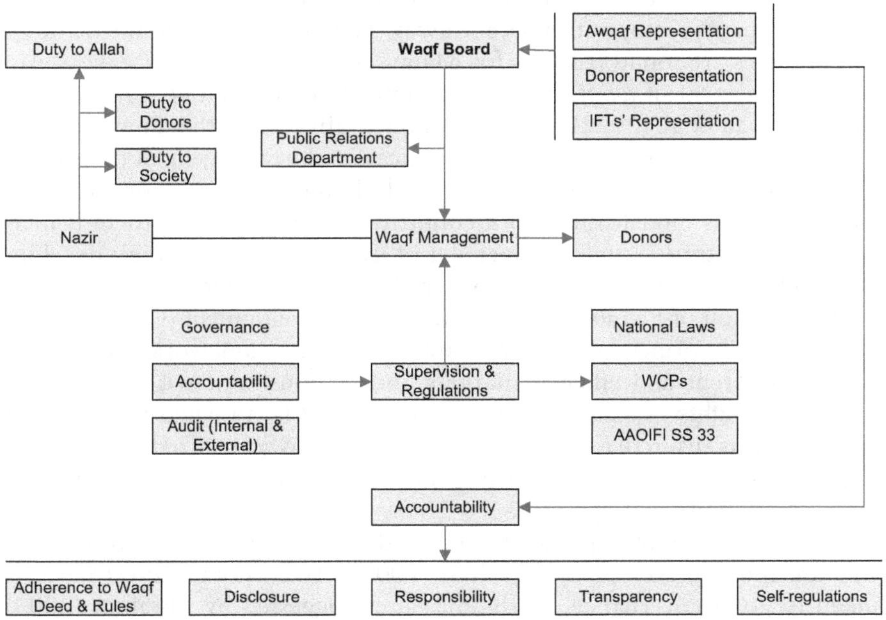

Figure 6.2 The Management and Governance Framework of *Waqf* Institutions.

IFP, Immediate Funds Transfer.

Source: Authors' own.

As the *awqāf* system for socioeconomic objectives has to be revived in almost all OIC member countries necessarily including Pakistan, it would also require strategic management of the evolutionary process. It might not be possible without strategic policy formulation and implementation at all levels.

Fortunately, the revitalization of *waqf* institutions has become top on the agenda of Muslim communities around the world for the past few decades. The awareness of *waqf* revitalization is increasingly gaining popularity amongst Muslim countries. The governments of most Muslim countries have realized the need for the revival of *waqf* as an important tool for creating a better society (e.g., Kuwait, Jordan, Sudan, Malaysia, Indonesia, and Bangladesh). In addition to this, many international *waqf* conferences were organized by the Islamic Development Bank (IDB) through its subsidiary, the Islamic Research and Training Institute (IRTI) (later renamed as IsDB Institute), and some universities in Malaysia and Indonesia also demonstrate a growing interest and awareness in *waqf* institutions and consider it as one of the tools of community development (Cajee, 2008; Ayedh & Ihsan, 2013).

6.2.1 Governance of Awqāf *vis-à-vis the Corporate Governance*

Good governance is a critical success factor for revitalizing *awqāf* institutions (Kahf, 2007; Saad et al., 2016; Cajee, 2007; Ayedh & Ihsan, 2013; Hassan Rusni et al., 2022) but the fact is that historically there was no framework for the not-for-profit sector until a decade away (Hyndman & McDonnell, 2009). Many studies are found (such as for Malaysia) that have gone a stage ahead for the assessment of *waqfs* by the government's councils that manage these *waqfs*. Hassan et al. (2022) conducted a qualitative study that compared the impact of good governance and best practices on the management of *waqf* by selected SIRCs in Penang, Perak, and Kuala Lumpur to Singapore, Kuwait, and the UAE as model framework countries. Studies find that there is ineffective administration and management of *waqfs* that hinders their development and expansion in terms of broader objectives of *waqf*.

Organization of Economic Cooperation and Development (OECD, 2005) has adopted six principles: (i) corporate governance framework should promote transparent and efficient markets and be consistent with the rule of law; (ii) the rights of shareholders are protected; (iii) an equal treatment of shareholders is ensured; (iv) the role of stakeholders is recognized; (v) accurate disclosure of the company's finances; and (vi) monitoring of the management and accountability by the board.

There are different aspects of accountability of nāzir where most relevant are those suggested by Ebrahim (2003). As corporate governance is linked to good governance, so the measures suggested by Ebrahim (2003) are compared with the King Report for Corporate Governance South Africa and OECD's corporate governance (OECD, 2005). Looking at the study by Ebrahim (2003) that provides five standards for accountability of nāzir, this book suggests, from the comparison of corporate governance, seven principles for the accountability of *nāzir*. These include disclosure statements and reports, performance assessment, participation, self-regulation, social auditing, adherence to the founder's objectives and protection of donors' rights, promotion of transparent and efficient *waqf* financial markets, and consistency with the rule of law. Abu-Tapanjeh (2009, pp. 17–19) has given a nice comparative position of Islamic principles of corporate governance with the revised principles of OECD.

King Report II on Corporate Governance for South Africa (2002) suggests a few principles for corporate governance for charities that include discipline, transparency, independence, accountability, responsibility, fairness, and social responsibility. It moved from the single bottom line (shareholders approach) to a triple bottom line, which embraces the economic, environmental, and social aspects of a company's activities It implies that for the good governance of charities, the word "corporate governance" is also used that refers to the structure of rules, practices, and processes used to direct and manage a company. A company's Board of Directors is the primary force influencing corporate governance.

Governance, in the context of *waqf* institutions, refers to the process and structure of directing and managing the affairs of the *waqf* institution toward enhancing the social welfare of the rightful recipients as well as demonstrating accountability to the *waqf* donor. Efficiency shows how well the institutions are using their resources to meet their objectives of socioeconomic justice like reducing poverty (Saad et al., 2016).

Saad et al. (2016) found that due to legislative lacunae, administrative lapses, lack of political will, indifferent attitude of the management of the *awqāf*, and lack of honesty/integrity, the commercial *waqf* properties are not being maintained efficiently and so they do not yield optimal level of benefits to the society.

As *waqf* and charitable organizations share similar characteristics (Sadeq, 2002), so the concept of its governance overlaps with that of the nonprofits, too. As the governance system in nonprofits (Western society in particular) encompasses the board of directors, the perspective of corporate management from the business sector can also be adopted (Hyndman & McDonnell, 2009). Here principal-agent theory might be relevant because the provider of funds wants money to be spent for the objective of the donation. Saad et al. (2016) compare two concepts, efficiency and governance, where efficiency is the measure of the use of resources to meet objectives while, governance, as explained by UNDP (1997), is how management power is exercised along with the accountability toward the donors.

The concept of accountability is the major difference between the conventional and Islamic codes of governance. Ayedh et al. (2018) identify the main historical stages of the development of accountability in *awqāf*. The first stage of *waqf* introduction and emergence at the time of the Prophet (PBUH) and his companions – ad hoc in nature mainly relying on the individual piousness and honesty of the *nāzir*. The second stage of "growth and development" witnessed the expansion of *waqf* in many aspects of the community such as religion, education, health, economic aid to the needy, etc. As accountability-related issues surfaced, mechanisms were developed as and when needed. These included: establishing *diwan al hisbah* for recording all transactions at the time of the second pious caliph (Omar Ibn Al khattab RA) especially for *awqāf* in the Fatimid period, and appointment the Qādi (judge) to supervise directly the *nāzir* and to ensure that the *waqf* is being used and managed in the right manner. The third "declining and collapse" stage started after the colonization of the Muslim areas in the world. The *waqf* properties were mismanaged, the role and contribution of *waqf* to the community shrunk to only worship places, and the institution lost the trust of the Muslim community.

6.2.2 Concept of Holistic Accountability in Awqāf

Accountability is a central theme in Islam because accountability to Allah and the community is paramount to a Muslim's faith (Lewis, 2006). Askary and Clarke (1997) asserted that the word *hisāb* which is interrelated with accounting, and accountable is repeated more than eight times in different verses in the Qur'an. In the Islamic perspective, the holistic accountability model is the most pertinent which was developed by Ihsan (2017) in his study on accountability practice in a *waqf* institution in Indonesia (Ayedh et al., 2018). This model of holistic *waqf* accountability based on studies by O'Dwyer and Unerman (2008) and Ebrahim (2003) encompasses upward and downward accountability.

In management of *waqf*, the religious dimension is added where the *waqf* money is devoted to Allah SWT in search of His favor for the welfare of human beings and all other creatures. In that way, the *waqf* governance extends the sphere of the term to some very broader levels. It increases the sphere of the external elements on one side by adding accountability, and the internal elements as it covers all aspects of administration.

Ebrahim (2003) reviewed five broad mechanisms of accountability to be practiced by the NGO. These are reports and disclosure statements, performance assessments and evaluations, participation, self-regulation, and social audits. Each mechanism, tool or process is analyzed along three dimensions of accountability: upward–downward, internal–external, and functional or strategic. He found that practically in the NGOs accountability emphasizes "upward" and "external" – accountability to donors while "downward" and "internal" mechanisms remain comparatively underdeveloped.

Ayedh et al. (2018) found that *nāzirs* tend to prioritize upward accountability instead of downward accountability. It means that they give more attention to the government and donors. Hence, the government's role must be well defined, and effective while avoiding interference regarding the *waqf* activities. Other measures may include: (i) regular issuance of financial reports, (ii) report of nonfinancial welfare activities, and (iii) conducting customers' (beneficiaries) satisfaction surveys.

There must be a focus on accountability in managing the system of *awqāf*. Accountability in the Islamic perspective means much more than the conventional conception of accountability. It is the most forceful and effective element in management as every believer has been held accountable to Allah SWT for all activities and actions (Qur'an, Al-Zalzalah 99:7). Haniffa (2002) takes the view while getting support from the Quranic verse (2:284), that the ultimate accountability in Islam is to Allah since all deeds will be counted in the *hereafter*. "To Allah belongs all that is in the heavens and on earth. Whether you show what is in your minds or conceal it, Allah will call you to account for it" (Qur'an, Al-Baqarah 2:284). Secondly, accountability is identified as part of *Ibādah* (servitude to Allah) and *amal sāleh* (virtuous deeds) in attaining *al-Falāh* (benefit for the people in this world and the hereafter) (Haniffa, 2002). Therefore, Ibrahim (2000) comes up with the concept of dual accountability whereby human beings are accountable to Allah SWT as well as to the people to fulfill any contract made among them. Shahul (2001) named it Islamic accountability which leads to some principles of good governance in Islam. Similarly, Zein et al. (2008) derived some good governance principles from Qur'anic verses and the principle of tawhid.

The first such principle is *amānah* which refers to a contract between God and man that determines the individual's relationship with society. If an individual understands the concept of *amānah*, the issues regarding rights and responsibilities can be resolved. The fulfillment of *amānah* would bring to *adālah* (justice), the second principle of good governance. According to Shahul (2001), *adālah* in an Islamic economic scheme is aimed at achieving social welfare. *Adālah* principle leads Muslims to work with full objectivity.

Other important aspects of accountability are functional accountability (accounting for resources, resource use, and immediate impacts) and strategic accountability (accounting for the impacts that an NGO's activities have on the actions of other organizations and the wider environment) (Ebrahim, 2003). Ebrahim (2003) also found that the NGOs and donors focused primarily on short-term "functional" accountability responses and not the longer-term "strategic" processes that are necessary for long-term social impact.

Ebrahim (2003) has indicated the key characteristics of the accountability mechanisms in the form of a table (Table 6.1).

6.2.3 Accountability of Nāzir *(Mutawalli or Manager)*

Accountability of *nāzir* is important in the management of *waqf*. *Nāzir* is accountable to (i) the *wāqif* (donor), (ii) government/*awqāf* institutions, (iii) the *waqf* beneficiaries, (iv) the related NGOs, (v) the similar *waqf* organizations, (vi) the society, and (vii) accountable to Allah SWT (Ayedah et al., 2018). Rashid (2008) contends that the phenomenon of lack of accountability in *waqf* is due to the decline of the standard of morality. Various

Table 6.1 Key Characteristics of Accountability Mechanisms

Accountability mechanism (tool or process)	*Accountability (upward, downward, or to self)*	*Inducement (internal or external)*	*Organizational response (functional or strategic*
Disclosures/ reports (tool)	– Upward to funders and oversight agencies – Downward (to a lesser degree) – Disclosures/ reports (tool) to clients or members who read the reports	– Legal requirement – Tax status – Funding requirement (external threat of loss of funding or tax status)	– Primarily functional, with a focus on short-term results
Performance assessment and evaluation (tool)	– Upward to funders – Significant potential for downward from NGOs to communities and from funders to NGOs	– Funding requirement (external) – Potential to become a learning tool (internal)	– Primarily functional at present, with possibilities for longer-term strategic assessments.
Participation (process)	– Downward from NGOs to clients and communities – Internally to NGOs themselves – Significant potential for downward from funders to NGOs	– Organizational values (internal) – Funding requirement (external)	– Primarily functional if participation is limited to consultation and implementation – Strategic if it involves increasing bargaining power of clients vis-à-vis NGOs, and NGOs vis-à-vis funders
Self-regulation (process)	– To NGOs themselves, as a sector – Potentially to clients and donors	– Erosion of public confidence due to scandals and exaggeration of accomplishments (external loss of funds; internal loss of reputation)	– Strategic in that it concerns long-term change involving codes of conduct

Table 6.1 (Continued)

Accountability mechanism (tool or process)	*Accountability (upward, downward, or to self)*	*Inducement (internal or external)*	*Organizational response (functional or strategic*
Social auditing (tool and process)	– To NGOs themselves (by linking values to strategy and performance) – Downward and upward to stakeholders	– Erosion of public confidence (external) – Valuation of social, environmental, and ethical performance on par with economic performance (internal)	– Functional to the extent it affects the behavior of a single organization – Strategic to the extent it affects NGO-stakeholder interaction, promotes longer-term planning, and becomes adopted sector-wide

Source: Ebrahim (2003).

authors suggest different aspects of accountability of *nāzir* (Jacobs, 2000; Brennan & Solomon, 2008; Ebrahim, 2003).

According to AAOIFI Shari'ah Standard no. (60) on Waqf, Para: 5/2 p.832/2015, the *nāzir* should perform the following tasks: (1) management, maintenance, and development of the *waqf*; (2) leasing of the assets or usufructs of the *waqf* and leasing of the *waqf* lands; (3) development of the *waqf* properties either directly through Shari'ah-sanctioned methods of investment or through financial institutions; (4) increasing the *waqf* money by investing it in Mudarabah and other similar forms; (5) changing the operational form of the *waqf* assets with the aim of maximizing the benefit generated for the *waqf* and its beneficiaries; (6) defending the right of the *waqf*; (7) settlement of the debts of the *waqf*; (8) payment of the entitlements of beneficiaries; (9) replacement of the *waqf*; (10) safeguarding the *waqf* properties against occupation or seizure by others; (11) using takaful to safeguard the *waqf* assets; and (12) preparation of the *waqf* accounts and the submission of statements and reports on them to the concerned authorities (IWG-2018).

There is another concept, "quality" used for the "quality management" (QM) with focus on the customer. Quality encompasses "aligning the product (as per the required internal standards) with the customer's needs (external demand)" and can be termed both as "doing things right" (efficiency) and "doing the right things" (effectiveness). So, the term "quality" implies both internal and external, as well as short-term and long-term perspectives. While efficiency emphasizes internal and short-term issues, effectiveness tends to emphasize long-term issues that are both internal and external.

6.2.4 Need for Standardized Waqf *Management Rules*

As can be inferred from the aforementioned discussion, accountability is a central theme in in the context of *waqf* management. Here, good governance is based on the concept of the absolute unity of Allah (*tawhid*) and belief in the life hereafter. The *waqf* charter, based on the Qur'anic guidance, originates a specific set of operational principles such *amānah* and *adālah* which reinforce the processes of governance. Critical academic studies have discussed various approaches for *waqf* that are based on the management of large commercial/financial corporations of Western origin. These approaches have high-end standards for transparency and accountability.

Waqf management protocols start from the formation of a *waqf* and the deed for creating a *waqf*. There is a need to find an appropriate set of tools for the standardized procedures for the creation and supervision of *waqfs*. Conditions for formation of *waqf*, as suggested by Hasan (2007), are given in Box 6.1.

Box 6.1 Major Conditions for *Waqf* Formation

1. The property must be a real estate or a thing with some meaning of perpetuity (e.g. land, buildings, vehicles, books, cash /liquid assets, tools, etc.)
2. The property should be given on a permanent basis (temporary *waqf* is only for family *waqf*).
3. The *waqf founder* must be an adult Muslim of good health and able to take such an action.
4. The founder must be the legal owner of the property and have the property in question under his/her possession.
5. The purpose of *waqf must,* at the end, be an act of charity from points of view of both Sharī'ah and the founder *(waqf* on the rich alone is not permissible because it is not charity).
6. The founder must use certain prescribed words and verb forms conventionally understood as signifying the notion of perpetuity, such as *waqf, hubs*, etc.
7. The object of the endowment must be property whose utilization will not result in its dissipation or consumption.
8. The creation of the *waqf* has to be declared formally according to the country's legal framework.

Source: Adapted from Hasan (2007)

A new thought process has evolved in respect of concepts and practices that fulfill the modern-day requirements for social welfare. Now, cash *waqf* has become a major institution within the overall concept of *awqāf* for helping the needy. The standards require a much deeper understanding of the working of *waqf* institutions with belief and knowledge of the specific stages of evolution of the *waqfs*. Impressive work has already been done on standardization and providing an effective framework for *waqf* operations in the modern age. AAOIFI issued its Sharī'ah Standard on *waqf* which indicates all Sharī'ah-related and many operations-related aspects. The IWG (2018) also suggested a comprehensive set of Core Principles for the operation and supervision of *awqāf* in October 2018. These WCPs have been structured around the basic building blocks of social finance focusing on "benevolence" and "mutual benefit" by harmonizing the alternative viewpoints regarding the three principles of perpetuity (preservation of the assets along with its purpose), inalienability, and irreversibility.

The WCPs allow the commingling of endowment funds with other philanthropy-driven funds with the condition that there is divine motivation and the *waqf* portfolio is restricted only to halal businesses. These principles pertain to the legal foundation, supervision, good governance, risk management, and Sharī'ah governance of any *waqf* and its activities. IWG's technical report is the main reference document for measuring the performance of *waqf* management that also accommodates the technical and operational aspects (IWG-2018).

By adopting the Basel Core Principles (BCPs), the WCPs represent an international standard of high-level principles to achieve and assess *waqf* supervisory practices. In case the banks create and manage *waqfs*, the BCPs that have already been adopted by banks in more than 150 countries, may represent the best model to emulate for *waqf* supervisory practices (IWG-2018).

Box 6.2 Basic Information Contained in an 18th-Century *Waqf* Register

1) The name of the *waqf*, locality, trustee.
2) The purpose for its establishment.
3) Original capital of the *waqf*.
4) Later additions to capital (either by individuals or by other *awqaf)*.
5) Annual return obtained from the capital (the *murabaha fi sene-I kamile*)
6) The purpose for which the annual return was designated.
7) Finally, information about the borrowers of the endowment capital:
8) The borrower(s)' name(s), locality, religion and gender.
9) The amount of capital they borrowed.

Source: Adapted from Hassan (2007, p. 214)

Quality is measured empirically also for *waqfs*. In a study of empirical measurement on one aspect of quality (reporting), Hanefah et al. (2021) found that in Malaysia, the quality of *waqfs* remained at a moderate level as it scored 40.29%. Though it seems quite a smaller (less than 50%) achievement, yet, in the times of the renaissance/re-emergence of Islamic social institutions, it is quite healthy, if it continues to grow with the process of emergence. However, as disclosure is the most effective corporate principle, lapses in the reporting of disclosures have to be removed. The basic information about any *waqf* in the Ottoman period is given in Box 6.2.

According to the WCPs, a temporary *waqf* donation can also fulfill its charitable objectives and result in two benefits – one for the beneficiaries as per the *waqf* deed throughout its specified period, and the other for the benefit of the *wāqif* who may need his property in the future (AAOIFI Sharī'ah Standard no. (33) Waqf p.832/2015).

There must be many additions to the list about the receipt of donations, investments, grants, *qarḍ hassan*, financing based on trade- and lease-based modes, and the benefits accruing to the nazir and the members of the *Waqf* Board.

Hanefah et al. (2021) measured five factors that influence quality *waqf* reporting practices. These are relevance, faithful representation, understandability, comparability, and timeliness. A similar study was conducted by Kamaruddin (2018) that found some lapses in the reporting of *waqfs* under investigation including many nondisclosures. There "information disclosed" is defined as, what the stakeholders desire, rather than what *nāzir* (*waqf* administrator) wants to disclose. This observation is closer to the fifth corporate principle of the OECD on disclosure and transparency, "accurate disclosure of the company's finances". So, corporate principles are employed for monitoring the *waqfs*.

6.3 Management of *Awqāf* in Some Jurisdictions

Waqf administration went through five stages during the Ottoman Caliphate starting from 1486, wherein each stage, the level of the caliphate's intervention increased while the *mutavallis'* powers and shares of *waqfs* in the revenues reduced.

Ottomans managed *waqfs*, in later stages, by centralization/nationalization in various stages. The system worked well, though some authors hinted at nationalization-related issues of performance, efficiency, and morality.[2] Internal management was performed by the *waqfs* themselves, as the *waqf* was an institution of the people for the people and managed by the people. It would have promoted self-governance and so should have inculcated the habit of self-rule while working under the laws of Sharī'ah, a set of ultimate principles of social justice.

6.3.1 Management of Cash Waqfs *in Ottoman Caliphate*

As cash *waqfs* are quite different from other *waqfs*, their management is also different. Cash *awqāf* became an institution of credit that was managed under the same administration led by *nāzirs*. Cash *waqf* made up 50% of the total number of *waqfs* in the 16th century with features of permanence, perpetuity, accountability, and most importantly, risk management. The role of *Qādi* in the administration and record keeping of the cash *waqfs*, as for other *waqfs*, was quite efficient and so impressive. As there was no concept of the financial *Qādi*/court, so the same *Qādi* used to examine, record, and provide decisions on the matters relating to the cash *waqfs*, under the Sharī'ah law.

Qādi used to record the *vakfname* (*waqf* deed) along with the operating procedures and accretion (return) rates. Three main kinds of cash *waqfs* "*neighbourhood avariz funds*", "*artisan guild funds*", and "*janissary funds*" were managed in the same way as there was no mention of kind specific rules.

The *waqf* trustees used to work just like the present-day fund managers of pool funds as a single authority. The amount endowed by each founder, the accretion rates (on trade- or lease-based financing) he or she finds appropriate, the rents received from the properties and the demanded services differed from one another. Within this view, the accounting of each *waqf* endowed to the funds was recorded in the same book but on separate pages.

Cash *waqfs* were like equity-based companies where they were administered by a single elected trustee as reported by Gürsoy (2018). The single trustee was appointed by the founder and recorded by the *Qādi*. Onwards, the assets were managed by a single trustee under the Sharī'ah law and the protection of the executive powers of the caliphate.

Vakfname (deeds) were important in managing the risks and uncertainties as there used to be necessary guidelines such as the characteristics of loan seekers (Gürsoy, 2018). Similar was the warning against advancing the loans without a strong guarantor and/or a valuable good(s) against uncertainties. Immovables taken as pledged assets were insured against potential natural risks. Devaluation risk was also managed by cash management, avoiding the use of multiple currencies and mentioning the currency type, as there were 36 different currencies in the early 19th century.

Vakfname also included the explicit mention of the voluntary supervision of the "reliable people" such as well-known people in the neighborhood, artisan masters, and Janissary headmen. There was a mechanism of public accountability too, as trustees were instructed to show all accountings to anyone who wished. The checking of the accountings at intervals by official supervisors was another risk-reducing precaution. Provided that no complaints were available against foundations accounting, they were not required to be checked by official authorities every year. In this way, the optimum output gained out of the risk-management processes manifested itself in all areas of the *waqfs*. Thanks to these risk-management practices the cash *waqfs* that started by the end of the 15th century continued their existence for about 450 years.

The risk management of the cash *waqfs* during the Ottoman period was an integral part of financial management. The purpose of such risk management is the sustainability of the endowed assets without decreasing and preservation of the *waqf* resources. The administrative risk also contained the possibility of malpractice and corruption (Gürsoy, 2018).

Although the maintenance of the optimum balance through a well-conducted analysis of the possible risks concerning the monetary foundations and funds was the task of the trustees, the necessary warnings were included in the endowment deeds against uncertainties. Among all, the characteristics of those asking for a loan were the leading warnings. While it was specifically suggested in the following statements that those in debt, the ill-natured people, the greedy, the extravagant, the arrogant, and the imposters should not be lent money, such people like soldiers, *kadis*, *ameers*, and governors were also included among those to be avoided in terms of lending (Suceska, 1990, p. 273).

Through the second warning within the context of risk management, it was requested that no money should be lent without the presence of a strong guarantor and/or a valuable good against the uncertainties. Special attention was paid in picking the guarantors from among the close acquaintances of the borrower such as relatives, spouses, or colleagues.

Through the third warning, precautions were taken against the risks likely to result from the potential devaluation of the endowed money over time. Through this warning which can also be associated with cash management, the loans lent in the markets in which multiple currencies were transacted were asked to be returned in the same kind of currency. The foundation expenses were also defined by the endowed currency type. As the income and expense balance in foundations were almost well suited, even the slightest fluctuation could lead to problems. Considering the transaction of 36 different currencies in the Ottoman economy in the early 19th century, the importance of the desire to transact upon the same sort of currency becomes apparent.

The warning system played an important role in preventing deficiencies and corruption. Also, the trustees had to show all foundation accountings to any requestor. The checking of the accounting at intervals by official supervisors was another risk-reducing precaution. Provided that no complaints were available against foundation accountings, they did not require to be checked by official authorities every year. Even though the concept of risk management was not directly used in foundations, precautions were taken in several transactions considering the potential risks. In this way, the optimum output gained out of the risk-management processes manifested itself in all areas of the trust institution.

6.3.2 Waqf *Management in Muslim India*

Mughal rulers of Muslim India were able to donate huge funds and lands to the *Sufi* shrines and *madrassas*. They also developed a well-developed monitoring institution of *Sadru-us-sudoor* for the supervision of *waqf* assets. They, however, could not take the steps that Ottoman Turks took to increase the central working of *waqfs*.

Under the Mughals, as Ernst and Lawrence (2002) reported, the State began to appoint a *mutawalli* who oversaw the financial aspects of dargahs including the endowment (*waqf*). The *mutawalli* was typically but not always a Muslim and was not necessarily related to the *sufi* or his descendants.

Islamic scholars and *sufis* that were managing the *waqfs* could have helped change the use of *waqf* funds donated to the shrines and *madrassas*. There were many cases and appeals regarding the shrines' assets in the past century, with decisions as recent as 2013. Documents regarding the *waqf* (endowment) and shrine administration dating from the 16th century onward were admitted as evidence in these cases, some of which are available as published legal proceedings while others could be found in colonial administrative archives.

6.3.3 Management of Waqf *in Malaysia and Indonesia*

Indonesia and Malaysia are currently going through the modern application of governance models of large corporations for *waqfs*. In the corporate-oriented governance models, according to Pitchay (2018), donors cannot intervene in the outcomes of *waqf's* productivity, because no channel should allow communication afterwards. Other issues of these governance models include, *inter alia*, the lack of reporting standards, lack of professionalism, and absence of strategies for the development of *waqf* assets (Masyita et al., 2005; Shaikh, et al, 2017)).

There are three processes of accountability-oriented governance: monitoring, Sharī'ah audit, and *shura*. The monitoring mechanism includes the office of *qādi*, the board of trustees, and the audit committee.

Rofiqoh et al. (2021) studied the establishment of a multicase model of Islamic Corporate Governance for Indonesian and Malaysian entrepreneurial cash *waqf* endowments and found that such governance models were built from a unique CSR based endowment membership scheme. Three points of the transferability of the governance model of cash *waqf* based on entrepreneurship are: (1) addition of *wāqif* (corporate partners), involving the general public, and the selection of permanent donors; (2) the productivity of endowment funds intended to finance *qard al hasan* on the qualifications of seedlings, shoots and business development and other financings; (3) job training in potential sectors (sewing, haircuts, and other job training) is a multibenefit project development strategy. The synergy of sustainable multibenefit projects in entrepreneurial money-based endowments is the key to the transferability of the governance model of cash *waqf* based on entrepreneurship endowments.

The governance of the *waqfs*, in Malaysia, faced various constraints such as legal, financial, and administrative. Legal constraints include loopholes in the legal framework that arise due to regulations of various state laws. There are *waqf* laws only in Selangor (since 1999) and in Malacca (since 2005). Also, the state jurisdiction creates various problems in understanding and interpretation of *waqf* operations that lead to contradictory fatwas across the states (Ibrahim, 2012). These situations resulted in the incoherent implementation of some of the Islamic laws including *waqf* practices (Alawiah, 2012).

The cash *waqf* is an impressive tool for the Islamic religious council in Malaysia to generate financial resources. It is more productive for the benefit of *waqf* institutions, and society in general at the macroeconomic level. Tax incentives have been given to the people to encourage them to dedicate property including cash *waqf* for charitable purposes (Ibrahim, Nor, & Mohammad, 2013). Because of the available potential of *waqf* assets in Malaysia, the Federal Government of Malaysia took a significant step to enhance SIRC's role in administering and developing *waqf* assets through the allocation of funds for developing *waqf* assets. In this respect, the Federal Government took initiative to implement projects with the cooperation of SIRCs.

6.3.4 Management of awqāf *in Kuwait*

Historically, *waqf* in Kuwait dates back to 1695, but notable development started in the 1930s and reached a significant stage in 1993 with the enactment of *awqāf* laws.

Before the governmental involvement in *waqf* management, Kuwait's *waqf* sector was administered by founders (*wāqfien*) or their representatives (*nāzir/mutawalli*) where the appointments of representatives were endorsed by judges of the court of law. But from the 1930s, a department of *waqf* was established followed by the establishment of *Waqf* Affairs Boards in the 1940s. After the independence of Kuwait in 1962, the Ministry of *Awqāf* and Islamic Affairs was established to perform several tasks including the responsibility of managing *waqf* properties (Al-Osman, 1997).

The *waqf* sector in Kuwait is administrated by the Kuwait Awqāf Public Foundation (KAPF) established in 1993 (Al- Osman, 1997). The Decree provided KAPF the status of a governmental body with relative autonomy in decision-making to regulate and manage the system to take care of *waqf* affairs internally and externally.

Waqf funds in Kuwait that have independent management are expected to contribute to the development of *waqf* practices to fulfill the community's needs. For that, KAPF established ten operational *waqf* funds broadly in three areas: social welfare-related funds, religious development funds, and education/scientific development funds (Khalil et al., 2014).

The main missions of the KAPF are to consolidate the concept of *waqf* as a developmental mechanism in the community and activate its role in achieving the objectives of the founders in addition to reinforcing the tendency of contemporary Islamic civilization. While the major responsibility of KAPF is to encourage people to establish new *awqāf*, managing them to allocate funds for activities and investment of the assets are its general tasks. In addition,

KAPF coordinates with governmental and nongovernmental bodies for the establishment of Sharī'ah-compliant *waqf* projects to achieve related objectives. This coordination includes specifically managing specialized funds in the *waqf* sector, regional institutions for the *waqf* development, and the management of family *waqf*.

For the sake of risk management that saves from the erosion of perpetuity, the KAPF developed a strategy based on three aspects: (i) real estate development (by establishing a company), (ii) long-term investments, and (iii) financial investments. Under the direct long-term investment, KAPF introduced to invest in charity educational institutions as well as providing consulting services in the areas of administrative and training programs. Besides, KPAF made investments in Sharī'ah-compliant investments such as investing in medium and long-term mutual funds.

As Afadli (1998) identified, KAPF ensures an appropriate distribution mechanism – the revenues of *awqāf* (and allied funds) are distributed as per the founder's conditions with the involvement of civil society institutions, and the involvement of families for family *waqfs*.

6.4 General Regulatory Framework of *Waqf* Management

The group working under IRTI-Bank Indonesia in their report of *waqf* core principles (IWG-2018) suggested a general regulatory framework for the management of *awqāf* (Figure 6.3).

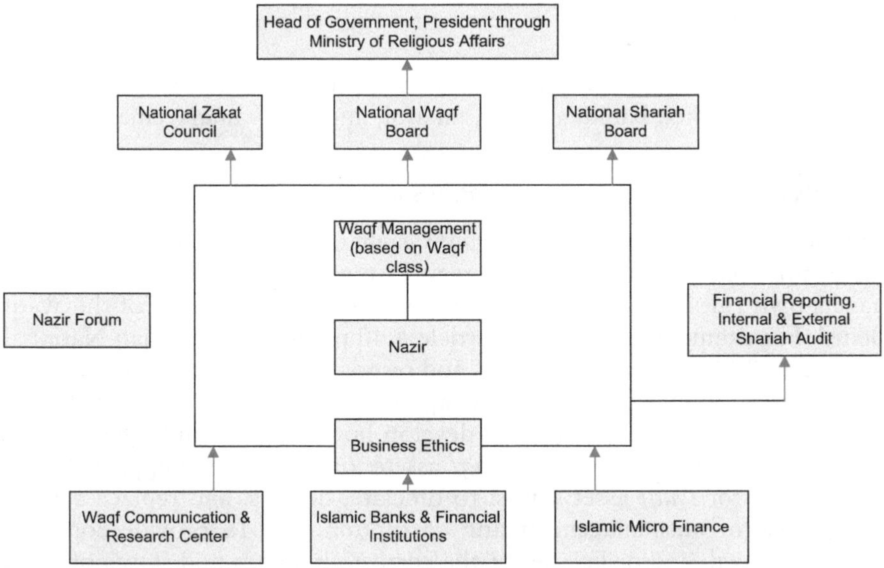

Figure 6.3 General Regulatory Framework for *Waqf* Management and Supervision.
Source: IRTI-Bank Indonesia (IWGWCP, 2018, p. 17).

However, *waqf* laws may differ widely across countries and jurisdictions. The most important task of the regulator is to supervise the *waqf* management, which includes ensuring Sharī'ah compliance, financial transparency, and economic efficiency. Therefore, there is a need to build a strong supporting system, such as strengthening the function of the Sharī'ah Supervisory Board, standardization of the *waqf* accounting and financial reporting system, assessment of *waqf* management performance, a monitoring system for operational efficiency, economic and social impacts for beneficiaries, and collaboration with financial institutions for Islamic microfinance.

The IWG (2018) has indicated two models for managing *waqf*, centralized and decentralized. Some countries such as Kuwait, Qatar, and various other MENA countries have applied the centralized model while others have applied the decentralized model, or a combination of both models at the same time, such as in the case of Indonesia. Following is the proposed institutional and regulatory framework for *waqf* management and supervision.

The regulations for *waqf* management institutions may comprehensively cover all operational aspects of the *waqf* institutions with the following objectives:

(i) Optimizing the collection based on supporting governing rules.
(ii) Maximizing the effectiveness of *waqf* management operations and to promote its governance.
(iii) Maximizing *waqf* roles in supporting equitable economic development and poverty alleviation.
(iv) To open the possibility of cross-sector financial activities such as the capital market, banking sector, takaful, and *zakāh* management.

6.4.1 Waqf Board and Its Duties – Strategies of Waqf Board

Another important element in the *waqf* system is the apex body, often termed the Waqf Board, which acts as a regulator and supervisor. Each country has its own rules about the power, composition, and functions of the Waqf Board. For example, according to article # 40 point (1) Indonesian National Act no. 41/2004 on *waqf*, the duties and responsibilities of a *Waqf* Board are as follows: (i) to improve the *nāzir's* capability for managing and developing *waqf* treasury. (ii) To manage and develop both national and international *waqf* treasuries and abandoned *waqf* assets. (iii) To provide approvals and permissions for *waqf* asset status; to officiate, dismiss, and replace a *nāzir* in the case of mismanagement and corruption. (iv) To provide consideration, approval, and/or license for the correct alteration and status of *waqf* treasury. (v) To provide advice and consideration for the government in the formulation of *waqf* policies. In the same article, point (2) states that in carrying out its duties, the Waqf Board collaborates with communities, mass organizations, experts, international institutions, and both local and national government bodies.

Strategies to accomplish the vision and mission of the *Waqf* Board include:

(i) To increase the competency and national and international networks of the Waqf Board.
(ii) To compose regulation and *waqf* management policies.
(iii) To enhance public awareness and willingness to contribute for *waqf*.
(iv) To boost the professionalism and honesty of *nāzirs* in managing and developing *waqf* assets.
(v) To coordinate and develop *nāzirs*.
(vi) To improve *waqf* asset administration.
(vii) To monitor and protect *waqf* assets.
(viii) To collect, manage, and develop both national and international *waqf* assets.

The main duties of the Waqf Board are to manage *waqf* assets through the nāzir both nationally and internationally. Additionally, the Waqf Board must collaborate with communities, mass organizations, experts, and international institutions.

The *nāzir* or *waqf* manager should have the following qualifications:

i. Being a *Muslim*.
ii. Being sane and passing the age of puberty.
iii. Being completely trustworthy.
iv. Having complete knowledge and understanding of the *waqf* rulings and regulations, as an essential requisite for senior management.
v. The relevant authorities may develop and perform a fit and proper test in order to confirm the quality of the senior management of the *waqf* institution.
vi. Being efficient and having the capability to manage *waqf* assets.

The *nāzir* should also pay attention to the following issues:

i. **Maslahah** (achieve benefit/avoid harm). The *nāzir* must prioritize aspects of *maslahah* as a form of responsibility to provide optimal benefits to *waqf* beneficiaries.
ii. **Transparency**. The *nāzir* has to manage cash/asset *waqf* transparently and under good governance regularly produce financial and performance reports that are accessible by the waqif.
iii. **Productivity**. The *nāzir* has to be able to manage the fund productively so that the *waqf* beneficiaries can benefit from the cash/asset *waqf* continuously.

iv. **Trustable.** The integrity of a *nāzir* is crucial. They must eschew any business opportunity and process that may give rise to moral hazard. All proposed business activities should be assessed based on Islamic law.
v. **Sustainability.** The *nāzir* must be able to maintain the sustainability of the value of *waqf* assets.

If a *wāqif* has determined the amount of a *nāzir*'s fee, then the cost of his services is adjusted to what has been determined by the nāzir. If this is not done by the *wāqif*, then the determination is based on the rules and regulations of the jurisdictions.

6.5 Core Principle of *Waqf*

Besides the principles for accountability of the nāzir, IRTI has developed core principles for the governance of *waqf*. Core principles of *waqf* have been suggested by a joint working group of the Bank Indonesia, in partnership with Islamic Research & Training Institute (IRTI) and Islamic Development Bank, Jeddah. The working group comprised experts from IRTI/IsDB, Bank Indonesia, and many *waqfs* (IWG, 2018).

The group has suggested optimal principles for *waqf* management for five dimensions: legal foundations, *waqf* supervision, good governance for nāzir, risk management, and Sharī'ah compliance. These make 29 WCPs. Each of these principles is important because it helps in achieving these dimensions. However, it should be kept in mind that these principles are developed for Indonesia. So, the IRTI document suggests time and again that these are context-specific. Each country can receive guidance from them and develop its own set of operational principles.

These principles tend to promote or maximize the benefits to others, inclusively for all humans and living beings, and emphasize the importance of maintaining public confidence high since the system is fully dependent upon the public's propensity to donate.

The WCPs have been formulated to address the objectives to provide a brief description of the position and roles of the *waqf* and management and supervisory system in the economic development program besides providing a methodology for setting the core principles in the *waqf* management and supervisory system.

6.5.1 Principles for Optimal Waqf *Management as per the IWG-2018*

The main areas of *Waqf* core principles are given in Table 6.2.

The Waqf Core Principles in Short:

A **Legal Foundations:** For legal foundations, six core principles are:
- WCP 1: Relating to Responsibilities, Objectives, Powers, Independence, Accountability, and Collaboration.

Table 6.2 Major Areas of *Waqf* Core Principles

No.	*Dimensions*	*WCP numbers*
A	Legal Foundations	WCP 1–WCP 6
B	*Waqf* Supervision	WCP 7–WCP 12
C	Good nāzir Governance	WCP 13
D	Risk Management	WCP 14–WCP 24
E	Shari'ah Governance	WCP 26–WCP 29

- WCP 2: Waqf Asset Classes: Assets classes may be based on (a) Commercial – Social; (b) Permanent – Temporary (c) Economic – Benefit; (d) Immovable asset; and (e) Movable assets.
- WCP 3: Permissible Activities: Activities have to be under the principles of sharī'ah and the management capacity of *waqf* institutions.
- WCP 4: Licensing Criteria: Licensing authority sets criteria for *waqf* institutions and *mutawallis* (*waqf* managers).
- WCP 5: Transfer of Waqf Management: *Waqf* supervisor can review, reject, and impose prudential conditions on proposals to transfer *waqf* assets from an existing *waqf* institution to another *waqf* institution (*waqf* manager).
- WCP 6: Takeover of Waqf Institution and Assets: The supervisor can approve/reject and impose prudential conditions on, any takeover or investments, against the prescribed criteria and to determine that affiliations or structures do not expose the *waqf* institution to undue risks or hinder effective supervision.

B ***Waqf* Supervision:** Six core *waqf* principles for supervision of *waqf* foundations.

- WCP 7: *Waqf* Supervisory Approach: The supervision mechanism must cover all aspects of *waqf*-collection, investment, management, and disbursement.
- WCP 8: *Waqf Supervisory Techniques and Tools*
- WCP 9: *Waqf* Supervisory Reporting.
- WCP 10: Corrective and Sanctioning Powers of *Waqf* Supervisor.
- WCP 11: Consolidated Supervision.
- WCP 12: Home–Host Relationships: The home and host *waqf* supervisors of cross-border *waqf* institutions must share information and cooperate for effective supervision of the group and the group entities.

C **Good *nāzir* Governance: One Core Principle:**

- WCP 13: Determining Governance Level: To determine that *waqf* institutions have robust and good governance policies and processes that cover sharī'ah compliance, strategic tools, the control environment, *waqf* management knowledge, and the responsibilities of the boards of *waqf* institutions – requirements relating to nazir.

D **Risk Management:**

- WCP 14: Risk Management: Among the core responsibilities of the administrator [details can be seen in the IRTI's document].
- WCP 15: Collection Management: Efficiency in collections management.
- WCP 16: Counterparty Risk: Includes prudent policies and processes to identify, measure, evaluate, monitor, report, and control or mitigate counterparty risk on a timely basis.
- WCP 17: Disbursement Management: The system of distribution for the profits of investments.
- WCP 18: Problem Waqf Assets, Provisions, and Reserves: Adequate policies and processes for the early identification and management of problem assets, and the maintenance of adequate provisions and reserves.
- WCP 19: Transactions with Related Parties
- WCP 20: Country and Transfer Risks
- WCP 21: Market Risk: Having an adequate market risk-management process that takes into account their risk appetite, risk profile, market and macroeconomic conditions, and the risk of a significant deterioration in market liquidity.
- WCP 22: Reputation and waqf Asset Loss Risk: It pertains to market risk and reputation and the loss risk to the endowment or the endower. It is to ensure that waqf institutions have an adequate management framework capable of handling any contagion, reputation, and waqf asset loss risks.
- WCP 23: Revenue/Profit-Loss Sharing Risk: Having an adequate risk-management process that considers their risk appetite, risk profile, and market and macroeconomic conditions. [The waqf supervisors need to put prudential limits to restrict *waqf* institution exposures to single counterparties or groups of connected counterparties.]

E **Sharī'ah Governance:** Sharī'ah governance is covered by four core principles relating to *waqf*.

- **WCP 25: Operational and Sharī'ah-Compliance Risk**: The *waqf* institutions should have proper operational and Sharī'ah-compliance risk-management processes to minimize potential fraudulent practices, anticipate system breakdown, and any other potential disturbance.
- **WCP 26: Sharī'ah Compliance and Internal Audit**: To have appropriate sharī'ah compliance and internal audit frameworks to establish and maintain a properly controlled operating environment in the light of sharī'ah.
- **WCP 27: Financial Reporting and External Audit**: To maintain reliable records of financial statements, annual publications, and the external audit function.
- **WCP 28: Disclosure and Transparency**: To regularly publish consolidated information that is easily accessible and fairly reflects their financial

condition, performance, risk exposures, risk-management strategies, and *waqf* governance policies
- **WCP 29: Abuse/Misuse of Waqf Services:** It is to control misuse of waf assets and abuse of *waqf*-related services.

6.6 Summary and Conclusion

The chapter provides a detailed background for the management of *waqf* institutions. Indeed, good governance is a success factor for *waqfs* where *nāzir* (administrator) remains in the center of the management though, in recent years, the board of trustees or the Waqf Board members also share many supervisory responsibilities.

As *waqf* and charitable organizations share similar characteristics (Sadeq, 2002), so the concept of governance of *awqāf* overlaps with that of nonprofit organizations. Standards of management revolve around four close concepts: efficiency, effectiveness, quality, and governance. There are recent empirical studies that assess various aspects of management around these aspects. Besides, there is accountability that requires deep understanding of the working for the sake of meeting the expectations of stakeholders in using the *waqf* resources to achieve the desired pious ends. For the manager of a nonprofit organization like *waqf – nāẓir*, it needs a clear mission, careful placement, and continuous learning and teaching, management by objectives and self-control, responsibility, and accountability to Allah SWT as well as the society regarding performance.

To maintain the integrity and a certain level of acceptability among the potential donors and the masses in general, the management of *waqf* must avoid bad governance and corruption, and maintain an image of serving the social cause. Systematic monitoring by the neutral monitors and external auditors should raise the confidence level and hence ensure the acceptance level among people while adding to the sustainability of the *waqf* organizations. An effective *waqf* management system would require close cooperation between the *waqf* management, supervisors, regulators, and auditors. Concerted efforts are needed to develop, implement, monitor, and enforce supervisory tools and policies on the optimal systems of management and governance.

Waqfs used to be managed under very high morals. However, the mismanagement started in the colonization period and played destabilizing role, especially in terms of the moral degradation of the *nāzir* that led to the misuse of *waqf* assets. The phenomenon of lack of accountability in *waqf* is due to the decline of the standard of morality. This issue must be taken into account while planning revival in a country like Pakistan.

Extra care and efforts are needed to develop the *awqāf* system in Pakistan with the objective of broad-based social and economic development. According to Transparency International's Corruption Perceptions Index (Corruption Perception Index, 2021), Pakistan dropped 16 points in the CPI over one year, ranking 140 out of 180 countries. The report revealed that the absence of "rule of law" and "state capture" resulted in a substantially low CPI score for Pakistan.[3] This trend could be the most serious hurdle in evolving the system of *waqf* in the country.

A specific code of conduct has to be developed and introduced for all personnel involved in *waqf* operations. Schweitz (2001, pp. 8–9) has suggested the following for the management of any NGOs working for public welfare:

> The most basic requirements of accountability stated in these codes are that the organization has (1) a specified purpose or mission, and (2) a transparent internal management system, free of conflicts of interest, discrimination, favoritism, secrecy, corruption, and all other unethical practices. Some of the codes explicitly require an elected, independent board of directors and specify its responsibilities. Another crucial aspect of accountability is proper, complete, and open financial accounting that … is stressed in all codes but with varying degrees of specificity.

Accountability is a central theme in Islam being part of belief. Here, good governance is based on the concept of the absolute unity of Allah SWT (*tawhid*) and getting His favor in this world and the hereafter. This foundational charter, when coupled with the Qur'anic guidance, provides a specific set of operational principles such as *amānah* and *adālah*.

Mutawalli (*nāzir*) is the main role player and a change maker for *waqfs*. Mainly, the dynamic leadership of *nāzir* could pave the road to the institutional evolution of *waqf*. Historic records suggest that *nāzir* used to have some flexibility that helped initiate institutional changes, such as the pooling of cash *waqf* assets, that too working under an environment of strict Sharī'ah law. But the flexibility for investments and financing the socioeconomic projects must be coupled with strict accountability and supervision.

The management of waqfs in modern days in Arab countries is quite innovative and effective. In the recent studies on *waqfs*, in some Muslim countries such as Malaysia, a moderate level of *waqfs*' working standards (above 40%) have been noticed, which, looking at the initial re-origination, is not a small achievement. However, important lapses in the reporting of disclosures in *waqfs* are also found as per some of the empirical studies that need to be taken care of.

Cash *waqfs*/endowed liquidity is a challenge to manage and maintain. The maintenance (the perpetual existence) not only is very difficult but also becomes a liability of the administrators, *awqāf* departments, and the state and society, at large. An innovative scheme of creating hard backing of the cash *waqf*s by the *awqāf* authorities must be devised. Further, the reliability and responsibility of *awqāf* establishments have to be improved by *awqāf* accounting, which is a proper tool to shape the truthfulness and accountability of *waqf* organizations.

Besides the principles for accountability of the *nāzir*, the WCPs for the governance of *waqf* entities need to be applied for the revival and growth of *awqāf* system in all countries having *awqāf*. These principles could maximize the benefits to human societies inclusively and emphasize the importance for keeping public confidence high since the system is fully dependent upon the public's propensity to donate. AAOIFI's standard on *waqf* also provides a crucial guideline for *waqf* and its regulatory framework.

Accountability for *waqf* organizations can be understood as a means through which individuals and organizations are held responsible for their actions. It is also a means by which *awqāf* managers, *nāzirs*, and other functionaries would be performing as per their welfare-oriented mission. The *waqf* authorities need to introduce: (i) disclosure statements and reports about assets, investments with a return thereon, expenses, grants, financing taken or given, etc.; (ii) performance assessment and internal and external evaluation reports; (iii) level of participation and consultation with stakeholders for indicating any lacunae and their removal; (iv) system for self-regulation by the managers, *mutawallies* and other personnel, and the beneficiaries; (v) social auditing that refers to a process through which an organization assesses, reports, and improves upon its social performance and ethical behavior, especially through stakeholders' dialogue.

Notes

1 The International Working Group on Waqf Core Principles' comprising experts from the IRTI (IsDB) Jeddah, Bank Indonesia, Indonesian Waqf Board, Padjadjaran University, Indonesia, Institute Pertanian Bogor, Kuwait Awqāf Public Foundation, Awqāf Bosnia Herzegovina, National Awqāf Foundation of Awqāf South Africa, Awqāf New Zealand, and an Observer from the World Bank Group. Its report was published in 2018.

2 Kahf states in his article "Kinds and Objectives of Islamic *waqf*" that *Awqāf* practically became part of the public sector, with all the known evils of waste of resources, lack of accountability, lack of motivation to improve performance and efficiency, slow and irresponsive decision making, favoritism, political interference in management and finally but not the least moral, financial, and economic corruption.

3 www.dawn.com/news/1671401

7 *Waqf*-Based Legal and Organizational Frameworks

7.1 Introduction

The role of *waqf* in funding religious, social, and general welfare related activities, public services like education and health, etc. could be effective only when the *waqf* system is based on an effective institutional, regulatory, and legal framework. All such subsystems must collectively provide an effective legal framework for organizing the *awqāf* system, creating and managing *waqfs*, and for accountability, transparency, and discipline of the *waqf* entities. Any legal framework must comprise the definitions, and categories of *waqf* – landed properties and liquid assets' *waqfs*; principles, rules, and the processes regarding the elements of *waqfs* – the subject matter of *waqf* also including the cash endowments, creation or establishment of *waqf*, rights and duties of the creators, the beneficiaries, *mutawallies*, and the role of administrators.

As a rule, a *waqf* is perpetual, although the *Mālikī* school of thought also accepted the temporary or time-bound *waqf* (Kader, 2021). This view is also held by Imam Abū Yūsuf as reported by *Ibn-e-Hammām* (*Fath-al-Qadeer*, Dar al Fikr, 2010, p. 89). This is contemporary thought as well as approved by the AAOIFI's SS on *waqf* (No. 60, Clause: 2/4/13). While the principle of perpetuity is at the heart of *waqf* law (Kahf, 1999), the English tradition of trust law supports the temporary establishment of charity foundations. Of course, according to contemporary *ijtihād*, temporary *waqfs* are also permissible and can be created, particularly cash *awqāf*. The sustainability of cash *awqāf* is made possible by investing at least a part of the endowment and using its return for welfare purposes as per the *waqf* deed. This aspect relating to the sustainability of cash *waqf* has been discussed in the earlier chapters.

Rules are also needed regarding the investment or lease of the *waqf* assets and the income of such assets, donations/endowments. A framework is needed for adjudication by the Sharīʿah courts (for Sharīʿah-related aspects) as well as the civil courts for civil suits (regarding wrongful possession and use of lease or sale of assets and allied matters of the use of *waqf* assets, appeals, and disposal of such appeals. For *waqfs* working as financial intermediaries, laws and rules need to be provided for various financial services,

DOI: 10.4324/9781003477549-7

profit-sharing ratios in sharing-based financing or profit rates on sale or lease based, tax-exemption rules regarding endowments, etc.

Waqf entities present the concept of beneficial ownership in addition to the title ownership. *Waqf* beneficiaries own a beneficial interest in the *waqf* asset, while the manager/administrator (*nāzir al-waqf*) holds the assets in the interest of the beneficiaries.

The four essential elements for the creation of *waqf* are: (i) the donor (*wāqif*), (ii) the *waqf* declaration deed (*ṣīghah*), (iii) the *waqf* property (*mawquf*), and (iv) the beneficiaries (*mawqūf ʿalaihim*). Regarding *ṣīghah*, legal provisions also need to be provided for *waqfs* created through the word of mouth. Jurists highly regard the assertion of *ṣīghah* which does not bear the opposite intention of *wāqif*. So, *waqf* is not legally binding with mere intention. Further, the establishment of *waqf* should not be attached to any condition in the future (Abbasi, 2012).

Waqf can also be in the form of "wills" (*waṣāya*) – testamentary *waqf*. It would require specific rules so that the Sharīʿah tenets regarding inheritance are not violated. As a rule, *waqf* asset or property cannot be subject to transfer, assignment, or transmission on the death of the *wāqif*. The rules are needed in case any *waqf* assets are required for any public use, or in the case of any unavoidable needs. Therefore, *istibdāl* or change of assets would also be covered by the legal framework. Equally important are the provisions of law or the rules relating to accountability of *nāzims/mutawallies*, the administrators and other functionaries involved in usage, lease, investment, *istibdāl* and maintenance of *waqf* properties, and accounting and auditing of the *awqāf* affairs.

7.2 Forms of *Waqfs* and Their Establishment

Waqf can be established in many forms depending on its purpose or nature of its outcome and the intended beneficiaries. The most common categories that may require different legal provisions are (i) Religious *waqfs*/philanthropic *waqfs*, and (ii) Public and private/family *waqfs*. Different rules are required for different categories of *awqāf* and the assets to be endowed. During the colonial period, the British judges declared the family *waqf* invalid because they regarded it as a family settlement, distinguished from a charitable trust. Mussalman Wakf Validating Act 1913 declared the family *waqf* valid. It was also provided that, unlike a private trust, a family *waqf* is perpetual and inflexible because its terms cannot be modified by either the administrator or beneficiaries. Therefore, it is rarely used in current times. Old family *awqāf*, however, may continue to operate.

Waqf can be made in all forms of wealth like orchards, arable land, commercial properties, agricultural machinery, cattle, cash (*nuqūd*), shares, rights or warrants in the companies, *ṣukūk*, medical equipment, books, money, universities or other buildings, a business, and any other form of wealth that could generate income.

Kahf (1998) lists several new forms of *waqf* such as the *waqf* of financial rights and *waqf* of usufruct. He derives this by using the term *māl*, which can include both financial rights, such as the publication right of a manuscript, and usufruct of a rented asset according to the majority of *fuqahā'* and the contemporary collective *fatāwa* of the OIC Fiqh Academy. The income so generated can be used for helping the sick, poor, needy, and jobless, rehabilitation and relief after any calamity, public or community services (utilities), and so on. All income-generating *waqf* objects must be valued in cash and the cash value should be considered the principal capital of *waqf*, or *waqf* value-capital. All efforts need to be made to safeguard the value-capital and to invest it.

Historically, there have been three types of *awqāf*: (i) a religious *waqf*, all revenue generated from such *waqfs* are spent on the operation and maintenance of mosques, *madāris*, and for the propagation of Islam, (ii) a philanthropic *waqf*, which aims at supporting the needy and the poor segment of the society and the activities of the community at large. Scientific research, education, health services, and other civic amenities, the environment, parks, roads, bridges, etc. are supported by philanthropic *waqfs*, and (iii) posterity or family *waqf* for the benefit of the donor's family and children.

The categories of *waqf* by its purpose include:

(i) *Waqf khayrī* – philanthropic *waqf*, its beneficiaries are the general public; one similar category of such *awqāf* is *Waqf* al-*sabil* meaning to set up and build the open utility assets like roads, parks, solar and other renewable power plants, water supplies, cemeteries, schools, and so on.
(ii) *Waqf-ahlī* – for posterity of the donor with the condition that the recipient could not sell or dispose of the property against the provisions of the *waqf* deed.
(iii) *Waqf al-awāridh* – the yield or income of *waqf* is held in reserve, to be used at times of emergency or unexpected events that negatively influence the livelihood and well-being of people. Such *waqf* could also be used to finance the maintenance of the utilities of a village or neighborhood.
(iv) *Waqf-istithmārī* – to be used for investment, the return from which is for use by any or specified beneficiaries – it is the most suitable category for promoting entrepreneurship for micro business and commodity sector in the economy.
(v) *Waqf mubāshar* – the *waqf* assets are used to generate services to the benefit of some charity recipients or other beneficiaries, like schools, capacity building centers and utilities for low-income groups in the society, etc.

Other relevant categories of *waqfs* regarding the beneficiaries and the managers are public *waqfs* (*waqf ʿām*) and private *waqfs*. The proceeds/usufruct of public *waqfs* can be used for public interest (*maṣlaḥah ʿāmah*) such as hospitals, mosques, public restrooms, and food centers, public water dispensers, and renewable energy plants for any area or community. Such endowed properties/assets cannot be disposed of either by the *waqf* creators – donors or by the beneficiaries.

In jurisdictions where *waqf* institutions have been developed on the line of the modern organization, another category of *waqfs* is *Incorporated Waqf*. Such *waqfs* are larger than a certain size in terms of the value of assets earmarked as endowments and have fully incorporated status necessarily subject to regulatory oversight.

Incorporated *waqfs* are further divided into Umbrella *waqf*, Private *waqf*, and Corporate *waqf*. The proceeds of private *waqf* are used to serve a specific group of beneficiaries such as students, travelers, sick, etc. *Waqf* assets of a corporate *waqf* are in the form of shares of companies that are issued and managed by a corporate body. Umbrella *waqf* is incorporated to provide administrative and legal support to an unincorporated *waqf* having properties/assets less than a specific size.

All endowments donated for the benefit of the general public or any specific groups from the public are governed by the public *awqāf* rules. The endowments made for any identified beneficiaries like posterity of the *wāqif* are covered under the private *awqāf* rules.

7.2.1 Rules Regarding Waqf *Management*

The legal framework of *waqf* must also provide the rules about various factors of *waqf* management. Such rules will govern the efficiency, governance, effectiveness, and quality of the management by the *waqf* board, *nāzir*, and other functionaries. The law would also provide the characteristics of the *wāqif* and the duties of the *mutawallī* as trustee of the *waqf*. A non-Muslim can also be an endower (*wāqif*) (AAOIFI Shari'ah Standard 60, Clause: 2/4/3/5; and IWG, 2018). *Wāqif* (donor) must be an adult natural sane person, with free will for making the declaration of *waqf* and not have been legally barred from transacting in the assets (Abbasi, 2012). These factors are shown in Figure 7.1.

7.2.2 Waqf *(under Islamic Law) and a Trust (under Common Law)*

In common law, a trust acts like a *waqf* with ownership bifurcated. The trust owns the assets in question that are administered by a trustee, who has a fiduciary duty to administer trust property for the beneficiaries' interest, who in turn, holds beneficial ownership in the trust assets.

Trusts are versatile contracts recognized both in English common law and Sharīʿah. They are an essential component of many modern Islamic financial instruments. Indeed, trust law is a pre-requisite for ṣukūk issuance. *Waqf* structures can be used for trusts under English common law (Wilson, 2016).

Donating any property as *waqf* for religious, pious, and charitable purposes would imply that a *waqf* once established, cannot be revoked unless

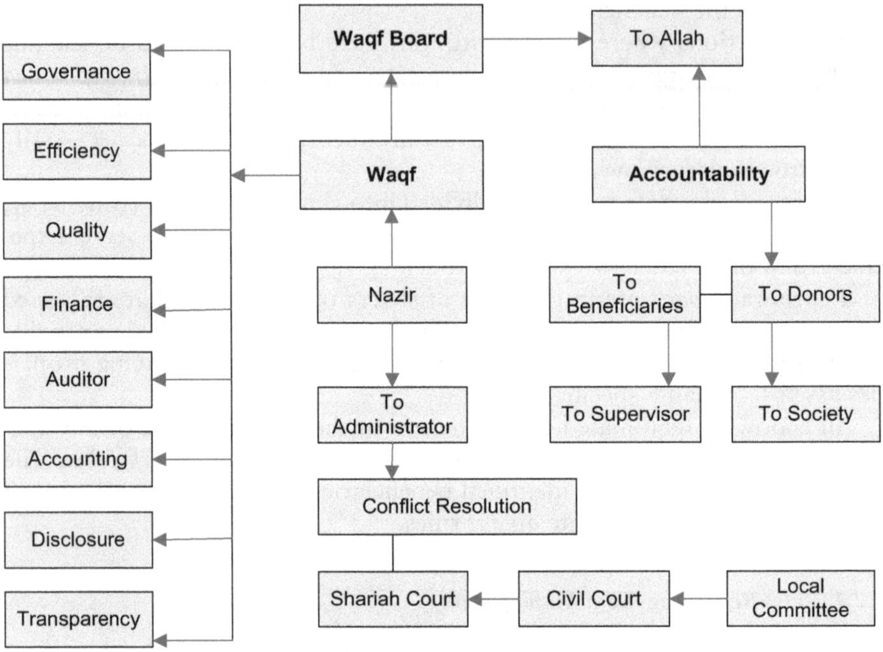

Figure 7.1 The Factors of *Waqf* Management.

Source: Authors' own.

it is a testamentary *waqf* based on the will وصيت, or cash *waqf* created for any specified period (IWGWCP, 2018 and AAOIFI, SS # 60).

In *waqf*, the ownership of the subject matter becomes suspended (Kahf, 1999). Based on the underlying divergence between *waqf* and trusts or other charities/*tabarruʿāt*, the former has more scope for innovation for longer-term welfare projects than in the case of the latter.

Trusts are sometimes established to avoid or minimize inheritance taxes with the wealthy transferring their assets into a trust which would not count as part of their estate (Wilson, 2016). Accordingly, in the case of properties given as trusts, or other *tabarruʿāt* given as charity, the ownership of the given subject matter transfers from the donor to the beneficiary.

Hasan (2007, p. 91) has explained in detail the difference between a trust and a *waqf*. The following points further clarify the difference between *waqf* and endowments as trusts or *ṣadaqah* in general Islamic civilization:

(a) The subject matter of *waqf* cannot be owned in absolute terms, while the subject matter of a trust as a charity is fully owned by the beneficiary.
(b) The stipulations of the *wāqif* must be adhered to as per the related *waqf* deed. In contrast, the stipulations of the donor of normal charity or trust

do not enjoy this status. Instead, any such stipulations would be taken merely as a suggestion and not as a mandatory condition (al-Shaybani, 1997, p. 250).

(c) If the *wāqif* becomes an apostate, his *waqf* would become void whereas the apostasy of the donor of *ṣadaqah* would not affect the legal status of *ṣadaqah* in any way (Abbasi, 2012, cf. Ibn ʿĀbidīn).

(d) The subject matter of a *waqf* could never be employed by the *nāzir* for Sharīʿah noncompliant purposes; however, a *ṣadaqah* could be used by its new owner in any manner.

(e) *Waqf* constitutes the property of the whole community, while *ṣadaqah* belongs to a particular individual.

(f) While *waqf* laws and the arising issues, their implementation is decided by the Sharīʿah courts (especially in Islamic countries), and trusts are governed by the civil law, or the common law (of England).

In English common law jurisdictions, the *waqf* trustees can apply for recognition as a registered charity. This means the trustees of the endowment might claim back any income tax paid by the donors provided the funds received are not used for commercial purposes. The *waqf* will also benefit from exemptions from corporate taxes and capital gains tax, although the latter exemption is hypothetical as *waqf* endowments cannot be sold. In the case of cash *waqfs*, any profits must be distributed for charitable purposes and the trustees are not permitted to benefit from any financial gain.

To further differentiate trust and *waqf*, we discuss here briefly the *waqf* and trust law in Malaysia to get a picture of the related issues. According to Malaysian law, *waqf* refers to the dedication of any property, usufruct, or benefit for any charitable purpose, or any welfare purpose. The registration of *waqf* lands must be a requirement to guarantee its sustainable management in the future as per the *waqf* deed. As per *waqf* law in Malaysia, all *waqf* assets are vested in the States' Islamic Religious Councils (SIRCs), which are state statutory bodies. A *waqf* must be created according to Islamic law which would come within the jurisdiction of the SIRC as the trustee. The *waqf*, *ipso facto*, does not have legitimacy in the eyes of secular law and does not fully qualify as a nonprofit organization. This centralization of control in the state reflects the European trend that existed in the 19th and 20th centuries in the management of trusts and foundation assets (Alias, 2013).

Of course, there is some confusion between the concept of *waqf* in Islam and the concept of trust under common law. Many businessmen and profit-making bodies in Malaysia (as in other Islamic countries) tend to treat the two alike (Kader & Norasiah, 2014). As indicated by Kader and Norasiah (2014), the profit-oriented bodies or individuals do not like to come under the control of the SIRC for fear of a lack of competent personnel, general distrust, and the desire to have full control over the management of the *waqf* property. They wish to place the *waqf* property under the governance structure of a registered society under the Societies Act, or in the case of a public company, a trust company under the Trust Companies Act 1949.

In the case of the Societies Act, a trust deed is drawn up to deem the property as a "trust property" under provisions of the Trustee Act 1949 and then the trustees may elect to form a body corporate in the form of a foundation registered under the Trustees (Incorporation) Act 1952. In such cases, any legal dispute relating to the properties under the foundation will be decided by the civil courts as opposed to *waqf* property which comes under the purview of the Sharī'ah court. A *waqf*-owned building or property cannot be used for activities that are contrary to the principles of Islam. Of course, it could come under the definition of "trust" within the meaning of the Trustee Act 1949 (Act 208). It may imply that a *waqf* could also be termed as a charitable trust, but all charitable trusts could not be *waqfs* simply because all operations and activities by any *waqf* must be according to the Sharī'ah principles.

To qualify for charitable status, *waqfs* must have their finances subjected to an independent audit at the end of each financial year, with their accounts submitted to the charity's commission promptly. The commissioners also require an institution applying for charitable status to submit its articles of association and the names and contact details of the trustees. In return for benefiting from favorable tax treatment, *waqf* endowments are required to be financially transparent with their accounts open for public inspection. Sound standards of corporate governance are also required, the evidence for this being the robustness of the articles of association and the formal minutes of meetings of the boards of trustees.

7.3 Existing *Waqf* Laws and Status in Pakistan

As little work has been done in Pakistan to revive the *awqāf* system as per the emerging trend as a social welfare institution, we discuss in detail the law and status of *awqāf* in Pakistan.

In Pakistan, there are only traditional religious *awqāf* with the exception of a few *waqfs* working with welfare objectives. The existing legal framework on *waqf* does not recognize cash *waqf* that could play a proactive role in general welfare. There has been the least progress in terms of the role of *awqāf* in the socioeconomic development and welfare of the community. There are hundreds of *madāris*/shrines-related *waqfs* that own land, buildings, and other properties but play almost little role in welfare or development. Of course, they might be playing some role in imparting religious education.

So far, the Constitution of the Islamic Republic of Pakistan and the *waqf*-related laws provide little room for promoting *waqf* and introducing a unified and comprehensive framework for *waqf* law that could play a role in socioeconomic growth and public welfare. The *awqāf* affairs are controlled by the provincial ministries of religious affairs. The ministry appoints a *waqf* administrator in each province to control, manage, and maintain the *waqf* properties. The system is operating mainly for building and maintaining mosques, *madrasas*, orphanages, and charitable institutions (IWGWCP, 2018).

Awqāf departments in provinces that govern the traditional religious *awqāf* own vast properties and lands, both farmland and buildings. Punjab with the largest province in terms of population has more than 74,000 acres *waqf* land. Similarly, Sindh, the second largest province owns 11,000-acre *waqf* land (Lashari, 2022). Opportunities are available for welfare-oriented uses of these properties. The *Awqāf* Departments are desired to be self-sufficient to have their own budgets and are not subsidized by the federal government, except for Baluchistan where the number of *waqfs* is very small and subsidy is provided for running the administrative expenses (Çizakça, 2000).

Awqāf departments in KPK and Baluchistan provinces are unable to generate income sufficient for their running expense. In KPK, the powerful land mafia occupies 78% of the precious land in the province (50,612 kanals out of 65,108 kanals) (Malik, 2020). The police, education and health departments have seized 1451 kanals of *awqāf* land in different cities of the KPK and not paying a single penny to the *awqāf* department. Out of 30,000 mosques constructed in the KPK on *awqāf* department's land, only 78 are managed by the department. The revenue of the department for 2019–20 was Rs 115.9 million while the expenditure was Rs 168 million having a deficit of Rs 52.51 million. There was a scheme to use commercial land in the province to construct mega plazas to generate extra revenue. Three commercial buildings were to be constructed in Peshawar immediately (Malik, 2020).

In Baluchistan, the Baluchistan *Waqf* Properties Act 2020 covers the management of *waqf* lands. Of course, many *waqf* properties had been abandoned since 2006 due to the law-and-order situation created by the terrorists, and the cases pending decisions. Recently the decision has been made on all pending cases of abandoned *waqf* properties in the province. As a result, the rent of more than Rs 10 million could be collected from abandoned *waqf* properties.

Following are the sources of earnings of the *awqāf* departments in Pakistan:

1. Cash boxes in shrines (about 50% of the annual income)
2. Income from gifts given in connection with vows, covenants, oaths, etc. (15%)
3. Income from attached businesses (5%)
4. Income from rented urban properties (15%)
5. Income from rented agricultural land (10%)

The main head of expenditure (around 60%) is the salary of the bureaucrats and staff of the *awqāf* department. Small amounts are spent for social purposes like education (merely 6.7%), and health (around 11%) of the total expenditure. Expenditure on maintenance of historical *waqf* buildings is declining (Islamic Market).

Ibad (2013) gives a brief account of the *waqf*-related laws in Pakistan, adopted from British colonial legislative processes that defined basic *waqf*-related concepts and framed related rules. The same concepts are continuing with minor changes regarding the language, concepts, terminologies, and the intended results. Rather, the manner of control got increased over time in all the subsequent laws with minimal space for the religious and/or welfare activities to be performed under the institution of *waqf*, thus crippling the main national source of welfare and poverty alleviation. It might be the reason that the most recent addition – the Islamabad *Waqf* Properties Act, 2020 has been criticized severely. It not only violates the widely accepted juristic principles of *waqf* but also against the human rights provisions of the Constitution of the Islamic Republic of Pakistan (Hassan, 2022).

7.3.1 State Control over Awqāf *in Pakistan*

Due to the impact of British India, the following *waqf* acts were in force in Pakistan before April 1959:

1. Mussalman Waqf Act 1923 and 1935 (Bombay Amendment)
2. The Qanoon-e-*awqāf* Islami, 1945 (Former Bahawalpur State)
3. The Northwest Frontier Province Charitable Institution Act 1949
4. The Punjab Muslim Awqāf Act, 1951
5. Mussalman Waqf Act (Sind Amendment), 1935!

The Mussalman Wakf Act 1923 provided for the compulsory registration of *awqāf* and for keeping a check on *mutawalli*s by requiring them to file annual accounts of *awqāf* with the officials. This Act did not apply to family *awqāf*. After Independence, various statutes were passed for the regulation of *awqāf*. West Pakistan Waqf Properties Ordinance, 1959, was issued to establish a new department to maintain and regulate prominent shrines, mosques, and other *waqf* properties. Accordingly, the *Awqāf* and Religious Affairs Department started its work in 1960. *Waqf* could be nationalized under "The Waqf Properties Ordinance, 1961". In 1972, the Department was made a provincial subject. Later in 1976, it was federalized but finally, in 1979, it was again provincialized, with the same status as after the 18th amendment.

The Waqf Properties Ordinance 1979 (of each province) governs the *awqāf* in all four provinces of the country. Under this Ordinance, the Chief Administrator of *Awqāf* is authorized to take over the administration and control of a public *waqf* by notification. This Ordinance does not apply to private/family *awqāf*.

According to Malik (1990), a statistical analysis covering the provinces of Punjab, Sindh, NWFP, now KPK, Baluchistan, and the Islamabad Capital Territory revealed that by the year 1984, 344 shrines, 648 mosques, 31,913 acres of culturable lands, 48,188 acres of unculturable lands, 2,215 shops, and 1,869 houses had been taken into official control through the departments of *awqāf*. Hundreds of *waqf* schools were brought under the control of the *awqāf* department.

The nationalization was made with the slogan like, "*Waqfs are misused by the pirs, mutawallis, sajjada nasheens and other parasites*" (Malik, 1990, p. 75). The motives behind this move of *waqfs* could be summarized as follows[1]:

1. The administration wanted to control the religious elements in the country since *waqfs* were often associated with religious activities.
2. The state had an eye on the financial resources of the endowments.
3. Centralization meant bureaucratization of the religious establishment, which was thus denied any opportunity for autonomy.

Due to the taking over of *waqf* land and properties by the government, people do not go for *waqf* even in the case of genuine needs of some (disabled) members of any family (where one may wish to create a *waqf* for permanent support of such family members). It is commonly understood, "*Waqf* means that you handed over your property to the *awqāf* department and then your property is gone", as indicated by a participant of the FGM, at IBA Karachi.

The nationalization of *waqfs* was against the *waqf* principles and the will of the Father of the Nation, Muhammad Ali Jinnah, who, in his opening address to the Indian National Congress in 1906, pleaded for the restoration of the right of endowers' control of Islamic endowments, which had come increasingly under influence of British jurisdiction since 1887 (Malik, 1990, p. 65).

The Council of Islamic Ideology (CII) also protested the confiscations as being directly against Islamic law. The CII resolved that the *waqf* estates must be exempted from the land reform of 1972. Of course, the Federal Sharī'aht Court (FSC) that examined the *Waqf* Ordinance of 1979 along with all the existing Acts ruled that nationalization was not against the Shari'ah. Section 16 of the Ordinance (1979), which pertained to *istibdāl* transactions, was considered to be justified as long as the original purpose of any *waqf* continued to be served (Malik, 1990, p. 85).

Accordingly, the *awqāf* department has been accused of doing a disservice to the traditional social aspects of *waqf* and replacing them with nothing (Malik, 1990, pp. 91–96). Thus, the *waqfs* were "neglected and misused" and no longer available for any social or economic and wellbeing role in society. It caused antisocial wastage of the unique institute of Islamic social finance, and that of resources endowed for pious purposes.

Dr. Ejaz Shafi Gilani, a specialist in public opinion research, the Pakistani affiliate of the Gallup International Association, and the Chairman of the Pakistan Institute of Public Opinion (PIPO), who was a participant of the Focus Group Meeting held at Islamabad for this research project contended that *waqf* used to be in the hands of common Muslim citizens; it was given under the state (authority) that deprived the common man of an independent institution of welfare. "*Muslims established this institution to get rid of unnecessary government intervention. Waqf is a part of Sharīʿah, complete Sharīʿah. If we take it out of it (complete Sharīʿah), and use it without Sharīʿah, it will be partial (implementation)*", he added. The forum suggested that the SECP or any other institution may provide facilitation for the establishment and registration of *waqfs*, but it should remain out of the clutches of the bureaucratic state institutions.

During the 1980s, some *waqfs* were returned to their original *mutawallis* in line with section 12 of the Regulations of 1961, section 16 of 1976, and 1979. It is considered, of course, that it also might be for reconciliation with the politically powerful shrine holders. It is also possible that such *waqfs* might be unprofitable.

7.3.2 Islamabad Capital Territory Waqf Properties Act, 2020

The Islamabad Capital Territory Waqf Properties Act, 2020 was passed in September 2020. This enactment was without proper deliberation and a comprehensive understanding of the principles underlying *waqfs* and the related issues (Madni, 2022). The rules regarding *awqāf* act were disseminated across all the provinces and advertised on national media.[2] As a subordinate law, it is not in alignment with fundamental rights in the Constitution of Pakistan on several grounds. The Act was severely criticized at the national level on the ground that it violated the Sharīʿah rules regarding *awqāf*.

The Act of 2020 covers all properties donated for any purpose recognized by Islam as religious, pious, or charitable, but does not include the properties of family *waqf* donated as per section 3 of the Musalmān Waqf Validating Act, 1913 [under which the benefit is claimable for himself by the person by whom the *waqf* was created or by any member of his family or descendants].

Under section 8 of the Act, the Chief Administrator Awqāf (CAA) can take over, by simple notification, any *waqf* property into control and assume the administration, management, and maintenance of that property. The takeover notification shall be served upon the management or the *mutawalli* and affixed on some prominent part of the property sought to be taken over. The "control" and "management" shall include control over the performance and management of the religious, spiritual, cultural, and ceremonies or *rasūmāt* at or in the *waqf* property. During the lifetime of the *wāqif*, of course, the take-over shall be subject to the consent of such person and on such terms and conditions as may be agreed upon between such person and the CAA. Section 6 of the Act requires that the *waqf* manager or *mutawalli* must register the *waqf* property in the prescribed circumstances and manner. Any property not registered with the CAA shall be deemed to have been notified under section 8 (taken over by the Chief Administrative – shall be considered as nationalized).

Section 10 pertains to the eviction of persons wrongfully in possession of *waqf* properties. Regarding the leased *waqf* lands, if the CA is satisfied that the lessee or tenant of any immovable *waqf* property has committed a breach of the conditions of the lease or tenancy, the administrator may order the termination of the lease or resumption of the tenancy. Section 11 pertains to the termination of tenancy. According to Section 12, any such building and crops raised on such *waqf* land would be liable for forfeiture/removal. Any appeal against forfeiture or termination of tenancy could be made within 60 days only to the CA Awqāf, who shall confirm, modify, or vacate the order made by the administrator (himself) under sections 10 and 11. Any such decision shall be final. Sections 26 and 27 of the Act provide for imprisonment for up to 5 years and heavy fines of up to Rs 25 million in case any *waqf* assets are not registered or information is not provided to the CA.

Madni (2022) contends in his analytical article the following regarding the Act, 2020: "*The Waqf Property Act has received a social backlash from ulama, the political fraternity & the public. It is said that the Act is not only against the Islamic law but is also against the Constitution of Pakistan*".

The challenges faced by the *awqāf* departments at provincial level include: (i) ad hocism and inconsistencies in policies; (ii) bureaucrat administrative heads (Chief Administrator *Awqāf*) are changed frequently affecting the policies of the management; (iii) development projects are prepared without proper feasibility and then abandoned without completion thus causing losses; (iv) traditional management practices and lack of strategic managerial practices, neglecting emerging concepts of public administration, and weak monitoring; (v) lengthy legal proceedings in courts – the courts grant statuesque in the case of leased land and buildings that affects the income – many cases are pending in different courts; (vi) no comprehensive policy and plan for the suitable use of *waqf* lands; (vii) encroachments and lose control over *waqf* properties, and weak will of the government functionaries to retrieve land; (viii) lack of capacity building for management – no trainings for the field staff; and (ix) most importantly, trust deficit of the community.

7.3.3 Rules Relating to Charities and Awqāf

Overall, a mix of the rules relating to charities and *waqf* laws and rules cover all activities that may come under *waqfs* or trusts. Before the enactment for Charity Commissions in 2021, the legal environment for charitable foundations in Pakistan included the following laws:

i. The Companies Act, 2017 – under section 42
ii. The Societies Registration Act, 1860
iii. The Charitable *Endowments. Act, 1890*
iv. The Trust Act, 1882
v. The Charitable and Religious Trusts Act, 1920

vi. The Social Welfare Act, 1961 [Voluntary Social Welfare Agencies Ordinance 1961]
vii. The Pakistan Madrasah Education (Establishment and Affiliation of Model *Dini Madāris*) Board Ordinance, 2001

If we take a case study for Punjab *awqāf*, generally the following laws/rule governed the affairs and activities of *waqfs*:

a) The Punjab Waqf Properties Ordinance, 1979
b) The Punjab Holy Quran (Printing and Recording) Act, 2011
c) The Punjab Waqf Properties (Accounts) Rules, 1982
d) The Punjab Auqaf Organization (Appointment & Conditions of Services) Rules, 1994
e) *For private and public trusts: Trust Act 1882 and The Punjab Trusts Act 2020*
f) The Punjab Waqf Properties (Administration) Rules, 2002

"*The Punjab Waqf Properties (Administration) Rules, 2002*[3]" provide the framework for managing *waqf* properties, particularly the land and buildings to be leased. With promulgation of these rules, "The *Waqf* Properties (Administration) Rules, 1960" were repealed. The main aspects that these rules cover include the appointment of managers, lease of *waqf* properties, consolidation of land holdings, auction of trees on *waqf* land, and appeal against the orders of zonal administrators. According to Rule 7, an auction committee is constituted for lease of *waqf* lands, and the lease has to be made through open auction after due publicity. The lease is governed by the following subrules: (a) the lease shall be in writing; (b) the period of lease shall be one year and shall not exceed three years with the following breakup: (aa) first year's money to be determined in the open auction; (bb) second year, 20% increase; and (cc) third year, 20% increase. Rules have been provided for further extension of the lease, but no extension in yearly lease can be granted beyond four years, making a total of five years including the auction year, on any ground of massive expenses by the lessee on improvement or installation of tube well, etc.

Doing charity, which is certainly a noble cause, must be an easy and problem-free activity. Corrupt are to be trapped at source rather than teasing the common man by clutches of revenue officials. As indicated by almost all participants of the research project for this book, particularly, Dr. Amjad Saqib of Akhuwat, tax-related issues and supervisory hurdles are the main hurdle in charity for welfare. Dr. Amjad pointed out:

> Tax issues are there. We have many people who come and say, "get money and we do not need any receipt with the name". If the government asks us to inform about all the donors, why should we tell? If someone wants a receipt with name and address, should get it, but the one who doesn't want

> to get, should not. The government's job is to catch the corrupt earner at the time of earning. But afterward, if someone wants to donate, then should be allowed. --- *We or other welfare entities are not tax inspectors, and so we have no right to know about the income, expenses, and source of earnings of the donor. The State should do this job at the sources of income.* ... People involved in community services like welfare trusts / NPOs say, "If NPOs have to work under such a law, then it is better we close down it and leave the country. Why should I work? My audited reports show our all receipts and expenses that you can see. I am registered under SECP's law, the most powerful regulator", what else is your genuine and valid requirement?

Dr Amjad referred to the Charity Commission in the provinces established in 2020 and contended that the commission reflected oppressive laws. He added:

> It implies that after the establishment of trust/*waqf*, a clerk of govt, upon a delay in report, would come with non-bailable warrants; they can change the trustees on their own. They want to occupy and take administration into their own hands. That will lead to the collapse of the charity-based welfare activities conducted already in the country, as it is happening in the other government departments including religious *awqāf* taken over by the Government.

7.4 *Waqf* Law and Rule in Selected Islamic Countries

Before we discuss the possible legal framework for evolving *waqf* system in any country like Pakistan that need to develop *awqāf* system, it would be worthwhile to see similar legal frameworks in a few selected countries where the institution of *waqf* is being revived.

During the first half of the 20th century, many Muslim countries issued *awqāf* laws which were based on the Ottoman laws. By the second half of the 20th century, most Arab and Muslim countries had gained their independence and enacted new laws that put *awqāf* under government control. Large areas of *awqāf* land were nationalized in Egypt, Algeria, Syria, Tunisia, Türkiye, and Palestine. The nationalization and the transfer of responsibility from private *mutawallis* to ministries of *awqāf* meant the demise of the independent identity of the *waqf* institution and made the *waqf* an instrument of government policy.

But then it was felt that *awqāf* must be autonomous functioning under the *waqf* boards or similar institutions so that every *waqf* could function for the objective it was created. The wave of laws that reversed the nationalization started in Egypt in 1971 when the Egyptian *awqāf* authority took over the management of *awqāf* properties from the Ministry of Awqāf (Dafterdar, 2011, p. 659). In Iran, the "*Waqf* and Charity Organisation" (WCO) was established in 1984 to develop, revive, expand, reconstruct, and rehabilitate *awqāf* properties. In Sudan, the "Federal Corporation of Awqāf" was established in 1987. Kuwait founded "*Awqāf* Public Foundation" in 1993. In Jordan, the Ministry of *Awqāf*, Islamic Affairs and Holy Places established "*Awqāf* Properties Investment Corporation". In Malaysia, at the federal level, the Prime Minister's Department established the Department for *Awqāf*, *Zakāh*, and *Hajj* (JAWHAR) in 2004 to coordinate the activities of the states' religious councils in matters relating to *awqāf* development. The "Qatar *Awqāf* Authority" was established in 2007 to take over the activities of the former Awqāf Department at the Ministry of Awqāf and Islamic Affairs.

In Türkiye, *waqfs* are termed as the Foundations that are regulated under the Foundation Law (Civil Law No. 5737, ratified by the Turkish Assembly on February 20, 2008; By-law on the Registration and Announcement of the Foundations, No. 28269, published in the Official Gazette on 26.04.2013) [Originally drafted in 1935 and modified at least 20 times]. The Foundations law embodies 82 articles and includes general provisions, provisions for Governing Foundations, Directorate General of Foundations, Foundations Council, Organization of the Directorate General, and recruitment and miscellaneous provisions. The objectives of Foundation law, as listed in article 1, are "to set out the rules and procedures relating to the management, operations and monitoring of the foundations; to ensure that their movable and immovable listed properties at home and abroad are to be registered, safeguarded, repaired and maintained; to ensure that the assets of the foundation are economically managed and used; and to define the organization, tasks, powers, and responsibilities of the Directorate General of Foundations". The following article gives the scope as:

> *This Law covers fused (mazbut), annexed (mülhak) and new foundations, non-Muslim community and artisans' foundations, and the Directorate General of Foundations. The international principle of reciprocity shall be reserved in the implementation of the law hereof.*

7.4.1 Legal Framework of Waqf *Entities in Malaysia*

During the British rule, in Malaysia, the Pahang Laws were enacted in 1596 (Rashid, 2012). *Waqf* mainly remained subject to court decisions and laws originating from British, French, and Ottomans sources leading to foreign norms that were superimposed upon the local practices during the 19th and early 20th centuries till the independence of Malaya (Alias, 2013). In Johor province, *Waqf* Prohibition Enactment 1911 was implemented, while in Kelantan Islamic Religious Council and Malay Customs Enactment 1938 was passed after which in Perak Control of *Waqf* Enactment 1951 was issued (Yacoob, 2013; Nooraini, 2015). Before 1950s, lands were donated as *waqf* for mosques, *surau*, religious schools, and cemeteries (Kader & Norasiah, 2014).

The *waqf* system in Malaysia is implemented through several laws, namely, the Federal Constitution 1957, the NLC 1965, the Administration of Islamic Law (Federal Territories) Act 1993 (Act 505), Selangor *Wakaf* Enactment (No. 7 of 1999), Trustee Act 1949 (Act 208), Malacca *Wakaf* Enactment 2005, Negeri Sembilan *Wakaf* Enactment 2005 and the respective Administration of Islamic Law Enactments of the various states as well as other laws having an effect on the administration of *waqf* like the Trustee Act 1949, Specific Relief Act 1950, Contracts Act 1950 and others (Shafii, Iqbal, & Tasdemir, 2016).

According to Malaysia's Federal Constitution, it is within the exclusive powers of the State government to legislate laws on the administration of *waqf* and that of *waqf* properties in each of the States by the SIRC. SIRC has been declared by the law to be the "sole trustee" of all general or specific *waqfs* in any state. *Waqf* properties are registered in the *waqf* register maintained by the *Waqf* Registrar in each SIRC. SIRC reports to the respective land offices for the endorsement of the statutory vesting on the registered document of title where the endorsement describes the SIRC as the sole trustee (Kader & Norasiah, 2014). The SIRC is under a statutory duty to annually publish a list of *waqf* properties, investments and assets under its jurisdiction in the State Gazette.

As provided in Section 25 of the Civil Law Act 1956, the administration of Muslim's property must be in accordance with Islamic law. There are 14 SIRCs, one for each of the 13 states and one for the Federal Territory. The first state law on the administration of Islamic Law in Malaysia, after independence, that contained provisions on *waqf* was passed by Selangor in 1952. The legal framework since 1952 is that all *waqfs* are registered in the name of the SIRC as proprietors following the National Land Code (NLC) 1965.

A Majlis under the SIRC has the authority to register, regulate, monitor, and manage consumptive *waqf* properties within the state. The Majlis has an advisory board and a *waqf* properties management committee. The advisory board consists of individuals, legal, and Sharīʿah experts appointed by the Majlis along with the Mufti, the secretary of the Majlis, the state legal adviser, and the State Director of Land as permanent members. Members normally include state financial officers, scholars, and practitioners in a profession relating to Sharīʿah, property management, and financial management (Tahir, n.d.).

Some states have specific laws for *waqf* administration like Johor's Wakf Rules 1983, Selangor's *Waqf* Enactment 1999, Negeri Sembilan's Wakf Enactment 2005 and Melaka's Wakaf Enactment 2005. The Selangor's Enactment has since been overtaken by the *Waqf* Enactments in Melaka and Negeri Sembilan. It also contains provisions relating to the appointment of a registrar of *Waqf*, a deputy registrar, and officers thereunder, the establishment of an Advisory Panel on the Management of *Waqf*, and the establishment of a *Waqf* Fund. Some of these rules also provide for forming a *waqf* management committee, powers of the SIRC, and *istibdāl* (provision for replacing any asset in the case of need for public use or making payment against that to the beneficiary).

Waqf of any immoveable property is for the beneficiaries named by the donor in the *waqf* deed. If provided in the deed, the property can be rented out and the income could be used to help and assist the beneficiaries. The *waqf* beneficiaries could be the underprivileged, poor or orphans, or even the general Muslim public[4] or the State if required for survival or welfare. With the condition of getting approval from the respective SIRC, the intended beneficiaries may sometime include the donor's heirs and descendants.

The laws relating to *waqf* at the states level are of two categories: (i) provisions in the state Administration of Muslim Law enactments, and (ii) specific rules or enactments relating to *waqf*. The Enactments exclude the concept of "trust" under the Trustee Act 1949 from the definition of *waqf*. It implies that the *waqfs* are out of the jurisdiction of civil courts, and their matters are decided based on the rules approved by the BNM's Shariah Advisory Council. Kader and Norasiah (2014) suggested that the provisions relating to *waqf* management in the Negeri Sembilan Wakaf Enactment could be used as a feasible template for the revision of *waqf* laws in other states in Malaysia.

Waqf Lands Administration Manual, 2010, was provided by the Department of *Waqf*, Zakāh and Hajj ("JAWHAR") for the management of the *waqf* lands in Malaysia. As the *awqāf* are under the control of the States, JAWHAR at the federal level oversees the streamlining of *waqf* management and administration in the country. It provides the official guidelines to streamline the administration of *waqf* lands and represents the best practice for managing *waqf* lands in Malaysia. The second chapter of the manual discusses various processes of registering *waqf* lands at the land office under the NLC. The third chapter deals with the processes for management and administration of *waqf* lands like assessment rates, the creation of leases and tenancies of the land/buildings, termination of such leases and tenancies, payment of quit rent, collection of rent of the *waqf* premise through counter payment, maintenance of the lands/buildings, application of state land for the creation of *waqf* for the public interest (*irsād*), replacement of *waqf* land (*istibdāl*), insurance of *waqf* property and claiming insurance, as well as applications to the land office for conversion from leasehold to freehold title. Guidelines are also laid down relating to court actions on *waqf* lands.

The National Land Code Amendment, 1992 (Act 832) facilitates the transfer of land to the *waqf* administrator and provides for endorsement of the statutory vesting of *waqf* land on the SIRC to be endorsed on the Register Document of Title at the land office. It was notified by the Director of Lands in 1999 (Directive No. 8/1999) that all *waqf* lands must be vested in the authority of SIRC by way of endorsement of the statutory vesting on the Register Document of Title. The procedure for endorsement of statutory vesting under s. 416c has also been laid down. SIRC gives a written application to the registrar, or the land administrator accompanied by the documents or witnesses to attest the *waqf* creation. The statutory provision of the respective law indicating the SIRC as the sole trustee of *waqf* is also attached. As *waqf* land falls under the jurisdiction of each state, the system lacks standardization and there are some inconsistencies in implementation. Hence, the directive to use the vesting order as the sole process of the endorsement of the vesting *waqf* on the SIRC is timely although it merely provides a short term solution to *waqf* land (Kader & Norasiah, 2014).

To ensure that *waqf* land is permanently protected, the land offices have provided several procedures to ensure that the land of any *waqf* is legally secured. One salient requirement is that the land must be registered under the name of the *waqf* administrator who acts for the designated beneficiaries or benefit of the ummah (in the case of the public *waqf*). Various forms have been provided like 14A, 12A, and 12B for effecting the transfer of *waqf* land in different situations. Sometimes, the concern is expressed as to what would happen if any land is not immediately reserved or gazetted as *waqf* land in a case where the *waqf* document goes missing from the land office or the office of the SIRC. [The authors are of the view that the emerging tool of Blockchain could be used for the preservation of the *Waqf* land and other records.]

By citing a Case Law decision (*Majlis Agama Islam Selangor v Bong Boon Chuen & Ors [2008] 6 MLJ 488*), Kader and Norasiah (2014) contended that the validity and formal recognition of *waqf* are still subject to provisions of the written law, although the creation of *waqf* land emanates from Sharīʿah principles. Implications could also arise in cases where a *waqf* is created and registered under the name of Imam or *Qadhi*, or the name of the head of the village, and they die.

7.4.2 Waqf *Law and Regulation in Indonesia*

In Indonesia, that presents great potential in terms of *waqf* assets and funds, the regulation for *waqf* was embedded in Act No. 5/1960 on agrarian matters. In 2004, Act No. 41/2004 on *waqf* was provided; the act consists of nine chapters which are divided into 71 sections. The birth of the Indonesian *Waqf* Board [Badan Wakaf Indonesia (BWI)], based on Law No. 41 of 2004 regarding *waqf*, played a crucial role in the development of *waqf* in Indonesia.

BWI is the embodiment of the mandate outlined in Law No. 41 of 2004 on *waqf*. BWI is an independent agency to develop *waqf* in Indonesia in carrying out its duties free from the influence of any authority and is accountable to the public. In 2010, the President of Indonesia launched the National *Waqf* Money Movement at the State Palace. The establishment of cash *waqf* in Indonesia was led by a nonprofit organization that was established in 1993 by a group of journalists with the mission to help the needy through *zakāh*, *infāq*, *sadaqah*, and *waqf*. Recognizing that cash *waqf* has the potential to provide the necessary funds for charitable projects, including poverty alleviation, the Indonesia *Waqf* Board launched a cash *waqf* scheme known as Tabung *Wakaf* Indonesia or the Indonesian *Waqf*-shares (Shafii, Iqbal & Tasdemir, 2016).

In Indonesia, trust law is also applied to manage *awqāf*. *Waqf* donors could appoint their own trustee to manage their *waqf* upon registration with the Indonesian *Waqf* Board through IWB branches, and representatives of the Indonesian Ulama Council. *Waqf* property is controlled by the state, and indirect endowments are considered part of national wealth (Article 33 clause 3 of the Constitution). If the *waqf* asset is impaired, *waqf nāzir* is responsible in the case of mismanagement to ensure that the *waqf* stream stays beneficial to the beneficiaries, even if it is sold and replaced with another asset. The legal system, monitoring and oversight systems of *awqāf* in different countries are given in Table 7.1.

Table 7.1 Law, Court Monitoring, and Oversight of *Waqf* in Selected Countries

SR #	*Enactment/Law*	*Türkiye*	*Indonesia*	*Malaysia*
1	Dedicated Law on *Waqf*/ Endowment	Foundations Law 2008	Indonesian *Waqf* Regulation 2007 and Cash *Waqf* Act 2009	Federal Law-Section 25 of the Civil Law Act 1956 – Each state has its own Enakmen Wakaf (13 states, 1 federal territory)
2	*Waqf*-related laws and provisions	Secondary rules and regulations amended by Directorate General of Foundations	No corporate *waqf* practice in Indonesia. Trust law is also applied to manage *waqf*. *Waqf* donor could appoint own trustee to manage his *waqf* upon registration with Indonesian *Waqf* Board through IWB branches, and representatives of Indonesian Ulama Council.	1. Companies Act 1965 (in the case of corporate *waqf*, the company managing *waqf* has to also observe Companies Act) 2. Trustee Act 1949 (via the concept of Amanah Hibah, *waqf* could be initiated) 3. Labuan Islamic Financial Services and Securities Act 2010 (LIFSSA) 4. Section 105 allows for the establishment of *Labuan Islamic Trust*

Table 7.1 (Continued)

SR #	*Enactment/Law*	*Türkiye*	*Indonesia*	*Malaysia*
3	Central Supervisory Authority	Directorate General of Foundations	Indonesian *Waqf* Board (IWB). Consists of supervisory board and board of directors (management)	No central regulator Majlis [State Islamic Religious Council (SIRC)] of each state. SIRC acts as a regulator and governing body that manages *waqf* in each state. *Waqf* Management Committee is established to manage *waqf* for its behalf. A Department at the Federal Level JAWHAR plays a coordinative and advisory role, as it does not the power to regulate *waqf* matters.
4	Sharīʿah/legal Court for Legal and Dispute Resolutions	As for Sharīʿah-related disputes, as Türkiye is officially a secular country, no such institution exists. For legal disputes, the authorized court is the one where the foundation is settled.	Sharīʿah court in each city	Mufti (Head of the Islamic Religious Council) of each state
5	Sharīʿah Advisory (in case mutawalli or managers are not sure of any Sharīʿah aspects of *waqf* operations)	Not available	Majlis Ulama Indonesia (MUI)	Fatwa Council in each state

Source: Adapted from Shafii, Iqbal, and Tasdemir (2016).

7.5 Proposed Framework for *Waqf* Law for Pakistan (as a Case Study)

Keeping in view various categories of *waqfs*, the donors, the purposes, and the beneficiaries of *waqfs*, the structure of the proposed framework is depicted in Figure 7.2.

Based on the current status in Pakistan that only religious *awqāf* are operating with a little role in social and economic development and welfare, the best option could be to develop a new stream of *waqfs* while keeping the current stream operating separately with some changes for improvement. Hence, the legal framework will comprise two parts, one for the religious *awqāf* currently operating or that might be created by individuals, the corporate bodies, or the state for *masājid*, shrines, or preaching Islamic values (*Da'awah awqāf*). The objective would be removing the lacuna and loopholes enabling the institution to play an effective role in serving the cause of Islam.

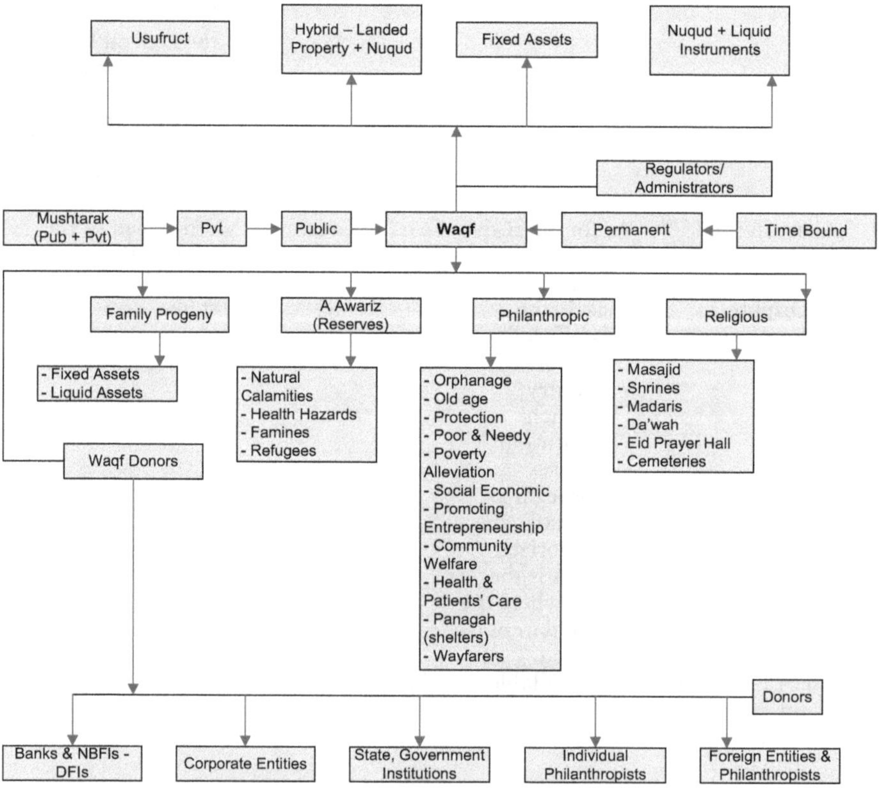

Source: Authors' own

Figure 7.2 *Awqāf* Structure to Be Covered in the Legal Framework.

Source: Authors' own.

The second part will be for the creation, registration and operations of the philanthropic/charitable *waqfs* that will include such *waqf* that could be created for the general welfare of the public or any specific groups, or specific sectors, and sectors like health, education, capacity building, and areas, and also *waqf al'awāriz*, and family/posterity/lineage *awqāf*.

7.5.1 Providing Constitutional Provision for Revival of Awqāf

The institution of *waqf* having the potential of eradicating poverty and enhancing the welfare of the society that would lessen the burden on the public sector for providing necessary civic facilities and social infrastructure would require a mandate from the Constitution of the Islamic Republic of Pakistan. A proviso could be added to Article 38 that requires the State to take policy measures for the promotion of the social and economic well-being of the people of Pakistan (Article 38). Currently, Article 38 mandates the following:

> The State shall — (a) secure the well-being of the people, irrespective of sex, caste, creed or race, by raising their standard of living, by preventing the concentration of wealth and means of production and distribution in the hands of a few to the detriment of general interest and by ensuring equitable adjustment of rights between employers and employees, and landlords and tenants; ... .. (e) reduce disparity in the income and earnings of individuals, including persons in the various classes of the service of Pakistan; (f) eliminate ribā as early as possible.

After the proviso (g) that was added earlier, the following proviso (h) needs to be added:

> (h) encourage and promote the establishment of religious and philanthropic *awqāf* [of fixed assets / landed properties, or Cash / liquid assets] and/or foundations by the resident individuals, the oversees Pakistanis, entities and corporate bodies, or the foreign philanthropists, or the State of Pakistan, for the welfare of the community and socio-economic development of the economy.

Welfare and broad-based growth of any society require all rich and well-off citizens to play their role in serving mankind. Hence, rich non-Muslims, individuals and entities, from within the country or abroad, would also be enabled and encouraged to establish charitable, foundations for community centers and any kind of social services in line with the culture and social values of the local society.

As *awqāf* fall under the provincial portfolio, the promotion of *awqāf* and revival of the role that it played in Islamic history for social and economic development would become an agenda item of the meetings of "The Council of Common Interest" (CCI). The CCI may make and implement plans for promoting *awqāf* through the *Waqf* Board Pakistan and the *Waqf* boards of the Provinces and AJ&K, or any other Federal units. A Parliamentary Committee would be playing role in the preparation of the *waqf*-related legal framework and the law.

The legal framework to be provided for the Federation of Pakistan and its units would also suggest an organizational framework containing a *Waqf Board Pakistan* (WBP) and the provincial *waqf* boards (PWB), policies and mechanisms for making any endowments, use of endowed resources as per the respective *waqf*/trust deeds, accounting, auditing, and accountability at different levels – from WBP to all personnel involved in the collection, use, and disbursement of the *waqf* funds.

The legal framework would also include sections on the organizational and administrative structure of the *awqāf* system at the federal and provincial levels. Of course, the role of the Federal Government will be to give an overall structure and framework for making endowments and possible uses of funds for different categories of *waqfs* and procedures for resolving Sharīʿah-related issues in *awqāf* and disputes regarding the use of *waqf* assets.

Therefore, the framework would also provide the procedure for resolving the Sharīʿah and procedural issues and their resolution by the Council of Islamic Ideology (CII) and the Federal Sharī'aht Court (FSC) for the Sharīʿah issues, and civil courts for resolving the procedural issues in management and use of *waqf* properties. Such a detailed framework to be provided by the State is a prerequisite for creating harmony and ensuring that all operations of the *waqf* institutions play a positive role in creating religious harmony in the country and maximizing the benefits without wastage of endowed resources.

7.5.2 Legal and Organizational Framework for Waqf

For the preparation of the legal and organizational framework of *awqāf* in Pakistan, or any other OIC member country, guidance can be taken from the AAOIFI's *waqf* standards (Sharī'ah (SS No. 33), Financial Accounting Standard FAS (37) and Governance (GSIFI-13); and the Core *Waqf* Principles (IWG, 2018) suggested by the International Working Group on *Waqf*. Malaysia and Indonesia have done a lot of work in providing a conducive environment for *awqāf* creation and management. The *waqf* law of Singapore is almost similar to that of *waqf* law in Malaysia. Hence, the legal framework operating in these countries can also be helpful in providing a legal framework effective for promoting *awqāf*. The Legal & Organizational Framework for *Waqf* (LOFW) may be provided having some parts, sections/provisions as suggested in the following.

7.5.3 Organizational Framework

The suggested framework for promoting *waqf* system to play an active role in the welfare of society and the development of the economy on a sustained basis also suggests an organizational framework for *waqf* that can be depicted as given in Figure 7.3.

The organizational framework suggests the Parliament through its Committee on *Waqf*, the Council of Common Interest (CCI), and the *Waqf* Board Pakistan at the federal level as the policymaking and implementing institutions for promoting *waqf* to realize the objective of broad based welfare in the country.

All provinces and administrative units shall be independent in creating and operations of *waqfs* through Provincial *Waqf* Boards (PWBs) as any individuals, entities, corporate bodies, government, and State institutions may like to establish under the law. PWBs will have offices at the district level or could be at Tehsil level, if so required. The authors suggest that the officials/staff of the WBP and the PWBs and their area offices should be of special cadre with a defined gap between the lowest and the highest paid personnel.

All philanthropic *waqfs* may be established under the Companies Act, 2017 and supervised by the *Waqf* Department to be created in the SECP. Religious or *da'wa waqfs* could be created under the Societies Act, or the Companies Act as the creator may like. Any *waqfs* of landed properties shall be registered with the related land record office in the provinces/capital territory.

The *waqf* creators or their nominees may generally be serving as *nazirs* (managers) of different *waqfs*. The respective *waqf* boards may be serving as *wakil* of the *waqfs* and their creators for efficient and fair management of the system for maximizing the benefits of the beneficiaries and the society at large.

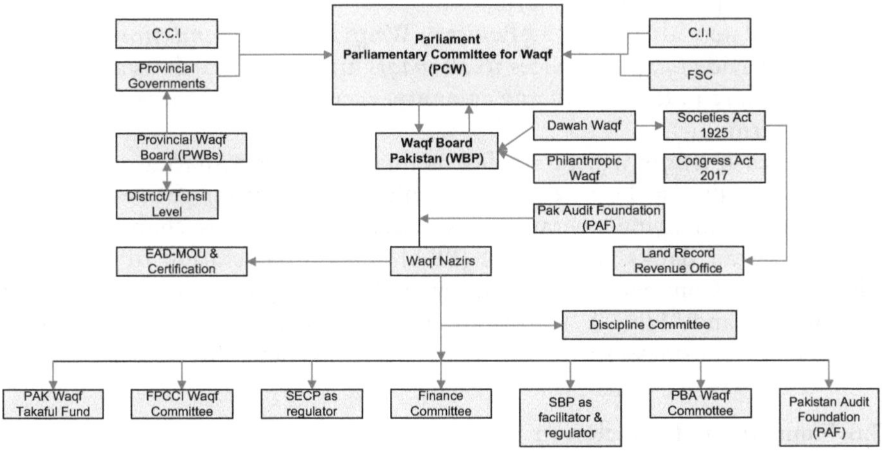

Figure 7.3 Suggested Organizational Framework for *Waqf* System in Pakistan.

Source: Authors' own.

While Finance Committee of the respective *waqf* boards will be playing a strategic role, under directions of the *waqf* boards, in receipt and investment of *waqf* funds, lease or use of *waqf* properties, and use of investment returns and *waqf* fund, the Discipline Committee would ensure that all personnel involved in *waqf* affairs fulfill their responsibilities taking it as a sacred duty.

Going forward, when the new *waqf* law is promulgated and the system starts functioning, the WBP may create the Pakistan Audit Foundation (PAF) that will undertake external audit of all *waqfs* and the *waqf* boards in the country. The PAF might give a rating to the *waqfs* after the audit based on performance, transparency, reporting, and governance of the *waqfs*. Different *awqāf* may also get a rating from any other recognized rating agency approved by the WBP. Such ratings could be used by the respective *awqāf* for getting *waqf* funds from the rich and philanthropies within the country or abroad. The Federal Board of Revenue or other taxation authorities in the country must not ask the *waqf* managers to provide them with information about those who make endowments or donate for the *waqf*. Tax authorities have to manage any wrongdoings, if any, at the income source level.

For getting donations/*waqf* funds from foreign countries, the respective *waqfs* would be required to get themselves registered with the "Economic Affairs Division" (EAD), Government of Pakistan. Different *waqfs* may register donors of small amounts, may be up to $10,000 per month, and issue them web-based cards through mobile Apps. Their scrutiny would be easy as in the case of Roshan Digital Accounts allowed over the last couple of years for the nonresidents. For the creation of new *awqāf* or foundations by overseas Pakistanis or foreign donors/institutions, a proposal for the establishment of *waqf*/foundation in any province or area has to be submitted to the EAD that would allow within a specified period of 3 months, and also inform the respective *waqf* board.

The WBP may also create a "*Pakistan Waqf Takaful Foundation*" (PWTF) that will provide *takaful* services to all *waqfs* and *waqf* boards as a loss mitigation measure in the case of any calamity, accident, or any other sources of damage/harm.

As the cash *waqfs* will be serving as financial intermediaries as well, the State Bank will also be involved in regulating such *waqf* entities, particularly in their financing operations as discussed in various chapters of this book. Pakistan Banks Association (PBA) and the Federation of Pakistan's Chambers of Commerce and Industry (FPCCI) may establish "PBA *Waqf* Committee" and "FPCCI *Waqf* Committee" to facilitate the banks and corporate bodies/businesses to create *waqf* as part of their CSR activities.

7.6 Summary and Conclusion

Revival of *waqf* enabling it to play its historic role in the welfare of Muslim societies must be backed by the legislation having an appeal for all, and the ability to provide a basis for the institutionalization of this unique "beyond market" segment of Islamic economics. Compared to the traditional *awqāf*, the *waqfs* being established currently also comprise *waqfs* of cash, stocks, securities, intellectual property rights, and other liquid and illiquid financial instruments by individual, institutional, and corporate *wāqifs* (Suhaimi, Rahman, & Marican, 2014; Hamad, 2015).

The inability of the state institutions to provide necessary civic, health, and education facilities to the public is causing serious harm to the balance of society that could be devastating in the long run to all groups including the rich. Development of *waqfs* on the emerging trends for broad-based social and economic development would lessen the burden on the government which is facing increasing debt servicing obligations, and budgetary and trade deficits. Therefore, *waqf-related* legislation must not only make philanthropy easy but also involve all members in society by wealth sharing for financial and social inclusion.

As indicated by the participants of the Focus Group Meeting (FGM) held at IBA Karachi, all Muslims wish to contribute for the sake of their *World Hereafter*. But the problem is that rules and regulations are too many and discouraging. "*People have stopped making waqf due to fear of confiscation by the government*", indicated Dr. Usman of IOBM Karachi in the FGM. It was strongly suggested that the legal and organizational frameworks must be facilitators to encourage contributions to the welfare of society. "*Any property endowed in the name of Allah SWT for the poor, needy, etc. as waqf cannot be confiscated by the government*", the participants added.

The nonresidents must be legally allowed to create a *waqf* in the native country like Pakistan through Roshan Digital Account, as one is allowed to purchase a house while sitting abroad. It can be done by adding a provision under Section 42 of the Companies Act, 2017. Similarly, SECP may set up a facilitation desk for creating cash and *ṣukūk waqfs* and work on providing facilitation for *waqf ṣukūk* to be taken by overseas Pakistanis and foreign philanthropists.

Waqfs, in the long run, will accumulate assets to the tune of multiple billions of rupees and so will require very professional administration while extremely careful legal provisions to encourage longer term charity for the formalized institution of public welfare. It would require highly technical legal and managerial frameworks akin to the ones promulgated for central banking and the banking and nonbanking financial sectors. It is because huge money will find the way out for the special welfare-oriented role for generations. Any disruption in the matters of independent and efficient functioning of this unique institution having a divine foundation would have serious economic, social, and political implications. Hence, *waqfs* cannot be left at the mercy of the bureaucratic culture, or the tribal structure prevalent in society.

Notes

1 https://islamicmarkets.com/education/waqfs-in-pakistan-bangladesh
2 Similar *Bills* were prepared by the provinces, but the same could not be passed by the respective provincial assemblies mainly due to severe criticism by the Sharī'ah scholars and many politicians on the federal territory waqf properties act (2020) that had many loopholes and rules against the waqf principles and the Constitution of Pakistan.
3 https://punjabcode.punjab.gov.pk/uploads/articles/the-punjab-waqf-properties-administration-rules-2002-pdf.pdf
4 Juristically, in historical perspective *waqf* funds, if there is a provision for general welfare, could be used for survival at the State level. In Ache Indonesia, *waqf* took a central point in providing funds for its struggle against the Dutch Colonial power, when it was used to purchase an aircraft for the national defense and facilitate interisland transportation (Nasir et al., 2019).

8 Summary Recommendations for Realizing the Potential of *Waqf* for Shared Growth and Sustainable Socioeconomic Development

8.1 Introduction

Economic behavior in any value-based system is based on ethical and belief-based social norms to ensure the well-being of individuals and mutual survival in society as per its own standards. Islam enjoins justice and fair dealings in business, and balance in the production of goods and services, consumption, savings, investments, and socioeconomic activities. Many persons and groups in any society might remain behind others due to the lack of opportunities, any inability, or functioning of the market economy forces, and hence might be unable to fulfill their basic needs. For a healthy, and harmonious society, therefore, a share of income and wealth must be passed on to those who might not be able to get resources sufficient for their co-survival in the relative term. The objective is to maximize the welfare of society as a whole and achieve success by gaining God's pleasure (Mahmood & Suhaib, 2019). It would lead to increasing financial and social inclusion that would help boost overall economic growth by promoting countercyclical economic policy and by helping poor people maintain human capital for the future and assist in the recovery of the economy (WB-IDB Report, 2016).

As deliberated in detail in the book, *waqf* is a multipurpose tool for social and economic development that played a role throughout Islamic history, of course with some gaps due to colonialism and the commercial mindset emerging from the Western capitalistic paradigm. The Prophet (PBUH) dedicated *waqfs* for all welfare-oriented purposes including, *inter alia*, the poor and needy, disaster relief, travelers, migrants, etc. (Cajee, 2022). While educational institutions, hospitals, and travelers' inns were included in the *waqf* beneficiaries' list soon after the Islamic state expanded in AD 8th and 9th centuries, the Ottomans started financing the traders, craftsmen businesses, and farmers from the *awqāf* funds. As contended by Hoexter (2002, p. 128), the contribution of *waqf* "*to the shaping of the urban space can hardly be overestimated… . A major part of the public environment in (Islamic) towns actually came into being as a result of endowments*".

While *waqf*, as an institution of social welfare, preceded the modern institution of "trust", the nonprofit sector involving endowments, charities, and

DOI: 10.4324/9781003477549-8

philanthropies in the West and also in the East are emerging increasingly. It made the *waqf* studies in the 21st century more relevant for resolving socioeconomic problems like poverty, hunger, lack of education, and health and civic facilities in developing Muslim societies (Omercic, 2018). The *waqfs* being established currently are also of cash, stocks, securities, intellectual property rights, and other financial instruments by individual, institutional, and corporate *wāqifs* (Suhaimi, Rahman, & Marican, 2014).

Waqf played the role of development in the past and it is valid for all times. "*There is no justification for the assumption that the modern Muslims would be less pious than their forefathers*". In case a suitable framework is provided, Muslims today would be just as keen as their forefathers to establish *awqāf*, as Çizakça (1998) indicated. The privately accumulated capital may be endowed by the well-to-do voluntarily to finance all sorts of social services to society. This way, *waqf* will help in realizing the socioeconomic goal of a better distribution of income and shared wealth in the economy.

Findings of this study, from the primary research as also interpretive analysis of the available material pertain to both theoretical/conceptual aspects as well as the practical/operational aspects of any economy. The researchers found that all activities of *awqāf* must be conforming to the tenets of Sharī'ah with the intention to get Allah's bounties through service to the cause of Islam and the welfare of the community. Sadr (2017) establishes that the key to the success of *waqf* is conformity with *waqf* operational practices with established Islamic regulations. This aspect differentiates *waqf* from other charities or endowments.

The main aspects of the findings are:

(a) As per the consensus view of the jurists, cash or liquid assets *waqfs* are also allowed. Spending for others' welfare, being a virtuous/noncommutative act, it cannot be limited to landed properties or assets.
(b) *Waqfs* could be created for instant and long-term help of the poor, and the needy in any society, as also for general welfare schemes in social and economic sectors like health, education, civic amenities, providing abode of certain minimum level to the poor, and creating reserves or buffer for rehabilitation measures at the time of any calamities.
(c) As provided by AAOIFI in its Sharī'ah Standard No. 60, *waqf*-based endowments could be made for a given period as well. Accordingly, time-based deposits and *ṣukūk* certificates could be issued and taken. *Waqf ṣukūk* may not differ from the structure of investment *ṣukūk* in the form but in the purpose. The former are for any noble welfare cause like helping others to please Allah SWT (Oubdi & Raghibi, 2018).
(d) *Waqfs* can also be created for setting up businesses at micro or community levels, capacity building and professional training, and even for financing the public sector needs of a social service nature. In this

perspective, *waqf* could work as a direct and indirect financial intermediary like investment banks, and fund managers, or like commercial banks, special-sector development banks, and microfinance institutions.

(e) In the operational perspective, a part, at least, of cash endowments may be used for investments or building such assets the usufruct of which could be leased out; the returns of investments and leases would be used for any welfare purposes as per the respective *waqf* deeds.

(f) As developed in Islamic history, *waqf* is a civil institution with its legal frameworks, objectives, beneficiaries, management, and regulations. Any framework for *waqf* must provide the *waqf* founders freedom to determine its objectives, management, usage, and distribution of income/produce, of course, within the confines of *Shari'ah*. Kahf (2012, p. 7) indicates that "*there is no room for the Imams, preachers, or other religious leaders to make any decision regarding a waqf property based on their own preferences*".

(g) Contributing to *waqfs*, or charity making for formal welfare activities must be made easy and hassle-free.

(h) *Awqāf* must be managed and operated as autonomous charity/welfare institutions. The state should provide effective and efficient organizational, legal, and management frameworks. The objective would be to formalize the welfare institution to maximize the benefits with transparency, as could be required for proper governance. However, no *waqf* can be nationalized or controlled by the state's bureaucracy. As suggested in the previous chapter, for Pakistan, as a case study, *waqf* boards at the center and the provincial levels will be supervising all autonomous *waqfs* in the light of the law approved by the Parliament, and consultation by involving the Council of Common Interest (CCI) and the federal and provincial institutions dealing with poverty alleviation, social services, and welfare activities.

(i) Going forward, when the system is developed, the *Waqf* Board Pakistan may like to establish the "Pakistan Audit Foundation" (PAF) by involving the audit companies, and in consultation with its Finance Committee and the Discipline Committee for ensuring proper governance.

Another finding of the research is that *waqf* is no doubt a crucial part of the model of financial inclusion that Islam suggested. Dr. Usman of IOBM, Karachi in the focus group meeting (FGM) held at IBA, Karachi, exclaimed:

> But in Pakistan, the government and common people think of waqf as limited to masjid, madrasah, and mazār. Everyone talks of financial inclusion, but no one thinks about the model of financial inclusion with the crucial role of waqf that Islam suggested.

Some details of the aforementioned findings are given in the following.

8.2 Promoting Charity at the Micro Level and Making Charity Giving Hassle-Free

Islam encourages the well-off citizens in society to donate and cooperate for overall development and welfare in terms of social and economic viability, and moral and spiritual supremacy. Spending habits of society need to be rationalized by avoiding extravagance, lavish spending for self-pleasure and miserliness, and encouraging spending for fulfilling the needs of others in the society (Qur'an 17:26–29; 25:67).

In addition to compulsory *zakāh* and other religious levies, Islam encourages *sadaqah* as charity, and suggests *waqf* as an endowment for any good cause involving the benefit and welfare of others. Thus, besides pursuing religious and philanthropic objectives it is also inherent for every *waqf* institution to accomplish broader socioeconomic objectives. The extravagance becomes irrelevant when one is purposefully spending for charity for improvement of the community and the propagation of the message of Islam.

In the Western perspective, Bekkers and Wiepkings (2011) identified all the core elements of the theoretical models of charity giving presented in the classical as well as modern approaches. They summarized eight mechanisms that influence giving behavior: (1) Awareness of needs, (2) Solicitation, (3) Costs and benefits, (4) Altruism, (5) Reputation, (6) Psychological benefits, (7) Values, and (8) Efficacy. All these factors may encourage Muslims to make endowments for the welfare of others and success in this world and the hereafter.

Humans are linked to one another through their obligations to God in the Islamic concept of faith and community. Further, a charitable act is neither simply an act of faith nor only an act of community; it is the building of community through faith, and the building of faith through the deepening of the community (Alterman, Hunter, & Phillips, 2005). From the Islamic perspective, of course, charity/sacrifice for others is considered one form of worshipping Allah by Muslims. Muslim donors get involved in charitable giving to seek the pleasure of Allah, general welfare contribution for self-purification of the wealth and soul, and for self-contentment.

Basically, the several types of charitable giving in Islam are mainly *sadaqāt*. These *sadaqāt* include *zakāt* [compulsory *sadaqah*] and *waqf* [voluntary *sadaqah*]. While *zakāt* is one of the five pillars of Islam, *waqf* is an act of specifying certain property and preserving it for the benefit of Muslim community (Kahf, 1998).

Motivating the rich people to create *waqf* is necessary. Therefore, *ulamā* including imams of mosques, and teachers of religious institutions should take initiatives fast because people believe them, and they have an immense influence on these people. So, if they consult with rich people and inform

Table 8.1 Theoretical Framework of Charity Giving in Islamic Perspective

Internal Mechanism	Achieve human ultimate success (*falāh*) • Self-purification of the wealth and soul • Self-contentment • Altruism • Moderatism • Proactivism
External Mechanism	• Seek the pleasure of Allah SWT • Inclusivity • Purposefulness • High standard of intention and quality
Social Impact	General welfare • Sufficiency • Charity culture begins at home
Anonymity	Secrecy: it is important, anonymity in giving as part of spiritual development – not to show off
Charitable Giving in Difficult Situations	Giving is encouraged even in difficult situations. It is a form of sacrifice.

Source: Mustafa Omar et al. (2016).

them about the divine benefits as well as earthly benefits of making *waqf*, it can bring a strong boost for the creation of *waqfs* by the well-off citizens in society.

In the following, we illustrate the framework of charity giving in Islamic perspective.

8.2.1 Using Fintech for Waqf*-Based Donations and Financing the Micro Businesses*

While many rich people are already working for social welfare, charity giving must be promoted at the micro level so that all members of society might take part in the formalized system of philanthropy and welfare. Digitalization of finance and fintech can play a role in this regard. Islamic fintech follows Sharī'ah-based principles and is hence a type of technology that is ethical and religiously acceptable. Through its very nature, it cares for the elements of the environment, social values, and corporate governance (ESG) as well. The alignment of certain Islamic financial products and environmental, social, and governance factors along with recent strides in digitalization may allow Islamic fintech to make a strong foothold in the market.

Islamic institutions and tools of social finance like *waqf*-based charity giving, *qarḍ hassan* and business financing could certainly be helpful in the redistribution of wealth leading to the common welfare. The fact that Islamic fintech and finance are Sharī'ah compliant does not just mean that they are acceptable to Muslims across the globe, but they also offer a different choice by avoiding *ribā* and *gharar* in terms of the ethical and moral implications that come with investment choices.

8.3 Promoting *Waqfs* – A Vital Requirement for Economies Like That of Pakistan

The second major finding of the study is need for reviving the system of *awqaf* in Pakistan to play its historical role in socioeconomic development for broad-based welfare. *Waqf* has been institutionalized in Islamic culture as a civic charity organization to serve society, to fulfill its numerous social and economic needs sustainably. Historically, it contributed with an expanded scope by covering education, health, civic facilities and public utility services, and other areas of social services (Kahf, 2012a).

The West learned about *waqf*-based charitable endowments during the Crusades. However, only the 20th-century welfare states popularized this trend of *waqf*-like institutions in their quest for development (Salamon & Anheier, 1997). Accordingly, many charitable institutions like foundations and endowments are running universities and other educational institutions. Hence, the potential of *waqf* in the 21st century has been recognized as a social sector institution that can be used to realize social and economic objectives (Omercic, 2018).

The list of the top 10 Wealthiest Foundations[1] in the world shows that huge amounts have been made available for welfare-related activities in the West. It contained only one Muslim foundation (Mohammed bin Rashid Al Maktoum, Dubai, UAE with an endowment of $10 billion). Although most of the OIC member states are facing serious financial problems due to debt-servicing obligations, hundreds of thousands of rich individuals and corporate entities must come forward for financing welfare activities for the public.

Recently, the *GlobalSadaqah*, an award-winning global platform for welfare activities, has established a crowdfunding platform (*EduSadaqah*), specifically for Islamic finance educational providers to raise funds to support their causes and activities. It aims at providing a secure and reliable way for Islamic finance education providers to raise funds for various causes including scholarships to deserving students, research grants, upgrade facilities, and purchase of new equipment or technology. The platform allows educational institutions to connect with donors, alumni, and community members who are looking to support their endeavors. They encourage educational institutions offering Islamic finance programs to join *EduSadaqah* to further publicize their needs and initiatives to potential donors and supporters.[2]

As far as Pakistan is concerned, there are ample opportunities for better use of the *waqf* properties – farmland can be utilized for olive farming, fish farming, moringa (*sohanjna*) farming, citric farming, vegetable farming, eucalyptus tree farming for timbre, cattle farming, etc. Islamic Financial Institutions (IFIs) can be involved in the utilization of *waqf* properties for development, and welfare projects can be involved in *waqf* projects. The joint venture, public-private partnership projects, and similar schemes are available for utilization of *awqāf* properties and assets by banks and financial institutions on commercial basis. In towns and urban areas, hundreds of acres are available for new commercial projects. The existing commercial *waqf* properties can also be upgraded. For community development, *awqāf* can offer *qarḍ hassan* for small farmers, micro businesses and cottage industries. Scholarships may also be provided for students on a need cum merit basis. Other possible welfare related steps are financial help for widows, and the establishment of orphanages, vocational schools and medical centers, etc.

8.3.1 Categories of Waqfs

In terms of general categories, we discussed in detail that a *waqf* could be of three categories, namely, *religious*, *philanthropic*, and *family*. All such *awqāf* may lead to socioeconomic welfare as any endowments for the cause of Allah (SWT), His creatures, and the welfare of human beings are covered under *waqf*. It may, *inter alia*, include feeding the poor and hungry, providing healthcare services, civic facilities, and public utilities for the betterment of society, facilitating education and research, financing small businesses and entrepreneurs, and taking care of wild animals. Family or posterity *waqf* that started in the time of the second Caliph of Islam to ensure that children and descendants of the *waqf* founder are not in problem in the future.[3] In terms of the objectives, *waqf* is divided into four categories, namely, *awqāf* for religious objectives, social objectives, cultural objectives, and economic objectives (Khan et al., 2019).

8.3.2 Sources and Use of Waqf *Funds*

Historically, private funds and capital had been the main source of institutional development of *waqf*. *Waqf* resources and funds were spent on mosques and attached *madāris*, that is, construction and renovation, payment of salaries for imams and teachers, lighting, carpeting, cleaning, water supply, etc. Subsequently, community assets were built from *waqf* funds. Many hospitals, universities, astronomical observatories, orphanages, water wells, ships, transportation infrastructure, etc. had been provided through the system of *waqf* by the Muslims individually or as a group (Omercic, 2018). It may imply that the usage of *waqf* funds depends upon the intention of the *wāqifs* as indicated in any *waqf* deeds. As Kahf (2012) observed, "*This independent source of financing enabled religious leaders and preachers to take positions in various social and political issues independent of that of the ruling class...*".

Uses of *waqf* funds include a large list depending upon the *waqf* founder's wish and cover generally the necessities of the poor, needy, sick, widows, orphans, students, those who are not able to pay their debts, travelers, etc. In addition to fulfilling the instant needs of people, *waqf* funds could be used for generating employment opportunities by providing finance, and capacity-building services. In the field of *Shari'ah*-approved embellishments (*Al-Tahsiniyyat*), *waqf* has good access to playing successful roles in managing and organizing *waqf*-based concerns, particularly those that are business oriented. In this manner, the *waqf* activities can promote development in various sectors, such as the local economy, industrial sector, and other commodity-producing and business sectors.

Cash *waqf* which initially emerged to fulfill the needs of some specific low-income groups in the religious-social sphere consequently answered the needs of entrepreneurs and investors in the shape of trade and partnership based financial structures (Bulut, 2021). To serve the purpose of shared growth, it proliferated in Ottoman geography, from Anatolia to West Asia and Africa, and to some extent in the Malay region to play a broader role of enabling and financing.

The resolution of the Jeddah-based International Islamic Fiqh Academy (IIFA) about the Sharīʿah permissibility of cash *waqf* [IIFA, Resolution No. 140 (6/15), p. 297][4] has confirmed that the *waqf* has come of age by evolving into a financial product. It enabled the community welfare programs to permeate at micro levels as it could be traced back to the 16th and 17th centuries. For example, during the Ottoman era, Muslim communities widely practiced *waqf*-based financial services. The *waqf* pools comprising numerous cash *waqf* donations from different individuals were employed through the mechanism of *istighlāl* to finance various clients (Çizakça, 2000, pp. 47–48). Additionally, *waqf* pools were vital in providing seed capital to SMEs on a *muḍārabah* basis as well as for providing funds for consumption purposes (Çizakça, 1998). The progress of evolution in *waqf* continued, and by the early 20th century, precisely in 1907, *waqf* of company shares was permitted by some leading scholars (Dafterdar & Çizakça, 2013, pp. 7–8).

Further, in the Ottoman world, the *waqf* system was considered as the third subsector of the financial system which carried out the health, education, civic and social help functions, and religious and social work investments in the country. As reported by Bulut (2021, p. 69), ban on luxurious consumption and wasting, led to the channeling of resources to social welfare by redistributing disposable incomes. Accordingly, *waqf* is among the leading economic frameworks that prevent accumulated wealth from wastage or remaining idle (Bulut, 2021).

Cash *waqf* funds may better be invested in diversified portfolios with proper risk-mitigation measures. The return thus generated would play a crucial role in augmenting the incomes from immovable properties of *awqāf*. The investment returns can be used for financing the entrepreneurs based on all valid modes like *qarḍ*, with or without the feature of discretional donations by the loanees as in the case of "*Akhuwat*", trade- and leased-based and partnership modes, and hybrid structures while ensuring that every financial contract has proper linkage with the real sector activity or business based on Islamic law of contracts.

8.4 *Waqf* for Various Socioeconomic and Cultural Functions

An important finding on the conceptual ground is that society must be made to adopt ethical and balanced approaches for earnings, spending, and investments. Extreme poverty hinders the satisfaction of basic needs, prevents exercising human rights, and limits the horizon of people's participation in society, as an individual or as a social group. It must be eliminated through social finance with a focus on *waqf*. Financial inclusion in an economy without social inclusion will not serve the problem of hunger and poverty on a sustained basis.

The slogan of financial inclusion must, therefore, be added up with social inclusion to realize the full, easy, and fair access to national resources and activities; the maintenance of social relationships with family, friends, and acquaintances, and the development of a sense of group belongingness (Aparicio, 2013). It would also involve activating "beyond market" institutions of mutual help and sacrifice for cooperative risk and reward and wealth sharing; and *waqf* is the most effective institution for realizing social inclusion.

Waqf can provide the best economic and social welfare services in present-day economies where capitalism has divided human beings into two extremes. It is through uplifting the members of a society in the spiritual, material, and social spheres. It is a unique part of the beyond market or third sector in an Islamic economy that permeates all facets of human life catering to both worldly as also spiritual needs of the human being.

Waqf benefited Muslims by increasing their socioeconomic status through the development of education. Such was the case in the past and prospects for the future are becoming brighter contemporarily (Omercic, 2018). As reported by Kahf (2012), the main beneficiaries of *waqf* included education, healthcare, the poor, needy, orphans, and prisoners. Healthcare services included the construction of hospitals, as well as spending on physicians, apprentices, patients, and medicines. The social environment in a system with the aforementioned facets brings a sense of community, fellowship, capacity building, and inclusive human relationships.

The *waqf* revenues were spent to help people go to Makkah and Madinah to perform pilgrimage and to assist girls getting married, and numerous other philanthropic causes. Zubaidah Harun al-Rashid gave all her property to build a road from Baghdad to Makkah. It played a strategic role in consolidating Caliphate affairs in Balkan Peninsula where it was used to build bridges between people of different religious denominations (Çizakça, 2000; Omercic, 2018).

Linking the globally emerging concept of "CSR" to the *waqf* institutions could be instrumental in enhancing socioeconomic welfare. The funds allocated by the corporate bodies, particularly, by the banking and finance companies may relate CSR funds to the *waqf*-based community development programs. As such, the concept of *waqf* might lead to more careful and responsible handling and use of funds. As we have suggested in Chapter 7 on legal and organizational frameworks, the pay/packages/remuneration of the managers of *waqf* shall have to be regulated with a defined gap between the lowest and the highest paid in any *waqf*.

8.4.1 Waqf *for Education and Human Capacity Building*

OIC member countries' aspiration to attain the status of a high-income developed nation is very much dependent on an innovation-based economy founded on high-level education, knowledge, and creativity. However, due to budgetary restraints, a very meager part of GDP in countries like Pakistan is spent on education. Technical, higher, and innovative education is particularly affected by financial restraints.

Sustainable funding for higher education requires alternative funding sources other than public/government funding. The institution of *awqāf*/endowments has the potential to be that alternative source. Among the alternative resources, the possible *waqf* funds could fill the gap while keeping the status of universities as knowledge centers, not corporate entities maximizing their own benefits under the so-called trusts as of now.

It would require incentivizing the creation of *waqf* funds, as well as encouraging contributions to higher education, for example, through the provision of matching grants for HLIs during the initial fund-raising period. Of course, to successfully develop and implement the *waqf* system for higher and technical education and capacity building, political will, qualified people, and appropriate policies are prerequisites. The parliament, Ministry of Law, the Ministry of Education, and the provincial authorities need to develop *waqf* for this purpose.

8.5 *Awqāf* as Financial Intermediaries – Promoting Entrepreneurship

Another major finding of this research project is the functioning of *awqāf* as financial intermediaries. In the past, the *waqf* institutions financed the households and merchants. The income thus earned was used to provide public services like soup kitchens for the poor, inns for travelers, water fountains, places for worship, educational services, and other basic infrastructural facilities (Alias, 2012). There is evidence that in addition to the use of the *awqāf* system and the *waqf* funds for health and education fields, *waqf* funds were used in the establishment of cooperative housing, industrial companies, libraries, laboratories, and research centers. From this perspective, *waqf* can be a good vehicle for promoting entrepreneurship and the development of business and production sectors in pursuit of general well-being. It thus has a direct effect on the promotion of economic growth and gross domestic product of the country.

In the "beyond market" sector, social entrepreneurship, which comprises both nonprofit and for-profit enterprises, is one of the major forms of operations. Social enterprises or organizations apply market-based business approaches to serve social needs and ensure economic sustainability. A social enterprise/business is a "cause-driven" entrepreneurship that applies commercial strategies to maximize improvements in human well-being rather than maximizing earnings (Huybrechts & Nicholls, 2012). The main philosophy of social entrepreneurship may be interpreted as running any for-profit or nonprofit organization to achieve several social-cum-philanthropic goals by applying market-based principles. It is based on the principle that can be described as "doing charity *by* doing trade" rather than "doing charity *while* doing trade" (Molla & Alam, 2013). Such social enterprises are business-like operations but not for business.

Entrepreneurship from the Islamic perspective is based on divine ethics or Islamic etiquette to best serve the cause of mankind. The motivating factor for these entrepreneurs is the well-being of mankind and pleasing Allah SWT. Such an approach leads to community well-being through an Islamic value-centric approach. The best tool for such a socioeconomic system is *waqf* which has to be developed and promoted according to its essential features and principles. Similar to the motives of social enterprises/businesses, entrepreneurship in Islamic perspective places the community as the primary stakeholder in the output of any entrepreneurial action (Azid, Asutay, & Burki, 2007).

All banks can make a joint *waqf*, or many such *waqfs*, each for different social and economic activities like education and capacity building, providing renewable energy, or affording abode, and financing the entrepreneurs. It was suggested in the FGM held at Karachi that the Pakistan Banks' Association (PBA) could play a role by establishing *awqāf* by different banks or by the PBA with financing from different banks for various socioeconomic activities. "*In some countries, many companies, Islamic banks, and financial institutions have earmarked certain margins in their profit for different waqfs. In their AGM, our banks may also get approval and create liquid waqfs as part of their TORs*", suggested a former central banker participating in the FGM, Karachi. The banks' clients both on assets and deposits sides may also be encouraged to contribute by way of liquid endowments for such *awqāf*. The State Bank of Pakistan has to ensure, as the regulator of the banking companies, that the banks' CSR money is integrated with the *waqf* system to realize the socioeconomic objectives.

The proceeds of Charity Accounts with Islamic banking institutions (IBIs) can also be allocated for different *waqf* funds to be spent for any welfare activities. Meezan Bank already has such three funds that currently are termed as "trusts" due to some legal complications; these are: (1) for staff, wherein Meezan bank adds an equivalent amount to the employees' contribution; (2) Meezan Foundation wherein Meezan Bank added Rs 200 million – each year they make Rs. 100 million (contribution); and (3) Ehsan Trust. Once the new *waqf* law for facilitating *awqāf* is provided, such trusts could be registered under *waqf* law that would create a sense of sanctity for doing good with people with the intention of pleasing Allah SWT.

8.5.1 Developing a Cash Waqf *Financing Model*

Lack of finance and avenues for capacity building for the younger population are the major causes of low levels of entrepreneurship in countries like Pakistan (of course, with some other infrastructure and policy-related factors) (Haneef et al., 2014). The improved capacity building and health infrastructure developed with financing from the cash *awqāf* can enhance the income-earning potential of *waqf* beneficiaries. Developing the cash *waqf* financing model would improve the financial services for micro and medium level entrepreneurs. Based on such financial infrastructure the micro-level businesses and production activities would overcome their financial challenges and obligation in business and commerce (Lahsasna, 2010).

Production of necessary goods and services at the most affordable prices is the main indicator of any welfare state. Financing small farms, micro businesses, and innovative ventures leading to the production of goods and services for human use could be a game-changer in import substitution and enhancing export proceeds. Cash *waqf* funds can play a vital role in this direction. An organized *waqf* system supported by information technology and compatible with other programs can be expected to serve as an additional vehicle of fund mobilization to support and significantly contribute to government economic development programs, particularly the programs for poverty reduction and comprehensive human development (IWG, 2018).

Income/employment-generating projects, medical facilities, and infrastructure projects are essential in alleviating poverty. In this case, *waqf* certificates can be helpful in financing primary and secondary poverty-alleviating projects. The idea is that any "*Waqf* Administration Body" issues *waqf* certificates of different denominations and puts them in the market for sale. Individuals and institutions buy them. The *waqf* proceeds are then used to establish the targeted poverty alleviation projects." This idea was proposed by Islamic Economist Prof. Dr. Abul Hasan M. Sadeq in his paper captioned, "*Waqf*, Perpetual Charity and Poverty Alleviation" in July 2000.

Waqf-based Islamic Microfinance Initiative (MFI) is widely acclaimed as a new approach to alleviate poverty and bring about development. So *waqf*-based Islamic MFI should be the future policy agenda in all OIC member countries (Ahmed, 2007). If we utilize *waqf* to finance MFI operations, it can reduce financing costs and improve the viability of these institutions.

8.6 *Waqf* as an Institution of Public Policy

This research project also found that *waqf* can serve as an institution of public policy. It played role in the building of and preserving the continuity of almshouses, reservoirs, fountains, roads, bridges, highway inns, harbors, libraries, lighthouses, mosques, schools, sidewalks, soup houses, waterways, weirs, etc. This system had many fringe benefits as well – it ensured the prevention of violations of property rights against potential government and state officials, in the preservation of rich Islamic architectural and cultural heritage, and prevented the breakup of land due to inheritance law (Bulut & Korkut, 2016). *Waqf* can also be used for providing pensions for the elderly and disabled, the establishment of basic social security, and mutual indemnification systems (*takaful*).

Oubdi and Raghibi (2018) contend that *waqf ṣukūk* provide an Islamic solution for public finance deficits. *Waqf* played a tremendous role throughout the history of Muslim civilization. It's time that *waqf* should go through innovative processes to maintain its viable role within Muslim societies. Indonesia and some other nations have adopted innovative ideas to issue "Cash waqf Linked Sukuk" (CWLS) to encourage social investments by the rich. It has been found that CWLS had a significant impact on the socioeconomic development of Indonesia. Hence, *ṣukūk* are suitable instruments that could enhance the role of *waqf* and make it a common and familiar

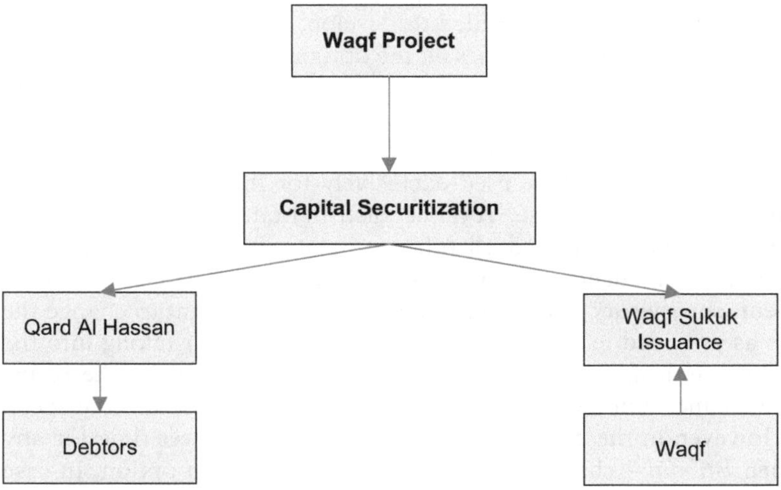

Figure 8.1 Structure of *Waqf* Ṣukūk Operation.
Source: Oubdi and Raghibi (2018).

tool for Muslims who seek divine blessing and mercy. It combines the flexibility of *ṣukūk* and the sustainability of *waqf*. Any other tool like *qard al hassan*/interest-free loans can be used to merge other forms of financing in the case of big projects. For that, *takaful* services can also be availed. Oubdi and Raghibi (2018) suggested a sukuk structure by which public authorities could raise funds for socioeconomic projects (Figure 8.1).

8.7 Management and Regulation of *Waqfs*

This research has specific findings regarding management, governance, and regulation of *awqāf* enabling the *awqāf* system to play effective roles in socioeconomic development. As we have discussed in detail in Chapter 6, good governance is the most crucial success factor for *waqfs*, and the *nāzir* of a *waqf* occupies a focal position in this context. In recent decades, of course, the board of trustees or the *waqf* board members also share many supervisory responsibilities. *Waqf* being a social welfare and divine institution, its management must revolve around efficiency, effectiveness, quality, and accountability not only to the donors and the intended beneficiaries but also to Allah SWT.

The *waqf* management must avoid bad governance and corruption and maintain an image of serving the social cause. For sustainability as a system of social welfare, it is crucial to maintain integrity and acceptability among potential donors and the masses in general. It would also require close collaboration between the *waqf* management, supervisors, regulators, and auditors. Concerted efforts are needed to develop, implement, monitor, and enforce supervisory tools and policies on the optimal systems of management and governance. The *Waqf* Board at the country level, as suggested, will need to introduce a specific code of conduct for all personnel involved in *waqf* operations, and other stakeholders of *waqf*.

Any *waqf* property must be used exclusively for the purpose for which it was endowed. The purpose, revenue distribution, management structure, supervisory authority, and all other stipulations by the founders are classified as the permanence of stipulations (Kahf, 2012a). Any government, management, supervisory authority, or any court has no right to change the conditions as provided in the *waqf* deed. Nationalization or taking into the State's control and management of *awqāf* by the bureaucrats is the recipe for bad governance and total loss of integrity as a sacred institution of social welfare. However, in the case a *waqf* becomes infeasible over time for any reason, then *istibdāl* – change of the *waqf* property – is an option. In case *istibdāl* is not feasible, the property, product, or income from the *waqf* property has to be spent on a closer available avenue. If such avenues are not available, the income and produce could be spent on the poor and needy as by-default beneficiaries of *waqf*.

There is a need to find an appropriate set of tools for the standardized supervision of *waqfs*. These standards require a much deeper understanding of the workings of institutions based on belief. So, every *waqf* will have its condition and background with which it would be dealt with. AAOIFI has provided the best such benchmarks for *waqf* as also Sharī'ah compliant and feasible contract structures in the form of Sharī'ah, corporate, and ethics standards.

The *Waqf* Core Principles (IWGWCPs, 2018) have been formulated to provide a brief description of the position and roles of the *waqf* and management and supervisory system in the economic development programs. They address various vital aspects like the *waqf* board's formation and its responsibilities as well as strategies. As the WCPs are developed for Indonesia, and the IsDB's Institute (formerly known as IRTI) document, these are context specific; so other countries may like to develop their own set of operational principles by getting guidance from AAOIFI's guidelines and IRTI's document.

8.7.1 Integrating Zakāh *and* Waqf *for Rural and Urban Support Programs*

While the Government might be making some efforts to alleviate poverty, it never took serious note of the institutions of Zakāh as a policy tool for fighting poverty as a national strategy. *Waqf* has also been the least explored institution in Pakistan's policy framework. As a lot of work has already been initiated in many Islamic countries as we discussed in various chapters, efforts must be initiated forthwith for the revival of *waqf* and integration of the *zakāh* system with *awqāf*. The objective must be poverty alleviation with socioeconomic development for enhancing social inclusion in society. In the first stage, extreme poverty could be removed from society through a joint operation of *waqf* and *zakāh*. It should lead to financial and social inclusion in the latter stage.

8.8 Recommendations and Concluding Remarks

In any ethics-based society, justice must be provided to all its members. Efficiency and profit maximization must be associated with the fulfillment of the basic needs of all, justice, common welfare, and sustainability. The treasures of a few in the current capitalistic paradigm have marginalized and impoverished the masses.

Greed, extravagance, and pride in one's richness in societies with a capitalistic mindset needed to be replaced with the welfare of all human beings through cooperation, responsible spending, benevolence, and sacrifice for others. All these features constitute the cornerstone of Islam's socioeconomic system and social finance. In Islamic history, *awqāf* played a central role in providing social goods, including education and civic amenities. Çizakça (1998) indicates that *waqf* can not only reduce public expenditures but at the same time cater to the social needs of a country. It can play a role in achieving the SDGs about the welfare of the people at large, and realizing *maqāsid al Sharī'ah* (Abdullah, 2018).

The inability of the state institutions in providing necessary civic, health, and education facilities to the public is causing serious harm to the balance of society that could be devastating in the long run to all groups also including the rich. Development of *waqf* system on the emerging trends for broad based social and economic development would reduce the burden on the governments which might be facing huge budgetary and trade deficits as in the case of Pakistan. Therefore, *waqf*-related legislation must not only make philanthropy easy but also involve all members of society at micro level by way of wealth sharing for financial and social inclusion.

It implies that in economies like that of Pakistan, the system of *awqāf* must be revived and promoted to play its role in a broader perspective as discussed in the book. For shrines and masque-based *waqfs* also, some innovative projects must be initiated. These may include Geo Mapping and digitalization of all *waqf* properties under shrines and masques, restoration of historical *waqf* properties, installation of digital cash boxes, and development of the welfare schemes. For the second stream of liquid *awqāf* and social finance, the *waqf* system has to be revived and promoted as suggested by the jurists for present-day Islamic societies.

The overseas may be legally allowed to create a *waqf* in their native countries through Roshan Digital Account, as recently allowed in Pakistan to purchase a house while sitting abroad. It can be done by adding a provision under section 42 of the Companies Act, 2017. Similarly, SECP may set up a facilitation desk for creating cash and *ṣukūk waqfs*, and work on providing facilitation for *waqf ṣukūk* to be taken by the rich and philanthropists with a country and abroad.

Final recommendations for reviving the institutions of *waqf* in countries like Pakistan with its expanded (socioeconomic) role (with some additions to what was suggested by Khan et al., 2019):

(a) The ultimate objective of the *waqf* system must be helping society in the upbringing and grooming of downtrodden and poor people of the community to contribute positively to society.
(b) The *waqf*-related framework must be developed by such a team that is well aware of the *waqf* rules in its historical perspective as well as the facets of socioeconomic development for balanced growth. They must also have some experience in philanthropic work and fulfill the requirements of morality and piety.
(c) The Sharī'ah scholars, researchers, academicians, and opinion makers in the electronic, social, and print media should highlight the need, significance, and benefits of *waqf* for community development, shared growth, and common welfare of the people.
(d) Awareness may be created among the public regarding the need for and the role of *waqf*-based endowments, preparation of the *waqf* deeds with operational details according to the needs of intended groups in the community so that the system could be improved to play its historical role with further reforms and innovations.
(e) There should be an anti-encroachment mechanism in the *waqf* organization to save the *waqf* properties from illegal occupation.
(f) The use of fintech for cash donations, financing, and other financial matters is needed. The installation of Cash Deposit Machines (CDMs) for cash deposits replacing traditional manual cash boxes for *waqf* donations will increase the trust of the people.
(g) In the case of shrines based *awqāf*, the teachings of the saints about religious harmony, interfaith peace, religious pluralism, and peace should be assimilated for the creation of a tolerant society.
(h) The commencement of any shrine based microfinance program, for example, "*Ali Hajveri Microfinance Waqf*" (AHMW) for entrepreneurs from the rural and urban poor, with the technical help of "Akhuwat Islamic Microfinance" is the need of the time. The devotees of the Shrine of Ali Hajveri (R) would be eager to contribute to the noble cause.
(i) There should be human resource development training on the use of Islamic fintech with a focus on the latest technical expertise involving e-platform for the collection and disbursement of funds, artificial intelligence, asset management, and other relevant fields
(j) The *waqf* board at the central levels, and the provincial *awqāf* organizations should overcome the issue of trust deficit and improve

image for gaining more trust of the people regarding the handling and usefulness of *awqāf* in the country.

(k) Ministries of planning, development and social initiatives may have a special division for preparing and implementing plans for community development through *awqāf*. Ministry of Religious Affairs, in collaboration with the Ministry of Law, may prepare conceptual, organizational, legal, and operational frameworks for approval by the State institutions and implementation by different ministries/institutions including also planning commission, central bank/monetary authorities and banks, NBFIs' entities working for poverty alleviation, and the corporate entities through the Securities Commission.

(l) The frameworks as suggested in the book may comprise two main segregated tiers, namely: (i) *awqāf* for *masājid*, attached madāris, shrines, and cemeteries, and (ii) for social and economic avenues like education, health, civic facilities, and financing micro enterprises and SMEs for promoting entrepreneurship. It must be free from sectarian issues and aspects to avoid any confusion that may harm the integrity of this sacred social system.

(m) Provision may be made in the framework for establishing and developing special *waqfs* to provide benefits to deserving groups like the extremely poor (to eliminate hunger), shelterless, widows, orphans, and the aged who might not get proper care and support.

(n) It is crucial to note in the context of the orphans and the old that might be in the problem, the Islamic paradigm does not deem it appropriate to establish special orphan and old-age houses because in such a situation they lose the family support that an Islamic society is supposed to provide. (This aspect was particularly highlighted by the renowned scholar Prof. Dr. Anis Ahmad during the interview with him for the research project.) Rather, the kin of the orphans, and the children of such old people must be obliged to take care of them. Of course, the *awqāf* could provide a stipend to such kin who are poor and unable to bear related expenses.

(o) For facilitating cash *waqfs*, the framework may include a "Cash *Waqf* Form" as suggested in the chapters on *awqāf* as financial intermediaries, and the legal and organizational framework, to guide and facilitate the contributors to indicate the purposes and the groups of beneficiaries of the funds being endowed by them. The *waqf* creators may also be given the option to indicate the investment options of the endowed money, the return from which would be used for the given purpose.

(p) Regarding the cultural and social aspects, it is crucial to fund such programs under *awqāf* so that the young generation is equipped with insightful understandings of the sociocultural values of Islam with the development of the intellect while avoiding the impurity of ideas and intellectual dirt.

(q) Education, knowledge creation, and capacity building are historically the topmost objectives of *awqāf*. It is for all sorts of education, namely, religious, scientific, technical, and social, as per widely accepted Islamic norms. The current system of creating trusts for running universities and professional education institutions may be changed to bring all such trusts under the *waqf* framework. It can be provided, as in Türkiye, that 70% of students at such universities would be getting free education on a need cum performance basis. It may also be provided that *waqf* management would be separate from the management of the University/training institutions, or any other institution run by the *waqf* as per the respective "*Waqf* Deed".

8.8.1 Contribution of This Research

The research culminating to the Book has given a compact review of contributions of *waqfs* in the past and a trend of *awqāf* and *waqf*-like institutions development. In other words, it has pointed out the growing attention given to the third sector of the economy, that is, "beyond market" economy. Some new categories of *waqf* and the relation of *waqf* institutions to the banks and education sector have been presented as a globally accepted juristic and practice related phenomenon. This research-based project will assist Islamic value-centric entrepreneurs, regulatory authorities, investors, and researchers to gain an overall insight into the potential of *waqf* as a tool for rendering social welfare services and developing economies of OIC member countries on a strong footing.

The suggested legal, organizational, and management frameworks would enable the State institutions including the ministries of planning, development, social initiatives, finance, religious affairs, law, lawmakers and judiciary, and the central bank and the Securities Commissions to introduce and implement the *waqf* system. It would enable individuals, corporate entities and different institutions to establish *awqāf* to which the well-to-do persons at micro level will also be contributing. The system could thus be evolved on sustainable bases. Regulators of financial system may like to announce some targets and/or encouraging measures enabling the banking and other companies to contribute to establishing *awqāf* for community development and shared growth, as also desired in the UN's SDGs.

The use of *waqf* or other social finance institutions for business entrepreneurial financing has not been a priority area mainly due to the impact of colonization and crony capitalism. Even at an academic level, there is a lack of comprehensive studies in the case of the application of *waqf* as a welfare institution in the context of Pakistan and many Islamic countries. Researchers should focus on the issue to uphold the divine role of *waqf* in poverty alleviation and peaceful co-survival.

The findings of this book would be helpful in improving the management of *awqāf*. The report recommends how the *awqāf* system can potentially spearhead the initiative of Islamic charities in realizing the maqāsid-oriented SDGs among Muslim-majority countries (Abdullah, 2018). As this study focuses on accountability, which, among other things, encompasses accounting and performance, the *mutawallis* are expected to improve their accountability and transparency in administering *waqf*. This is crucial as the demand for accountability and transparency has increased tremendously. Thus, the *waqf* regulators might come together with state authorities to improve *waqf*-related accountability.

Notes

1 Namely (i) the Bill & Melinda Gates Foundation ($42.3 billion); (ii) Stichting INGKA Foundation ($36.0 billion); (iii) Welcome Trust ($25.9 billion); (iv) Howard Hughes Medical Institute ($16.9 billion); … . and (ix) William and Flora Hewlett Foundation ($8.7 billion) (Omercic, 2018; p. 142).

2 https://globalsadaqah.com/edu-sadaqah

3 To reach a higher level of piety, many Companions of the Prophet assigned several portions of their properties as *waqf*. A few of them included a condition that a certain portion of their fruits and revenues must be assigned to their own children and descendants and the remaining portion should be spent as *waqf*.

4 https://iifa-aifi.org/wp-content/uploads/2021/12/Resolutions-Recommendations-of-the-IIFA-Official-Edition-Oct-2021.pdf

Bibliography

Abattouy, M., & Al-Hassani, S. T. S. (2013). The role of awqāf in developing Islamic civilisation: Definition, history, functions and articulations with society. Article Contributed by the Foundation for Science.

Abbasi, M. Z. (2012). The classical Islamic law of Waqf: A concise introduction. Arab Law Quarterly, Vol. 26, No. 2, pp. 121–153.

Abbasi, Z. (2019). Waqf in Pakistan: Rebirth of a Traditional Institution. Available at SSRN: https://ssrn.com/abstract=3327092 or http://dx.doi.org/10.2139/ssrn.3327092

Abdul, H., N., Ahmad, S., & Oseni, U.A. (2013). *Alternative Dispute Resolution in Islam*. Kuala Lumpur: IIUM Press.

Abdülaziz, B. A. Y. I. N. D. I. R. (1992). Bey 'bi'l-Vefâ. *Türkiye Diyanet Vakfı İslâm Ansiklopedisi (DİA)*, pp. 20–22.

Abdullah, A., & Yaccoub, H. (2012). Legal and sharī'ah issues in the application of wakalah-waqf model in takaful industry: An analysis. Procedia. Social and Behavioral Sciences, Vol. 65, pp. 1040–1045. *International Congress on Interdisciplinary Business and Social Science. ICIBSoS-2012.*

Abdullah, M. (2015). A new framework of corporate governance for waqf: A preliminary proposal. Islām and Civilizational Renewal, Vol. 6, No. 3.

Abdullah, M. (2018). Waqf, Sustainable Development Goals (SDGs) and Maqasid al-Sharī'ah. International Journal of Social Economics, Vol. 45, No. 1, pp. 158–172. https://doi.org/10.1108/IJSE-10-2016-0295

Abdullah, M. (2020). Classical waqf, juristic analogy and framework of awqaf doctrines. ISRA International Journal of Islamic Finance, Vol. 12, No. 2, pp. 281–296.

Abdurrashid, Khalil K. (2019). Financing kindness as a society: The rise and fall of Islamic philanthropic institutions (Waqfs). Available at Yaqeen Institute for Islamic Research: Retrieved from https://yaqeeninstitute.org/khalil-abdurrashid/financing-kindness-as-a-society-the-rise-fall-of-islamic-philanthropic-institutions-waqfs/

Abu-Tapanjeh, A. M. (2009). Corporate Governance from the Islamic Perspective: A Comparative Analysis with OECD Principles. Critical Perspectives on Accounting, Vol. 20, No. 5, pp. 556–567.

Adams, D. W., & Von Pischke, J. D. (1992). Microenterprise credit programs: Deja vu. World development, Vol. 20, No. 10, 1463–1470.

Afadli, D. (1998). Experience of the advancement of the developmental role of waqf in Kuwait, a working paper prepared by Deputy Secretary General of Kuwait Awaqaf Foundation; for the conference, Waqf Fund Management in Kuwait and Egypt: Can Malaysia Learns from Their Experiences.

Affandi, A., & Nufus, D. N. (2010). Analysis on cash waqf return fund allocation in Indonesia: A case study in Indonesian waqf deposit. *Paper presented in Seventh International Conference – The Tawhidi Epistemology*: Zakāh and Waqf Economy, Bangi.

Ahmad, A. S. (1988). *Pakistsani Society: Islam, Ethnicity and Leadership in South Asia*: Anjuman Taraqi-e-Urdu through Royal Book Company.

Ahmad, M. (2015). Cash waqf: Historical evolution, nature and role as an alternative to riba-based financing for the grass root. Journal of Islamic Finance, Vol. 4, No. 1, pp. 063 – 074.

Ahmad, S., & Muhamed, N. D. (2011). Institusi Wakaf dan Pembangunan Ekonomi Negara: Kes Pembangunan Tanah Wakaf di Malaysia. Wakaf institutions and national economic development: A case on wakaf land development in Malaysia. Prosiding Perkem VI, Vol. 1, pp. 138–147.

Ahmed, H. (2007). Waqf based microfinance: Realizing the social roleof Islamic finance. International Seminar on Integrating Awqaf in the Islamic Financial Sector, March 6–7, Singapore.

Ahmed, H. (2011). Waqf as sustainable social enterprise: Organizational architecture and prospects. In *Fourth World Congress of Muslim Philanthropists* (March, pp. 23–24), Dubai.

Ahmed, H., & Khan, A. (1998). *Strategies to Develop Waqf Administration in India* (No. 50). The Islamic Research and Teaching Institute (IRTI).

Ahmed, T., & Haseeb, B. (2021). Global Islamic Fintech Report 2021. Available at: www.capitalmarketsmalaysia.com/wp-content/uploads/2021/06/Global-Islamic-Fintech-Report-2021.pdf

Akhter, W., Pappas, V., & Khan, S. U. (2017). A comparison of Islamic and conventional insurance demand: Worldwide evidence during the global financial crisis. Research in International Business and Finance, Vol. 42, December 2017, pp. 1401–1412.

Al-Jaowhary (2001). Investment versus endowment. *Journal Majammal Fiqh al Islami*. Vol. 13. No. 13.

Al Rahahleh, N., & Bhatti, M. I. (2022). Empirical comparison of Shariah-compliant vs conventional mutual fund performance. *International Journal of Emerging Markets*, Vol. 18, No. 10, 4504–4523.

Alam, M. M., Shahriar, S. M., Said, J., & Elahi, M. M. (2018). Waqf as a tool for rendering social welfare services in the social entrepreneurship context. *Global Journal Al-Thaqafah*, Special Issue, pp. 87–98. (Online) www.gjat.my/gjat2018si/SI2018-06.pdf

Alshater, M., et al. (2022). Fintech in Islamic finance literature: A review. *Heliyon.*

Alawiah, S. (2012). An empirical investigation into the accounting, accountability and effectiveness of waqf management in the State Islamic Religious Council (SIRCs) in Malaysia, Thesis for the requirement of Doctoral degree, Cardiff University.

Ali, H., Mohamed, H, Hashmi, H. S., & Abbas M. H. (2019). Global Landscape of the Islamic Fintech: Opportunities, Challenges and Future Ahead. COMSATS Journal of Islamic Finance, Vol 4, No. 2, pp. 29–53.

Ali, K. M., & Hassan, M. K. (Eds.). (2019). *Revitalization of Waqf for Socio-Economic Development* (Eds.). Volume II. Switzerland: Springer International Publishing.
Alias, T. A. (2012). Venture capital strategies in waqf fund investment and spending. ISRA International Journal of Islamic Finance, Vol. 4, No. 1, pp. 99–126.
Alias, T. A. (2013). *Introduction of Family and Public Waqfs into the Malay States in the 19th and early 20th Centuries and External Influences on the Norms Affecting Waqfs of Malaysia up to 1957*. Middle East Studies Association of N.A. Conference.
Al-Osman, A. (1997). Experience of waqf management in Kuwait. In the symposium about the developmental role of waqf conference.
Al-Rahahleh, N., & Bhatti, M. I. (2022). Empirical comparison of sharī'ah-compliant vs conventional mutual fund performance. International Journal of Emerging Markets, ahead-of-print. https://doi.org/10.1108/IJOEM-05-2020-0565
Alshater, M., et al. (2022). Fintech in Islamic finance literature: A review. *Heliyon*, Vol. 8, No. 9. https://doi.org/10.1016/j.heliyon.2022.e10385
Alterman, J. B., Hunter, S., & Phillips, A. L. (2005). The idea and practice of phkilanthropy in the Muslim world. Bureau for Policy and Program Coordination; P. No. 5. The Muslim World Series, USAID. https://csis-website-prod.s3.amazonaws.com/s3fs-public/legacy_files/files/media/csis/pubs/the_idea_of_philanthropy_in_the_muslim_world.pdf
Alvi, Z. A. (2020). *President, Tahreek e Tahafaz e Masājid wa Madāris* (TTMM). *Islamabad* waqf Imlāk Act, 2020; Sharī'ahe and Qanooni Jaiza – Asrāt wa Natāiej *(Urdu)*. Islamabad: Sharī'ah Academy, IIU.
Amenta, E., & Ramsey, K. M. (2010). Institutional theory. In K. T. Leicht, & J. C. Jenkins (Eds.), *Handbook of Politics: State and Society in Global Perspective* (pp. 15–39). Springer. https://doi.org/10.1007/978-0-387-68930-2_2.
Amuda, Y. J. (2013) Empowerment of Nigerian Muslim households through waqf, zakat, sadaqat and public funding. International Journal of Trade, Economics and Finance, Vol. 4, No. 6, pp. 419–424.
Ansari, A. H., Jamal, P., & Oseni, U. A. (2012). Sustainable development: Islamic dimension with special reference to conservation of the environment. Advances in Natural and Applied Sciences, Vol. 6, No. 5, pp. 607–620.
Ansari, M. A. (1974). *Social Life of the Mughal Emperors, 1526-1707*. Allahabad: Shanti Prakashan.
Aparicio, R. (2013). Measuring social public policies: Inclusiveness and Impact. Paper for workshop (25–26 March), Paris: UNESCO. www.unesco.org/new/fileadmin/MULTIMEDIA/HQ/SHS/pdf/Workshop-Social-Inclusion_CONEVAL.pdf
Arshad, M. N. M., & Haneef, M. A. M. (2013). Repositioning issues of waqf as a third sector organisation into the mainstream economy. Journal of Chemical Information and Modeling, Vol. 53, No. 9, pp. 1689–1699. http://doi.org/10.1017/CBO9781107415324.004
Arshad, M. N. M., & Haneef, M. A. M. (2015). Reositioning issues of waqf as a third sector organisation into the mainstream economy. *Asia Pacific Awqaf Congress Organized by Awkaf Australia & Sydney University Law School*, 15–17 April 2015. Sydney, Australia.
Asadullah, M., Hassan, M., & Siddiqui, Z. A. (2021). Comparison of takaful and non-takaful insurance companies of Pakistan: Under pre, during, and post economic crisis 2008. Etikonomi, Vol. 19, No. 1, pp. 201 – 212.

Askary, S., & Clarke, F. (1997). Accounting in the Koranic verses. *International Conference, The Vehicle for Exploring and Implementing Sharī'ah Islami'iah in Accounting, Commerce and Finance*. Macarthur: University of Western Sydney.

Asrohah, H. (2012). Waqf and its contribution in education in historical perspective. El-Qist: Journal of Islamic Economics and Business (JIEB), Vol. 2, No. 2, pp. 279–292.

Auda, J. (2015). *Membumikan hukum islam melalui maqasid syariah*. Bandung: PT Mizan Pustaka, pp. 32–35.

Awqaf Properties Investment Fund (2019). The Development Impact of the Awqaf Properties Investment Fund - A Model for Sustainable Development, December 2019. www.isdb.org/apif/sites/apif/files/2020-03/APIF%20Impact%20Report%20%28English%20Version%29.pdf

Awqāf Properties Investment Fund (2022). Islamic Development Bank Jeddah; www.isdb.org/apif/about-apif

Ayedh, Abdullah A., & Echchabim, Abdelghani. (2018). Waqf accountability in the Republic of Yemen: An empirical analysis. Qudus International Journal of Islamic Studies. QIJIS, Vol. 6, No. 2.

Ayedh, A., & Ihsan, H. (2013). *Hal Nahtaj Ela'a Ma'aiir Mohasbah lel-Waqf*" [Do we need for Accounting Standards for Awqaf]. *9th International Conference on Economics and Finance (ICIEF)*, Türkiye.

Ayub, M. (2017). Takaful as a means for social welfare: Transforming it to Musharaka al- ta`awuniyyah Model. In *Financial Inclusion and Poverty Alleviation Perspectives from Islamic Institutions and Instruments*. London: Palgrave Macmillan, 2017.

Ayub, M. (2018). Institutionalising '*Waqf*' for realizing the shared development objective by Islamic banks and financial institutions. Journal of Islamic Business and Management (JIBM), Vol. 8, No. 2, pp. 330–343. https://doi.org/10.26501/jibm/2018.0802-001

Ayub, M. (2019). Islamic bankers to have the prior right to justice and fair treatment. Journal of Islamic Business and Management (JIBM), Vol. 9, No. 1. https://doi.org/10.26501/jibm/2019.0901-001

Ayub, M. (2020). Learning to abide the rules of nature. Journal of Islamic Business and Management (JIBM), Vol. 10, No. 1, June. https://jibm.org/archieves/volume10-issue1/editorial/

Ayub, M. (2022). *Economics and Economic Policy: Islamic Perspective*. Islamabad: Riphah International University and International Institute of Islamic Thought (IIIT), IPS Press Islamabad. www.ips.org.pk/economics-and-economic-policy-islamic-perspective/

Azad, M. A. K. (2018). *Cash Waqf: A Multi-Dimensional Islamic Finance for Economic Development*. Dhaka: Jagannath University Dhaka.

Azganin, H. (2019). Redevelopment of idle *waqf* property through financial technology: Case of Malaysia. International Review of Entrepreneurial Finance, Vol. 2, No. 1, pp. 42–58.

Azid, T., Asutay, M., & Burki, U. (2007). Theory of the firm, management and stakeholders: An Islamic perspective. Islamic Economic Studies, Vol. 15, No. 1, pp. 1–30.

Aziz, et al. (2021). Bibliometric analysis of literatures on digital banking and financial inclusion between 2014-2020. Library Philosophy and Practice, pp. 1–31.

Aziz, M. (2021). *Islamic Fintech Dialogue: Mobilizing Funding for Islamic Fintech. Islamic Fintech Dialogue Series 2021*. Malaysia: Digital Economy Corporation. https://mdec.my/wp-content/uploads/FinTech-Report.pdf

Aziz, M. R. A., & Yusof, M. A. (2013). The inclination of student and public towards the establishment of Islamic Waqf Bank. World Applied Science Journal, Vol. 26, No. 4. www.researchgate.net/publication/287417733_The_Relief_of_Higher_Education_Loan_Through_Islamic_Waqf_Bank

Aziz, M. R. A., Johri, F., & Yusof M. A. (2013). Cash waqf models for financing in education. *iECONS 2013*.

Aziz, M. R. A., Yusof, M. A., Johari, F., Ramli, A., & Sabri, H. (2014). The relief of higher education loan through Islamic waqf bank. Asian Social Science, Vol. 10, No. 22, pp. 175–181.

Babacan, M. (2011). Economics of philanthropic institutions,regulation and governance in Turkey. Journal of Economic and SocialResearch, Vol. 13, No. 2 , pp. 61–89.

Barber, M., & Shahzad M. (2022). *Frameworks for a Developmental Welfare State: Lessons from Pakistan's Ehsaas Program*. Stanford: CDDRL. https://fsi.stanford.edu/publication/frameworks-developmental-welfare-state-lessons-pakistans-ehsaas-programme

Barrowclough, D. (2019). Benefiting more from national and international resources for financing the sustainable development Goals: Old challenges and new options. In Bagci, Kenan K., & Türbedar, Erhan E.. (Eds.), *Financing for Development: Alternative Perspectives on Challenges and Opportunities of Financing Development*. The Statistical, Economic and Social Research and Training Centre for Islamic Countries (SESRIC). Organization of Islamic Cooperation.

Bayraktar, O. (2009). *Why Was the Ottoman Empire 'An Economic Loser' in The Period 1850-1918*. Unpublished term paper, Norwegian School of Economic and Business Administration.

Bekkers, R., & Wiepking, P. (2011). A literature review of empirical studies of philanthropy: Eight mechanisms that drive charitable giving. Nonprofit and Voluntary Sector Quarterly, Vol. 40, No. 5, pp. 924–973.

Berakon, I., Aji, H. M., & Hafizi, M. R. (2022). Impact of digital sharī'ah banking systems on cash-waqf among Indonesian Muslim youth. Journal of Islamic Marketing, Vol. 13, No. 7, pp. 1551–1573. https://doi.org/10.1108/JIMA-11-2020-0337

Bhattacharyya, J. (2004). Theorizing community development. Journal of the Community Development Society, Vol. 34, No. 2, pp. 5–34. DOI: 10.1080/15575330409490110

Bowles, S. (2004). *Microeconomics: Behavior, Institutions, and Evolution*. Princeton, NJ: Princeton University Press.

Braun, V., & Clarke, V. (2006). Using thematic analysis in psychology. Qualitative Research in Psychology, Vol. 3, No. 2, pp. 77–101. doi: 10.1191/1478088706qp063oa

Bremner, R. H. (1956). *From the Depths: The Discovery of Poverty in the United States*. New York, NY: New York University Press.

Brennan, N. M., & Solomon, J. (2008). Corporate governance, accountability and mechanisms of accountability: an overview. Accounting, Auditing & Accountability Journal, Vol. 21, No. 7, pp. 885–906.

Bryman, A. (2016). *Social Research Methods* (5th ed.). Oxford University Press.

Bukhārī, Muḥammad ibn Ismāʿīl, Al-Sahih; Hadith # 893. Available at https://hamariweb.com/islam/hadith/sahih-bukhari-893/

Bulut, M. (2020); Civilization, economy and waqf in Ottoman Europe. Journal of Nusantara Studies, Vol. 5, No. 2, pp. 48–67. http://dx.doi.org/10.24200/jonus.vol5iss2pp48-67

Bulut, M. (2021). Cash waqf in Ottoman Europe, Istanbul Zaim University, translation from Turkish to English by Salim Korkmaz [Editor].

Bulut, M., & Altay, B. (2016). Rethinking economic mentality of the Ottoman Empire with respect to education, culture, cash waqf and financial relations. *International Symposium on Waqf and Higher Education (ISWHE 2016)*. Malaysia: Centre for Islamic Economics (CIE). Kulliyyah of Economics and Management Sciences (KENMS). International Islamic University Malaysia (IIUM).

Bulut, M., & Korkut, C. (2016). Comparison between Ottoman Cash Waqfs (CWs) and modern interest-free financial institutions. Vakiflar Dergisi – Aralik.

Bulut, M., & Korkut, C. (2017). A look at cash waqfs as Islamic Financial Institutions and Instruments. In V. Efendić, V., et al. (Eds.), *Critical Issues and Challenges in Islamic Economics and Finance Development*. Islamic Research and Training Institute. DOI 10.1007/978-3-319-45029-2_4

Bulut, M., & Korkut, C.E.M. (2019). Ottoman cash waqfs: An alternative financial system. Insight Turkey, Vol. 21, No. 3, pp. 91–112.

Cajee, Z. (2022). Awqaf – Promoting Self-Reliance and Sustainability, Muslim Views, September. P. 20; Awqaf, S. A.

Cajee, Z. A. (2007). Revitalizing the institution of *awqaf* in developing the community. Singapore: Singapore International Waqf Conference.

Cajee, Z. A. (2008, November). *The Revival of Waqf in Muslim Communities: Implementation of the Recommendations of the International Waqf Conference South Africa*. Cape Town: International Conference on Waqf and Islamic Civilization.

Chancel, L., Piketty, T., Saez, E., & Zucman, G. (2022). *World Inequality Report*. World Inequality Lab., UNDP.

Chojnicki, Z. (2010). Socio-economic development and its axiological aspects. Quaestiones Geographicae, Vol. 29, No. 2, pp. 7–17.

Choudhury, M. A. (2009). Islamic perspective of socioeconomic development. Journal of Islamic Economics, Banking and Finance, Vol. 6, No. 3. [*Paper presented in the 6th Biannual Conference in Islamic Economics and Finance, Tehran, Iran: Tarbiat Modares University*]. www.ibtra.com/pdf/journal/v6_n3_article2.pdf

Cizakca, M. (1998). Awqaf in history and its implications for modern Islamic economies. Islamic Economic Studies, Vol. 6, No. 1, pp. 43–70.

Çizakça, M. (1995). Cash waqfs of Bursa, 1555-1823. Journal of the Economic and Social History of the Orient, Vol. 38, No. 3, pp. 313–354.

Çizakça, M. (2000). *A History of Philanthropic Foundations: Islamic World from the Seventh Century to the Present*. Istanbul: Bogazici University Press.

Çizakça, M. (2004a). Cash waqf models for financing in education., *The Fifth Islamic Economic System Conference*, Kuala Lumpur.

Çizakça, M. (2004b). Ottoman cash awqāf revisited the case of the Bursa, 1555–1823. Foundation for Science Technology and Civilization, June 2004, Publication ID: 4062.

Çizakça, M. (Ed.). (2004c). Incorporated cash waqfs and mudarabah, Islamic nonbank financial instruments from the past to the future? *International Seminar on Non-bank Financial Institutions*, January 26–28, 2004. Kuala Lumpur.

Çizakça, M. (2014). Risk sharing and risk shifting: An historical perspective. Borsa Istanbul Review, Vol. 14, No. 4. http://www.sciencedirect.com/science/article/pii/S2214845014000258

Çizakça, M. (2018). From destruction to restoration – Islamic waqfs in modern Türkiye and Malaysia. Endowment Studies, Vol. 2, No. 2, pp. 83–106. https://doi.org/10.1163/24685968-00202001

Corruption Perception Index (2021). Retrieved from https://images.transparencycdn.org/images/CPI2021_Report_EN-web.pdf

Cravoy, T. A., Gourlayy, A., & Beckery, B. (2009). SMEs and regional economic growth in Brazil. Working Paper (No. ISSN 1750-4171), Loughborough University.

Curry, T. J. (2016). *Supporting Responsible Innovation in the Federal Banking System: An OCC Perspective*. Washington, DC: Office of the Comptroller of the Currency.

Dafterdar, M. H. (2011). Toward effective legal regulations and an enabling environment for inalienable Muslim endowments. ICR Journal, Vol. 2, No. 4, pp. 654–668. https://doi.org/10.52282/icr.v2i4.604.

Dafterdar, M. H. (2015). The role of awqāf in modern economic development. Islamic Banking and Finance Review, Vol. 2, No. 1, pp. 41–57.

Dafterdar, M. H., & Çizakça, M. (2013). *The Role of Awqāf in the 21st Century: An Update on the Development of Islamic Foundations*. Berlin: Maecennata Institute.

Dar, H., & Azami, T. (2010). Takaful & retakaful. *Global Islamic Finance Report (GIFR)*. Cambridge.

Daud, W. N. W., & Arifin, N. M. (2018). A comparative study of the Takaful Rules and Regulation for Malaysia and Indonesia Act. International Journal of Academic Research in Business and Social Sciences, Vol. 8, No. 12, pp. 1249–1264.

De Haan, G., Boonstra, N., Huijsmans, I., & Kuipers, E. (2021). Exploring the meaning of health for older adults with low socioeconomic status: A qualitative study. International Journal of Nursing Studies, Vol. 120, p. 103983. doi: 10.1016/j.ijnurstu.2021.103983.

Durrani, M. & Boocock, G. (2006). *Venture Capital, Islamic Finance and SMEs*. New York: Palgrave Macmillan.

Dzuljastri A. R., et al. (2016). A study on sources of waqf funds for higher education in selected countries. Adam Akademi, Vol. 6, No. 1, pp. 113–128.

Ebrahim, A. (2003). Accountability in practice: Mechanisms for NGOs. World Development, Vol. 31, No. 5, pp. 813–829.

Egbert, H. (2008). *Islam, Civil Society and Social Work*. Netherland: Amsterdam University Press.

Eriksson, P., & Kovalainen, A. (2008). *Qualitative Methods in Business Research*. Los Angeles, CA: Sage Publishing.

Ernst, C. W., & Lawrence, B. B. (2002). *Sufi Martyrs of Love: The Chishti Order in South Asia and Beyond*. New York: Palgrave Macmillan.

Farfor, A. (2001). Daora Al-Waqf fia Al-Islam, Majalat Mljaama Al-Fiqh AlEslamy, Al-Daorah Al-thalathah Ashar. Vol. 13.

Farooqi, N. R. (1986). Mughal-Ottoman relations: A study of political and diplomatic relations between Mughal India and the Ottoman Empire, 1556-1748 (South Asia, Middle East). Doctoral dissertation, University of Wisconsin-Madison.

Faroqhi, S. (2004). *The Ottoman Empire and the World Around It: The Library of Ottoman Studies*. London: N. Y. I. B.

Fauzi, P. N. F., & Arifin, A. (2016). Takaful: A review on performance, issues and challenges in Malaysia. Journal of Scientific Research and Development, Vol. 3, No. 4, pp. 71–76.

Fauzia, N. N. (2021). Developing cash waqf model as an alternative financing for social enterprises to support decent work and economic Growth in Indonesia. Turkish Journal of Islamic Economics (TUJISE), Vol. 8, Special Issue. DOI: 10.26414/A2759; www.tujise.org/content/7-issues/16-special-issue-06-2021/1-a2759/tuj2759.pdf.

Federal Shariat Court. (2022). Judgment on Riba (Shariat Petition No.30-L of 1991, April 28. www.federalshariatcourt.gov.pk/Judgments/Shariat%20Petition%2003-I%20of%202016%20Prof%20M%20Ibrahim%20Khan%20-%20Women%20Protection.pdf.

Frenkel, Y. (2009). Awqāf in Mamluk Bilād al-Shām, Middle East Documentation Center. The University of Chicago. https://doi.org/10.6082/M1Z036BM

Gaudiosi, M. M. (1987). Influence of the Islamic law of waqf on the development of the trust in England: The case of Merton College. University of Pennsylvania Law Review, Vol. 136, pp. 1231.

Gennardi, P. (1921). Ministère des Affaires Étrangères, Nantes, Fonds Syrie/Liban, 1er versement (abbreviated as MAE): MAE251.1/Dossier Arrêté 753/1.2.

George, M. (1981). *The Rise of Colleges: Institutions of Learning in Islam and the West*. Edinburgh: Edinburgh University Press, p. 48.

Ghani, S. A., Nordin, R., Jalal, B., Mohamad, M. H., Mohamed, H. H. A., Awang, M. M., & Ahmad, A. R. (2019). Empowering the social economic status of higher education institution in Malaysia through waqf fund. In Noordin, N., & Ngadnon, N. (Eds.), *Sustainable Development and Societal Wellbeing in the Current Technological Era*. Padang: Redwhite Press, pp. 18 – 22. doi:10.32698/GCS.0165.

Gibson, W., & Brown, A. (2021). Using narrative research to explore the experiences of student-athletes in college sports. Qualitative Research in Sport, Exercise and Health, Vol. 13, No. 1, pp. 74–88. https://doi.org/10.1080/2159676X.2019.1704594

Giloth, R. (2019). Philanthropy and economic development: New roles and strategies. Economic Development Quarterly, Vol. 33, No. 3, pp. 159–169.

Greif, A., & Laitin, D. D. (2004). A theory of endogenous institutional change. American Political Science Review, Vol. 98, No. 4, pp. 633–652.

Gürsoy, Ç. (2018). The financial analysis of the Ottoman cash waqfs. In H. Dincer et al. (Eds.), *Global Approaches in Financial Economics, Banking, and Finance, Contributions to Economics*. Springer International Publishing AG, pp. 389–413. https://doi.org/10.1007/978-3-319-78494-6_19

Gustafsson, B. (1987). The rise and economic behaviour of medieval craft guilds: An economic-theoretical interpretation. Scandinavian Economic History Review, Vol. 35, No. 1, pp. 1–40.

Habib, I. (1992). *The Agrarian System of Mughal India, 1556-1707* (3rd ed.). Oxford India Perennials Series. India: Oxford University Press.

Hamad, A. (2015). The new waqf (Islamic trust) law in the Emirate of Sharjah Law. www.tamimi.com/en/magazine/law-update/section-7/june-5/the-new-Waqf-islamic-trust-law-in-the-emirate-of-sharjah.html

Hanbal, Ahmad. b; al-Imam (2001). *Musnad*. Published by Muassasah Al Risalah; Vol 8; Hadith # 4880. www.sifatusafwa.com/en/classical-collections-of-hadeeth/al-musnad-of-imam-ahmad.html

Haneef, M. A. (2016). Funding of higher education in Malaysia - The potential role of awqāf and endowments, CIE, Malaysia. In *Proceedings of International Symposium on Waqf and Higher Education*, 28–30 May, Istanbul, pp. 20–25.

Haneef, M. A., Muhammad, A. D., Pramanik, A. H., & Mohammed, M. O. (2014). Integrated Waqf Based Islamic Microfinance Model (IWIMM) for poverty alleviation in OIC member countries. Middle-East Journal of Scientific Research, Vol. 19, No. 2, pp. 286–298.

Hanefah, M. M., et al. (2021). Empirical analysis on quality waqf reporting practices of waqf institutions in Malaysia. In Alareeni, B., Hamdan, A., & Elgedawy, I. (Eds.), *The Importance of New Technologies and Entrepreneurship in Business Development: In The Context of Economic Diversity in Developing Countries*. ICBT 2020. Lecture Notes in Networks and Systems, Vol. 194. Cham: Springer.

Haniffa, R. (2002). Social reporting disclosure: An Islamic perspective. Indonesian Management & Accounting Research, Vol. 1, No. 2, pp. 128–146.

Haniffa, R., & Hudaib, M. (2007). Exploring the ethical identity of Islamic banks via communication in annual reports. Journal of Business Ethics, Vol. 76, No. 1, pp. 97–116.

Hapsari, M. I., M.A. Bin-Mohd, T. T., & Mohammed, J. D. (2022). A qualitative investigation into crowdfunding framework as a source of financing for waqf land development. Journal of Islamic Accounting and Business Research, Vol. 13, No. 3, pp. 425–443.

Hartini, A, Azrai, et al. (2015). The possible role of waqf in ensuring a sustainable Malaysian federal government debt. *International Accounting and Business Conference 2015, IABC 2015*. Procedia Economics and Finance, Vol. 31, pp. 333–345.

Hasan, S. (2006). Muslim philanthropy and social security: Prospects, practices, and pitfalls. *6th ISTR Biennial Conference*, Bangkok.

Hasan, S. (2007). *Philanthropy and Social Justice in Islam: Principles, Prospects, and Practices*. Malaysia: A. S. Noorudeen.

Hasibuan, S. (2010). Poverty alleviation: The Islamic way. *Paper presented in the Seventh International Conference – The Tawhidi Epistemology*: ZakāhZakat and Waqf Economy, Bangi, pp. 244–259. www.ukm.my/hadhari/wp-content/uploads/2014/09/proceedings-seminar-waqf-tawhidi.pdf#page=249

Hassan, A., & Shahid, M. M. A. (2010). Management and development of the awqāf assets. In *Seventh International Conference—The Tawhidi Epistemology*: Zakāh and Waqf Economy, Bangi, pp. 309–328.

Hassan, R., Abu Bakar, N. M., & Akmal Abu Bakar, N. H. (2022). A review on governance and best practices in waqf management for sustainable development in selected Malaysian states and other countries. Towards a Post-Covid Global Financial System: Lessons in Social Responsibility from Islamic Finance, pp. 161–184.

Hodgson, G. (1998). The approach of institutional economics. Journal of Economic Literature, Vol. 36, No. 1, pp. 166–192.

Hoexter, M., Eusenstadt, S. N., & Leutzion, N. (2002). *The Public Sphere in Muslim Societies*. New York: State University of New York.

Husain, A., & Rashid, S. K. (1979). *Wakf Laws and Administration in India*. Lucknow: Eastern Book Company.

Hüseyin, A., & Akar Ş. K. (2019). Finance in Ottoman Istanbul (History of Istanbul, Vol. 6), article translated from Turkish version of History of Istanbul to be published in a digitalized form. https://istanbultarihi.ist/571-finance-in-ottoman-istanbul

Huybrechts, B., & Nicholls, A. (2012). Social entrepreneurship: Definitions, drivers and challenges. In *Social Entrepreneurship and Social Business*, Springer Gabler. DOI: 10.1007/978-3-8349-7093-0_2

Hyndman, N., & McDonnell, P. (2009). Governance and charities: An exploration of key themes and the development of a research agenda. Financial Accountability & Management, Vol. 25, No. 1, pp. 5–31.

Ibn majah, Abu Abdullah Muhammad Bin Yazid (1998). Sunan, Darul Hadith al-Qāhirah; Chapter 50, Hadith # 33409. Available at https://sunnah.com/ibnmajah:3349

Ibn Nujaym. (n.d.). *Al-Bahr Al-Raiq Sharh Kanz Al-Daqaiq*. Cairo: Dar Al-Kitab Al-Islami.

Ibrahim, H., Nor, E., & Muhammad, J. (2013). Cash waqf and its development in the north region of Malaysia. *International Conference on Business Economic Research,* March 4–5, Golden Hotel, Bandung, Indonesia.

Ibrahim, L. (2018). Waqf-A contributory tool for bridging infrastructural deficit in Nigeria. European Journal of Islamic Finance (EJIF), No. 11, December.

Ibrahim, M. (2012). *Waqf Land Administration: Comparative Studies between State Islamic Religious Councils (SIRCs) of Johor and Selangor*. Research Report, Kuala Lumpur, Malaysia.

Ibrahim, S. H. M. (2000). The need for Islamic accounting: Perception of Malaysian Muslims accountants and academicians on the objectives and characteristics of Islamic accounting. Unpublished PhD thesis. University of Dundee, UK

Ihsan, H. (2007). *An Exploratory Study of Waqf Accounting and Management in Indonesian Waqf Institutions: The Cases of Dompet Dhuafa and Uii Waqf Foundations*.

Ihsan, H., & Ayedh, A. (2015). A proposed framework of Islamic governance for awqaf. Journal of Islamic Economics, Banking and Finance, Vol. 11, No. 2, pp. 117–133.

Ihsan, H., Sulaiman, M. B., Mohammad Alwi, N., & Adnan, M. (2017). A study of accountability practice in Dompet Dhuafa Waqf of Indonesia. Journal of King Abdulaziz University: Islamic Economics, Vol. 30, No. 2.

Imber, C. E. (1997). *The Islamic Legal Tradition*. Edinburgh; Stillman, N. Op. cit.

International Accounting and Business Conference. (2013). Accounting and business challenges: Gearing towards Islamic resurgence.; *Proceedings of the Conference* (April 23–24]. Johor Bharu, Malaysia. https://ir.uitm.edu.my/id/eprint/39074/1/39074.pdf

International Working Group on Waqf Core Principles. (2018). *Core Principles for Effective Waqf Operation and Supervision*. Bank Indonesia, IRTI, IsDB, Jeddah. www.bwi.go.id/wp-content/uploads/2019/10/102018-Core-Pinciples-for-Effective-Waqf-Operation-and-Supervision.pdf

Ira, M. L. (1991). *A History of Islamic Societies*. Cambridge University Press. pp. 165

IRTI. (2014). Islamic social finance report. https://doi: 10.1017/cbo9780511617614.005

Islahi, A. A., (1992). Provision of public goods: Role of the voluntary sector (waqf) in Islamic history. (Financing Development in Islam: Seminar proceeding series IRTI & IDB).

Islahi, A. A. (1989). Stages of socio-economic development: Shah Wali-Allah's concept of al-irtifaqat. MPRA No. 29628. Available at: https://mpra.ub.uni-muenchen.de/29628/. MPRA Paper No. 29628, posted 19 Mar 2011 19:15 UTC.

Islam, M. M, (2015). Cash-Waqf: New financial instrument for SMEs Development in Bangladesh. World Vision Research Journal, Vol. 9, No. 1, pp. 111–120.

Ismail Abdel Mohsin, M. (2009). *Cash Waqf: A New Financial Product*. Prentice Hall.

Ismail, A. M., (2013). Financing through cash-waqf: A revitalization to finance different needs. International Journal of Islamic and Middle Eastern Finance and Management, Vol. 6, No. 4, pp. 304–321. https://doi.org/10.1108/IMEFM-08-2013-0094

Ismail, A. R. (1992). *Pendidikan Islam Malaysia. Kumpulan Kertaskerja 19 Universiti Kebangsaan Malaysia*. Bangi: Kumpulan Penerbit Universiti Kebangsaan Malaysia. ISSN Print: 0976-6308 and ISSN Online: 0976-6316.

Ismail, W. M. W. (2021). Significance of technology to cash waqf collection: Application of unified theory acceptance and use of technology (UTAUT). International Journal of Academic Research in Business and Social Sciences, Vol. 11, No. 1, pp. 777–788.

IWGWCP-International Working Group on Waqf Core Principles. (2018). Core principles for effective waqf operation and supervision; Bank Indonesia, IRTI, IsDB, Jeddah. www.bwi.go.id/wp-content/uploads/2019/10/102018-Core-Pinciples-for-Effective-Waqf-Operation-and-Supervision.pdf

Jacobs, K. (2000). Evaluating accountability: Finding a place for the Treaty of Waitangi in the New Zealand public sector. Accounting, Auditing & Accountability Journal, Vol. 13, No. 3, pp. 360–380.

Jalil, A., & Romli, A. M. (2010). Waqf instrument for contruction contract: An analysis of structure. In *Seventh International Conference* –the *Tawhidi Epistemology*: Zakat and Waqf Economy. Bangi: Insitut Islam Hadhari, UKM.

Jeffrey, S., & Berthold, R. (2003). Dynamics of formal and informal institutional change in the EU. Journal of European Public Policy, Vol. 10, No. 6, pp. 858–883.

Joseph, S. (2014). Waqf in historical perspective: Online fatāwā and contemporary discourses by Muslim scholars. Journal of Muslim Minority Affairs, Vol. 34, No. 4, pp. 425–437.

Julia, T. (2022). *An Overview of the Activities of the Islamic Development Bank (IsDB): Türkiye and Bangladesh* (Research Report No. 26). Istanbul: Research Center for Islamic Economics (IKAM).

Kader, S. A. S. Z. (2021). Analysis of the law applicable to the creation of waqfs during the British era in Penang. In: *Waqf: Past, Present and Future*. Kuala Lumpur, Malaysia: International Islamic University Malaysia, pp. 16–30. ISBN 978-967-2641-80-3.

Kader, S. Z. S. A., & Mohamed, N. A. (2014). Legal framework for management of waqf land in Malaysia. Shariah Law Reports, Vol. 4, No. 1, pp. 1–23.

Kahf, M. (1992). Waqf and its Socio-political Aspects. Draft Discussion paper. Jeddah: Islamic Research and Training Institute. Retrieved from: monzer.kahf.com/papers/english/WAQF_and_its_Soci opolitical_Aspects.pdf

Kahf, M. (1998). Financing the development of awqāf property. *Paper presented at the Seminar on Development of Awqāf organized by IRTI*, Kuala Lumpur, Malaysia.

Kahf, M. (1999). Fiqhi Issues on the revival of awqāf. *Paper presented in the Harward Forum on Islamic Finance and Economics*, October, 01. www.awqafsa.org.za/wp-content/uploads/2012/07/Fiqhi-Issues-in-Waqf-Monzer-Kahf.pdf

Kahf, M. (2003). The role of *waqf* in improving the *ummah* welfare. *Paper presented at the International Seminar on Waqf as a Private Legal Body*, January 6–7, Medan, Indonesia. http://monzer.kahf.com/papers/english/ROLE_OF_WAQF_IN_THE_WELFARE_OF_THE_UMMAH.pdf

Kahf, M. (2007). The role of waqf in improving the ummah welfare. dalam *Singapore International Waqf Conference 2007*. Singapura: Majlis Ugama Islam Singapore.

Kahf, M. (2012a). Role of Waqf in Sustainable Development (Part One): Kinds and Objectives of Islamic Waqf, 4 January 4., Available at: www.onislam.net/english/Sharī'ah/contemporary-issues/islamic-themes/452483-kinds-andobjectives-of-the-islamic-waqf.html

Kahf, M., (2012b). Role of Waqf in Sustainable Development (Part Two): Waqf and Sustaining Economic Development, 11 January. Available at: www.onislam.net/english/Sharī'ah/contemporary-issues/islamic-themes/452593-waqf-andsustaining-economic-development.html

Kahf, M. (2012c). Role of Waqf in Sustainable Development: Reforming the Waqf Institution. Available at: http://www.onislam.net/english/shariah/contemporaryissues/islamic-themes/452731-reforms-enabling-islamic- waqf-play-its-role.html

Kahf, M. (2014). *Notes on Islamic Economics: Theories and Institutions*. California: Al-Manhal Publisher.

Kahf, M. (n.d.). *Waqf: A Quick Review*. Available at: www.iiibf.org/papers/english/WAQF_A_QUICK_OVERVIEW.pdf

Kahf, M., & Mohomed, A. N. (2017). Cash waqf: An innovative instrument of personal finance in Islamic banking. Journal of Islamic Economics, Banking and Finance, Vol. 13, No. 3, pp. 13–29.

Kalmykova, E., & Ryabova, A. (2016). Fintech market development perspectives. *SHS Web of Conferences*, Vol. 28, No. 1051, pp. 4–8.

Kamaruddin, M. I. H. (2018). A case study on waqf reporting practices for governance, performance and socio-economic impact in Malaysia. International Journal of Management, Accounting and Economics. Vol. 5, No. 9, pp. 693–714.

Karagedikli, G., & Tuncer, A. C. (2018). Microcredit in the Ottoman Empire: A review of cash waqfs in transition to modern banking. *Financing in Europe: Evolution, Coexistence and Complementarity of Lending Practices from the Middle Ages to Modern Times*. London: Palgrave Macmillan, pp. 239–268.

Kassim, S., & Khouildi, M. Y. (2019). Socially responsible investment sukuk as an innovative funding mechanism to promote the development of Islamic microfinance. *Financing for Development: Alternative Perspectives on Challenges and Opportunities of Financing Development*. Ankara, Turkey: SESRIC, pp. 75–83.

Kazgan, H. (1997). *Osmanlı'dan Cumhuriyet'e Türk Bankacılık Tarihi*. İstanbul: Türkiye Bankalar Birliği.

Khalil, I. A., Ali, Y., & Shaiban, M. (2014). Waqf fund management in Kuwait and Egypt: Can Malaysia learn from their experiences. *International Conference on Masjid, Zakāh and Waqf. (IMAF 2014)*, 1–2 December 2014, Kuala Lumpur, Malaysia.

Khan, F. (2010). Waqf: An Islamic instrument of poverty alleviation – Bangladesh perspective. *Paper presented in Seventh International Conference – The Tawhidi Epistemology*: Zakāh and Waqf Economy, Bangi.

Khan, M. B., Ghafoorzai, S. A., Patel, I., & Shehbaz, D. M. (2021). Waqf based Islamic fintech model for agriculture Sector of Indonesia. International Journal of Business Ethics and Governance (IJBEG), Vol. 4, No. 1, pp. 73–85.

Khan, M. F. (2016). Islamic social finance: Inclusive financial development. *International Conference held in Makkah on 15–8 March 2016, under the auspices of Ummul Qura University*, Makkah.

Khan, M. M., & Ramzan, M. (2015). Perceptions of stakeholders on Islamic banking in Pakistan. Journal of Islamic Business and Management, Vol. 5, No. 2, pp. 99–116.

Khan, M. N., & Ahmed, M. M. (2019). Waqf and its role in achieving the objectives of Shari'ah: An analytical and applied study. Al-Aijaz Research Journal of Islamic Studies & Humanities, Vol. 3, No. 1, pp. 443–460.

Khan, T. (2015). Historical role of Islamic waqf in poverty reduction in Muslim society. PDR, Vol. 54, No. 4 (Winter), pp. 979–996.

Khan, Z (2020). Reviving the waqf tradition: Moral imagination and the structural causes of poverty. Available at: https://yaqeeninstitute.org/read/paper/reviving-the-waqf-tradition-moral-imagination-and-the-structural-causes-of-poverty.

Khan, Z., Siddique, M., & Muhammad, M. (2018). Minimizing operating cost of Islamic microfinance institutions: A case of Akhuwat. Journal of Islamic Business and Management, Vol. 8(S), pp. 320–329.

Khoo, K. K. (1980). Perkembangan pelajaran Agama Islam [Development of Islamic studies]. In Awang Had Salleh, A. H. (Ed.), *Pendidikan ke Arah Perpaduan: Sebuah Perspektif Sejarah*. Kuala Lumpur: Penerbit Fajar Bakti.

King. (2002). *King Report on Corporate Governance for South Africa*. Johannesburg, South Africa: Cliffe Dekker Hofmeyr.

Köprülü, F. (1942). Fuad Köprülü. "Vakıf Müessesesinin Hukuki Mahiyeti ve Tarihi Tekamülü." Vakıflar Dergisi, Vol. II, pp. 1–35.

Koulu, A. (2016). Blockchains and Online Dispute Resolution: Smart Contracts as an Alternative to Enforcement. *SCRIPTed-A Journal of Law, Technology & Society*, Vol. 13, No. (1), pp. 40–69.

Kuran, T. (2001). The provision of public goods under Islamic law: Origins, impact, and limitations of the waqf system. Law and Society Review, Vol. 35, No. 4, pp. 841–898.

Lahsasn, A. (2010). The role of cash waqf in financing micro and medium sized enterprises (MMES): A new Islamic financial approach by using cash waqf model. *Paper presented at the Seventh International Conference – The Tawhidi Epistemology*: Zakāh and Waqf Economy, Bangi, pp. 97–118.

Lashari, A. M. & Usman, M. (2022). Public waqf in Punjab Province Pakistan: Challenges and opportunities. Journal of Contemporary Business and Islamic Finance, Vol. 2, No. 2, pp. 173–185.

Lawal, I. M. (2018). Waqf-A contributory tool for bridging infrastructural deficit in Nigeria. European Journal of Islamic Finance, Vol. 2018, No. 11, pp. 1–7.

Lewis, M. K. (2006). Accountability and Islam. *Paper presented at the 4th International Conference on Accounting and Finance in Transition*, Adelaide, Australia.

Lindawati, L. (2019). Kekuatan Cerita dalam Bisnis Sosial (Sociopreneur is A Storyteller). Jurnal Studi Pemuda, Vol. 7, No. 2, p. 100. https://doi.org/10.22146/studipemudaugm.39643

Madni, H. H. (2022). Waqf Properties Act 2020 and the Constitution of Pakistan: A critical study. Journal of Islamic Thought and Civilization, Vol. 12, No. 1, pp. 279–290.

Mahamood, S. M. (2006). *Waqf in Malaysia: Legal and Administrative Perspective*. Kuala Lumpur: University Malaya Press.

Mahamood, S. M., & Rahman, A. A. (2015). Financing universities through waqf, Pious Endowment: Is it possible? Emerald Insight, Vol. 31, No. 14, pp. 430–453.

Mahmood, T., & Suhaib, A. (2019). The theme of holy Quranic verses for consumers' welfare regarding weighing & measurement. The Journal of Middle East and North Africa Sciences, Vol. 5, No. 5, pp. 1–5.

Malik, A. A. (2020). Powerful land mafia occupies 78pc of Awqāf Land in KP. *The News*, August 17. Available at: www.thenews.com.pk/print/701716-powerful-land-mafia-occupies-78pc-of-auqaf-land-in-kp

Malik, S. J. (1990). Waqf in Pakistan: Change in traditional institutions. *Die Welt des Islams* New Series, Bd. 30, No. 1/4, pp. 63–97. www.jstor.org/stable/1571046

Mambu. (2021). Global Islamic banking consumer survey. *Mambu Research*. Available at: https://mambu.com/insights/press/more-than-half-of-millennial-and-gen-z-muslims-would-adopt-islamic-banking-if-it-were-more

Mannan, M. A. (2005). The role of waqf in improving the ummah welfare. *International Seminar on Islamic Economics as Solution, organized by Indonesian Association of Islamic Economists and Mua'malat Institute*, Jakarta Medan, Indonesia.

Mannan, M. A. (2011). *Cash Waqf: Living by Giving and Sharing. Towards Establishment of World Social Bank. A New Strategy of Interest-Free Micro-Credit to the Poor and Profitable Investment Option for the Rich*. Dhaka, Bangladesh: Mannan Charitable Trust (HMCT).\

Mannan, M. A. (1998). *Cash Waqf, Enrichment of Family Heritage Generation to Generation*, Social Investment Bank Publication Series No. 1, 1st edition.

Masyita, D. (2012). *Sustainable Islamic Micro finance Institutions in Indonesia: An Exploration of Demand & Supply Factors and the Role of Waqf*. PhD Thesis, Durham University.

Masyita, D., Tasrif, M., & Telaga, A. S. (2005, July). A dynamic model for cash waqf management as one of the alternative instruments for the poverty alleviation in Indonesia. In *The 23rd International Conference of the System Dynamics Society*, Massachusetts Institute of Technology (MIT), pp. 1–29.

McGregor, S.L.T., & Murnane, J. A. (2010). Paradigm, methodology and method: Intellectual integrity in consumer scholarship. International Journal of Consumer Studies, Vol. 34, No. 4, pp. 419–427.

Merriam, S. B., & Tisdell, E. J. (2015). *Qualitative Research: A Guide to Design and Implementation*. Hoboken, NJ: John Wiley & Sons.

Mikail, S. A. (2018). *The Concept of Beneficial Ownership Highlights on Sharī'ah Issues in Its Application in Islamic Finance, in Islamic Commercial Law Report, 2016*; ISRA and Thomson Reuters.

Miles, M. B., Huberman, A. M., & Saldaña, J. (2014). *Qualitative Data Analysis: A Methods Sourcebook*. Los Angeles, CA: Sage Publications.

Misas-Rubio, Maria. (2020). Ownership structure and financial stability: Evidence from takaful and conventional insurance firms. Pacific-Basin Finance Journal, Vol. 62, p. 101355.

Moghul U. F., & Safar-Aly, S. (2014). Green ṣukūk: The introduction of Islam's environmental ethics to contemporary Islamic finance. The Georgetwon Int'l Event Law Review, Vol. 27, No. 1.

Mohamed Ariff, (1991). *The Islamic Voluntary Sector in Southeast Asia: Islam and the Economic Development of Southeast Asia* (Ed.) Singapore: Institute of Southeast Asian Studies.

Mohammad, M. T. S., Iman, M., & Hamid, A. (2006). Obstacles of the current concept of waqf to the development of waqf properties and the recommended alternative. Malaysian Journal of Real Estate, Vol. 1, No. 1, pp. 27–38.

Mohsin, M. I. A. (2008). Cash waqf: A new financial product model aspects of sharī'ah principles on its commercialization. In *Islamic Banking and Finance Conference, 2008*, Kuala Lumpur, Malaysia, pp. 28–29.

Mohsin, M. I. A. (2013). Financing through cash-waqf: A revitalization to finance different needs. International Journal of Islamic and Middle Eastern Finance and Management, Vol. 6, No. 4, pp. 304–321.
Molla, R. I., & Alam, M. M. (2013). A third sector–led economic model: Scopes of Islamic entrepreneurship. American Journal of Islamic Social Sciences, Vol. 30, No. 1, pp. 73–91.
Moumtaz, N. (2021). Waqf and the Modern State, Capitalism, and the Private Property Regime. Available at: https://islamiclaw.blog/2021/04/22/waqf-and-the-modern-state-capitalism-and-the-private-property-regime/
Muhammad, I. N. (2010) Scholars, merchants and civil society, Imperatives for waqf based participatory poverty alleviation in Kano, Nigeria. Humanomics, Vol. 26, No. 2, pp. 139–157.
Muhamad, M. F., et al. (2017). Pondok educational system in malaysia-Its effectiveness and limitations. Social Sciences. Research supported by Intensification of Research in Priority Areas (IRPA) 1996-2000.
Mujani, W. K. (2013). The economic effects of the Julban riots during the Mamluk period (1468–1517). Acta Histriae, Vol. 21, No. 1–2, pp. 1–14.
Mujani, W. K., Abdullah, I., & Bakar, I. A. (2012). The role of the Al-Azhar University in the dissemination of Islamic religious knowledge in Malaysia. Advances in Natural and Applied Sciences, Vol. 6, No. 8, pp. 1411–1413.
Mujani, W. K., Rifin, M. K. I., Resad, I. S. M., Jamsari, E. A., Palil, M. R., Ahmad, M. Y., & Taib, M. S. M. (2017). Strengthening and enhancing economy and education through waqf in Malaysia. International Journal of Civil Engineering and Technology, Vol. 8, No 12, pp. 600–613. Available at: https://iaeme.com/Home/issue/IJCIET?Volume=8&Issue=12
Mujani, W. K., Ibrahim, I. A., & Safiai, M. H. (2012). Observatories in Islamic history. Advances in Natural and Applied Sciences, Vol. 6, No. 8, pp. 1370–1373.
Mujani, W. K., Muttaqin, A., & Khalid, K. A. T. (2014). Historical development of public institutions of higher learning in Malaysia. Middle-East Journal of Scientific Research, Vol. 20, No. 12, pp. 2154–2157.
Mustafa, O. M., Nizam, M. B., Yusof, S. A., & Amin, R. M. (2016). Developing a framework for charitable giving from an Islamic perspective. In "Waqf and Higher Education; Comparative Best Practices; Challenges and Way Forward". *International. Symposium*, 28–30 May, Istanbul Zaim University and IIUM, pp. 26–32. www.academia.edu/26890967/Waqf_and_Higher_Education
Nafar, N. (2019). Islamic re-distributive instruments and financing infrastructure development. In Bagci, Kenan K., & Türbedar, Erhan. (Eds.), *Financing for Development: Alternative Perspectives on Challenges and Opportunities of Financing Development*. The Statistical, Economic and Social Research and Training Centre for Islamic Countries (SESRIC), OIC.
Nahar, M. M. A., & Haneef, M. A. (2016). Third sector socio-economic models: How waqf fits in? Institutions and Economies, Vol. 8, No. 2, pp. 75–93. www.researchgate.net/publication/301749088_Third_Sector_Socio-Economic_Models_How_Waqf_Fits_In
Nasir, A., et al. (2021). Conceptual and influential structure of takaful literature: A bibliometric review. International Journal of Islamic and Middle Eastern Finance and Management, Vol. 14, No. 3, pp. 599–624.
Nasir, F. M., Kader, S. Z. S., Ali, Z., & Jappar, G. (2019). Waqf in selected Asian countries. *Paper presented at 7th Global Waqf Conference*, November 11–13, Kuala Lumpur, Malaysia.

Nazir, M. M. (2013). UAE's DMCC commodity murabaha trading platform. International Financial Law Review. Available at: www.iflr.com/Article/3248060/UAEsDMCCcommodity-Murabaha-trading-platform.html?ArticleId=3248060.

Nenova, T., Niang, C., & Ahmad, A. (2009). *Bringing Finance to Pakistan's Poor: A Study on Access to Finance for the Underserved and Small Enterprises.* Working paper. Washington, DC: World Bank.

Nixson, F., & Cook, P. (2005). Small and medium sized enterprises in developing economies, In *Finance and Development.* Cheltenham: Edward Elgar Publishing.

Nooraini, H. Mohiddin. (2015). *Waqf development in Malaysia and Singapore: A comparative study.* Doctoral thesis, Durham University.

Norinah M. Ali, Rahman, M., Ahmad R., & Mahdzan N. S. A. (2015). The need of an effective business model for Waqf land development in Malaysia. *Paper presented at the 20th International Research Conference on Business, Economics, and Social Sciences (IRC-2015),* Istanbul, 5–6 December.

North, D. (1990). *Institutions, Institutional Change and Economic Performance.* Cambridge: Cambridge University Press.

Nurhayati, S. (2021). Sharī'ah cooperatives' productive waqf management model through financial technology services in Bandung city area to promote the people's economy. International Journal of Science, Technology & Management, Vol. 2, No. 1, pp. 272–280.

Nurjanah, S., & Hasanah, U. (2021). Cash waqf as source of funding for financial technology startups. International Journal of Islamic Economics, Vol. 3, No. 01, pp. 47–70. doi:10.32332/ijie.v3i1.3467.

Obaidullah, M., & Khan, T. (2008). Islamic Microfinance Development: Challenges and Initiatives (May 1). Islamic Research & Training institute Policy Dialogue Paper No. 2. http://dx.doi.org/10.2139/ssrn.150607

O'Dwyer, B., & Unerman, J. (2008). The paradox of greater NGO accountability: A case study of Amnesty Ireland. Accounting, Organizations and Society, Vol. 33, No. 7–8, pp. 801–824.

OECD. (2015). *G20/OECD Principles of Corporate Governance.* Paris: OECD Publishing, Paris. http://dx.doi.org/10.1787/9789264236882-en

OECD, G20. (2020). How Islamic finance can help achieve the sustainable development goals. *OECD Development Co-operation Policy Papers.* Paris: OECD Publishing, p. 30.

Omerčić, J. (2018). Socio-economic potential of waqf in Bosnia and Herzegovina. CNS, Centar za napredne studije. Bosnia.

Oseni, U. A., & Omoola, S. O. (2015). Banking on ICT: The relevance of online dispute resolution in the Islamic banking industry in Malaysia. Information & Communications Technology Law, Vol. 24, No. 2, pp. 205–223.

Oseni, U. A., & Ali, S. N. (2019). *Fintech in Islamic Finance: Theory and Practice.* London, UK: Routledge Taylor & Francis.

Othman, M. Z. (1983). Origin of the institution of *waqf.* Hamdard Islamicus, Vol. 6, No. 2, pp.3–20.,

Oubdi, L., & Raghibi, A. (2018). Ṣukūk-Waqf: The Islamic solution for public finance deficits. European Journal of Islamic Finance, Vol. 2018, No. 9, pp. 1–7.

Öztek, S. Ömür. (n.d). The foundation and the first 50 Years of "türkiye cumhuriyeti ziraat bankasi" (the Agricultural Bank of the Turkish Republic) (1863–1929).

Peter, C. H. (2004). *The Birth of a Legal Institution: The Formation of the Waqf in Third Century A.H. Hanafi Legal Discourse.* Boston: Brill, p. 169.

Philip. K. H. (1974). *History of the Arab*. London: Macmillan Press Ltd., pp. 627–628.
Pirson, M. A., & Lawrence, P. R. (2010). Humanism in business–Towards a paradigm shift? Journal of Business Ethics, Vol. 93, No. (4), pp. 553–565.
Pitchay, A. A. (2018). Cooperative-waqf model: A proposal to develop Idle Waqf Lands in Malaysia. ISRA International Journal of Islamic Finance, Vol. 10, No. 2, pp. 225–236.
Pitchay, A. A., Kameel, M. M., & Yusuf, S. (2014). Priority of waqf development among Malaysian cash waqf donors: An AHP approach. Journal of Islamic Finance, Vol. 3, No. 1, pp. 13–22.
Pitchay, A. A., Meera, A. K. M., & Saleem, M. (2015). Factors influencing the behavioral intentions of Muslim employees to contribute to cash-waqf through salary deductions. Journal of King Abdulaziz University: Islamic Economics, Vol. 28, No. 1, pp. 63–98.
Pitchay, A. A., Rahman, M. N. Y. A., Thaker, M. A. M. T., Azhar, Z., Mydin, A. A., & I'sa Abd Jalil, M. (2018). Proposing awqaf alternative plan (AAP): The way forward & sustainable higher education financial system. International Journal of Islamic Economics and Finance (IJIEF), Vol. 1, No. 1, pp. 39–58.
Qaradawi, Y. A. (2008). *Poverty Alleviation in Islam*. Dhaka, Bangladesh: Central Sharī'ah Board for Islamic Banks of Bangladesh. www.csbib.org
Radushev, E., Ivanova, S., & Kovachev, R. (2003). *Inventory of Ottoman Turkish Documents about Waqf Preserved in the Oriental Department*. Sofia: St St. Cyril and Methodius National Library.
Raissouni, A. (2001). *Islamic Waqf Endowment: Scope and Implications*. Rabat, Morocco: ISESCO.
Ramli, A. M., & Jalil, A. (2013). Corporate waqf model and its distinctive features: The future of Islamic philanthropy. *The World Universities Islamic Philanthropy Conference*. Menara Bank Islam, Kuala Lumpur. Available at: www.researchgate.net/publication/311494911_CORPORATE_WAQF_MODEL_AND_ITS_DISTINCTIVE_FEATURES_THE_FUTURE_OF_ISLAMIC_PHILANTHROPY
Rashid, S. K. (2004). Alternative dispute resolution in the context of Islamic law. The Vindobona Journal of International Commercial Law and Arbitration, Vol. 8, No. 1, pp. 95–118.
Rashid, S. K. (2007). Issues Inherent in the Development of Waqf Properties. *International Waqf Conference Southern Africa*. Cape Town, South Africa, (August).
Rashid, S. K. (2008). Reason for decline of awqaf and how to bring about their revival. *International Conference on Waqf and Islamic Civilization,* Isfahan, Iran, pp. 135–168.
Rashid, S. K. (2012). Siti Mashitoh Mahamood, (2006), Waqf in Malaysia: Legal and administrative perspective. IIUM Law Journal, Vol. 16, No. 2. https://doi.org/10.31436/iiumlj.v16i2.56
Riazuddin, R. (2022). Pakistan's economic potential. *Daily Dawn*, September 8, 2022.
Rifinitiv. (2022). *Islamic Finance Development Report [IFDR]*. Available at: www.refinitiv.com/en/islamic-finance
Rizvi, S. K. A., & Naqvi, B. (2018). Is Pakistan ready to embrace fintech innovation? Lahore Journal of Economics. Vol. 23, No. 2 (Winter), pp. 151–182.
Rizvi, S. K. A., Naqvi, B., & Tanveer, F. (2017). Mobile banking: A potential catalyst for financial inclusion and growth in Pakistan. The Lahore Journal of Economics, Vol. 23, No. 2 (Winter), pp. 251–281.

Rodgers, D. T. (1998). *Atlantic Crossings: Social Politics in a Progressive Age.* Cambridge, MA: Harvard University Press.

Rofiqoh, S. N. I., Ratnasari, R. T., Sukmana, R., & Ala'uddin, M. (2021). Model of Islamic corporate governance cash waqf based on entrepreneurship: A multi case study in Indonesia and Malaysia. Multicultural Education, Vol. 7, No. 2, pp. 145–155.

Saad, N. M., & Anuar, A. (2009). Cash waqf and Islamic microfinance: Untapped economic opportunities. Islam and Civilisational Renewal (ICR), Vol. 1, No. 2, pp. 337–354.

Saad, N. M., Kassim, S., & Hamid, Z. (2016). Best practices of waqf: Experiences of Malaysia and Saudi Arabia. Journal of Islamic Economics Lariba, Vol. 2, No. 2, pp. 57–74.

Sadeq, A. M. (2002). Waqf, perpetual charity and poverty Alleviation. International Journal of Social Economics. Vol. 29, No. 1/2, pp. 135–151, 2002.

Sadr, S. K. (2017). The optimum size of rotating Qard Hasan savings and credit associations. ISRA International Journal of Islamic Finance, Vol. 9, No. 1, pp. 15–26.

Saeed, M. (2019). Effect of takaful models on performance of takaful operators. Empirical Economic Review, Vol. 2, No. 2, pp. 55–80.

Safari, M. (2013). Contractual structures and pay of patterns of sukūk securities. International Journal of Banking and Finance, Vol. 10, No. 2, Article 7. Available at: htp://epublications.bond.edu.au/ijbf/vol10/iss2/7

Sait, S., & Lim, H. (2006). *Land, Law and Islam Property and Human Rights in the Muslim World. UN-HABITAT.* London & New York: Zed Books. www.academia.edu/32940421/Land_Law_and_Islam_pdf?email_work_card=view-paper

Saiti, B., Afghan, M., & Noordin, N. H. (2018). Financing agricultural activities in Afghanistan: A proposed Salam-based crowdfunding structure. *ISRA International Journal of Islamic Finance*, Vol. 10, No. 1, pp. 52–61.

Salamon, L. M., & Anheier, H. K. (1997). *Defining the Nonprofit Sector: A Cross-National Analysis.* London: Manchester University Press.

Salarzehi, H., Armesh, H., & Nikbin, D. (2010). Waqf as a social entrepreneurship model in Islam. International Journal of Business and Management, Vol. 5, No. 7, pp. 179–186.

Samiul, H. (2007), *Philanthropy and Social Justice in Islam, Principles, Prospects, and Practices.* A.S. Noordeen, Gombak, Kuala Lumpur, Malaysia.

Sanep Ahmad, & Nur Diyana Muhamed. (2011). Institusi wakaf dan pembangunan ekonomi negara: Kes pembangunan tanah wakaf di Malaysia.

Sarker, A. A. (2019). Role of cash waqf deposit (CWD) as an instrument for socio-economic development: Bangladesh perspective. In: Ali, K., Hassan, M., & Ali, A. (Eds.), *Revitalization of Waqf for Socio-Economic Development*, Volume I. Cham: Palgrave Macmillan. https://doi.org/10.1007/978-3-030-18445-2_2

Saxena, N. A. (1995). *Facets of Socio Economic Development.* New Delhi, India: Discovery Publishing House.

Schuster, R. (2021). The earliest waqf legacy in the world is deciphered: Two villages in Palestine. Available at: www.haaretz.com/archaeology/2021-12-06/ty-article-magazine/earliest-waqf-legacy-in-the-world-is-deciphered-two-villages-in-palestine/0000017f-f860-d044-adff-fbf95e250000

Schweitz, M. L. (2001). NGO network codes of conduct: Accountability, principles, and voice. *Paper presented to the International Studies Association Annual Convention*, Chicago, Illinois.

Sensoy, F. (2016). The philanthropies of the Sultan's daughter Ayse Sultan from the beginning of the 17th century, and her waqf's accounting records. *Fourteenth World Congress of Accounting Historians* (pp. 357–402). Pescara.

SESRIC. (2015). *Integration of Waqf and Islamic Microfinance for Poverty Reduction: Case Studies of Malaysia, Indonesia and Bangladesh* (9th Feb). Ankara, Turkey: SESRIC.

Shafii, Z., Iqbal, Z., & Tasdemir, M. (2016). Governance regulatory framework for waqf in selected countries. In Johari, F., & Abdul Rahman, A. (Eds.), *Muktamar Waqf Iqlimi III (IQLIMI2016) proceedings in Ban Nua Mosque.,* Songkla, Thailand, 2016 (Paper ID: IQLIMI2016-044). Universiti Sains Islam Malaysia (USIM), Negeri Sembilan, Malaysia.

Shahid, M. (2022). Pakistan's economic potential. *Daily Dawn*, August 11.

Shaikh, S. A., Ismail, A, G., & Shafiai, M. H. M. (2017). Application of waqf for social and development finance. ISRA International Journal of Islamic Finance, Vol. 9, No. 1, pp. 5–14; DOI 10.1108/IJIF-07-2017-002.

Shaybani, M. I. H. (1997). *Sharh Kitab al-Siyar al-kabir*. Beirut, Lebanon: Dar al-Kutub al-`Ilmiyyah.

Shirazi, N. S., Ali, S. S., & Obaidullah, M. (2017). *Practical Means of Integrating Zakāt and Waqf into Poverty Reduction Agenda of OIC Member Countries.* Jeddah, Kingdom of Saudi Arabia: Islamic Research Training and Institute.

Shirazi, N. S., Obaidullah, M., & Haneef, M. A. (2015). Integration of waqf-Islamic microfinance model for poverty reduction: Case of Pakistan. *IRTI Working Papers Series 1.*

Shukor, S. A., Anwar, I. F., Aziz, S. A., & Sabri, H. (2017). Muslim attitude towards participation in cash waqf: Antecedents and consequences. International Journal of Business and Society, Vol. 18, No. (S1), pp. 193–204.

Shukri, S. (2020). *Islamic Fintech Dialogue Report 2020.* Malaysia Digital Economy Corporation.

Shulthoni, M. N. M., Saad, K. S., & Ariffin, M. I. (2018). Waqf fundraising management: A proposal for a sustainable finance of the waqf institutions. Journal of Islamic Monetary Economics and Finance, Vol. 3, Special Issue (2018), pp. 153–178.

Sıddiqi, M. N. (1982). *Recent Works on History of Economic Thought in Islam: A Survey*. Jeddah: International Center for Research in Islamic Economics, Research Series in English, No. 12.

Siddiqi, M. N. (2004). *Riba, bank interest and the rationale of its prohibition.* Jeddah: Islamic Research and Training Institute.

Sideris, J. (2022). Fintech take-off in the Middle East. *The Papers*. Available at: https://thepaypers.com/expert-opinion/fintech-take-off-in-the-middle-east--1258535

Sinclair, H. (2012). Confessions of a Microfinance Heretic: How Microlending Lost Its Way and Betrayed the Poor. Oakland, CA: Berrett-Koehler Publishers.

Singer, A. (2008). *Charity in Islamic Societies*. New York: Cambridge.

Smith, A. (1976). *An Inquiry into the Nature and Causes of the Wealth of Nations* [First published in1776]. London: Oxford University Press.

Solimán, M. M. (2017). Islamic Finance: An Innovative Avenue for Financing the Sustainable Development Goals. Available at: www.huffpost.com/entry/islamic-finance-an-innovative-avenue-for-financing_b_58b97c82e4b02eac8876cd83

South Commission. (1990). *The Challenge to the South*, Report. New York: Oxford University Press.

Spahić, O. (2014). *The Mosque as a Community Center: A Concept and Evolution.* Kuala Lumpur: A. S. Noordeen. ISBN 9789830653587.

Stacey, J., & Rittberger, B. (2003). Dynamics of formal and informal institutional change in the EU. Journal of European Public Policy, Vol. 10, No. 6, pp. 858–883.

State Bank of Pakistan. (2020). *Handbook of Statistics on Pakistan Economy 2020.* Karachi, Pakistan: Sate Bank of Pakistan.

SBP (State Bank of Pakistan) (2021). *Monthly Statistical Bulletin*, September 2021.

Stefini, T. (2014). Cash Waqfs as a source of entrepreneurial credit for merchants: Some evidence from Venetian archival sources. *Paper submitted at the History Project, Annual Conference*; Institutions, Credit and the State, Yale University.

Stemplowskir. (1987). Rozwój jako przedmiot dyskusji. In: *Ameryka Łacińska.* Dyskusja o rozwoju. Warszawa.

Stewart, R., van Rooyen, C., Dickson, K., Majoro, M., & de Wet, T. (2010). *What Is the Impact of Microfinance on Poor People? A Systematic Review of Evidence from Sub-Saharan Africa.* Social Science Research Unit, Institute of Education, London, United Kingdom.

Suhaimi, F. M., Rahman, A. A., & Marican, S. (2014). The role of share waqf in the socio-economic development of the Muslim community: The Malaysian experience. Humanomics: The International Journal of Systems and Ethics, Vol. 30, No. 3, pp. 227–254. https://ideas.repec.org/a/eme/humpps/v30y2014i3p227-254.html

Sukmana, R. (2020). Critical assessment of Islamic endowment funds (Waqf) literature: Lesson for government and future directions. Heliyon, Vol. 6, No. 10, e05074. DOI: https://doi.org/10.1016/j.heliyon.2020.e05074

Sulaiman, S., Hasan, A., Mohd Noor, A., Ismail, M. I., & Noordin, N. H. (2019). Proposed models for unit trust waqf and the parameters for their application. ISRA International Journal of Islamic Finance, Vol. 11, No. 1, pp. 62–81. https://doi.org/10.1108/IJIF-02-2018-0019

Sundqvist, E., Backlund, F., & Chronéer, D. (2014). What is project efficiency and effectiveness? Procedia – Social and Behavioral Sciences, Vol. 119, pp. 278–287.

Syakir, M. M. T., Mujani, W. K., & Rozali, E. A. (2015). Wakaf Pendidikan Tinggi Pertama Di Malaysia. *Kertas Kerja Persidangan Antarabangsa Fiqh Semasa & Perundangan Islam 5 (PAFSPI2015),* organized by Faculty of Islamic Studies, Universiti Kebangsaan Malaysia, Johore College of Islamic Studies (MARSAH) and Institut Agama Islam Sultan Thaha Saifuddin Jambi Indonesia. Hotel Allium Batam Indonesia, 19 December.

Szawlowski, M. (2022). The growth of sharī'ah-compliant financial technology. The Business Year. Available at: www.thebusinessyear.com/article/islamic-fintech-2022-saudi-arabia/

Tahir, S. (n.d.). Proposal for a new comprehensive waqf law in Malaysia. Available at: www.google.com.my/search?q=wakaf+enactment+2003&sugexp=chrome,mod=5&sourceid=chrome&ie=UTF-8

Tajudin, M., Omar, R., Smedlund, A., & Aziz, R. P. (2020). Financing with heart and intelligence: Augmenting intimacy and sustainability through Islamic fintech. International Journal of Engineering and Advanced Technology, Vol. 29, No. 9 (Special Issue), pp. 1638–1664.

Tirmidhi, A. I. M. (n.d). Sunan at-Tirmidhi (Jami at-Tirmidhi) 2341, 4/150. Beirut, Lebanon: Dar al-Kutub al-'Ilmiyyah.

Tohirin A. (2010). The cash *waqf* for empowering the small businesses. *Seventh International Conference – The Tawhidi Epistemology*: Zakāh and *Waqf* Economy, 6–7 January 2010, Bangi, Malaysia.

UNCTAD. (2017). *Trade and Development Report: Beyond Austerity: Towards a Global New Deal.* Geneva and New York: United Nations.

United Nations Development Programme. (1997). *Governance for Sustainable Human Development: A UNDP Policy Document.* New York: United Nations Development Programme.

Vision in Action Advisory Group. (2011). Report on Christian-Muslim interfaith dialogue on "*Engaging Structural Greed Today*". In Kota Kinabalu, Sabah, Malaysia, September 25–30.

Watanabe, H., Fujimura, S., Nakadaira, A., Miyazaki, Y., Akutsu, A., & Kishigami, J. (2016a). Blockchain contract: Securing a blockchain applied to smart contracts. In *2016 IEEE International Conference on Consumer Electronics, ICCE 2016,* Kyoto, Japan, pp. 467–468.

Watanabe, H., Fujimura, S., Nakadaira, A., Miyazaki, Y., Akutsu, A., & Kishigami, J. (2016b). Blockchain contract: A complete consensus using blockchain. In *2015 IEEE 4th Global Conference on Consumer Electronics, GCCE 2015,* Las Vegas, USA, pp. 577–578.

WB-IsDB (2016). *Global Report on Islamic Finance, Islamic Finance: A Catalyst for Shared Prosperity*. DOI: 10.1596/978-1-4648-0926-2

Weber, M. (1978). *Economy and Society: An Outline of Interpretive Sociology.* Barkeley, CA: University of California Press.

White, A. (2006). Breathing new life into the Islamic waqf: What reforms can fiqh regarding awqāf adopt from the common law of trusts without violating shari'ah? Real Property, Probate and Trust Journal, Vol. 41, No. 3, pp. 497–528.

William, H. R. (2005). A framework for the analysis of stability and change in formal institutions. Journal of Economic Issues, Vol. 39, No. 3, pp. 665–681. DOI:10.1080/00213624.2005.11506839

Wilna, M. (1999). Islam versus western modernity: A contrast in educational thought. British Journal of Religious Education, Vol. 21, No. 3, pp. 158–166. DOI: 10.1080/0141620990210307

Wilson, R. (2016). *The Use of Trust in Waqf and Ṣukūk, in Islamic Commercial Law Report.* ISRA and Thomson Reuters.

World Bank. (2017). *Pakistan Development Update Growth: A Shared Responsibility.* Washington, D.C.: World Bank Group.

World Bank. (2020). *Leveraging Islamic Fintech to Improve Financial Inclusion.* Washington, DC: World Bank.

World Humanitarian Summit (WHS). (2016). Special Session Summary, 24 May. Available at: https://reliefweb.int/report/world/world-humanitarian-summit-islamic-social-finance-special-session-summary-istanbul-23-24

Wynen, A.V. T. (1949). Note on the origin of uses and trusts – WAQFS. SMU Law Review, Vol. 3, No. 2. https://core.ac.uk/reader/147636660

Yaacob, H., & Hisham Yaacob, H. (2013). Waqf history and legislation in Malaysia: A contemporary perspective. Journal of Islamic and Human Advanced Research, Vol. 3, No. 6, pp. 387–402.

Zain, N. R. M., Mahadi, N. F., & Noor A. M. (2019). The potential in reviving waqf through crowdfunding technology: The case study of Thailand. Al-Shajarah, 2019 (Special Issue Islamic Banking and Finance 2019), pp. 89–106.

Zakaria, A. A. M., Samad, R. R. A., & Shafii, Z. (2013). Venture philanthropy waqf model: A conceptual study. Jurnal Pengurusan, Vol. 38, pp. 119–125.

Zaman, A. (2018). An Islamic approach to inequality and poverty. Journal of King Abdulaziz University: Islamic Economics, Vol. 31, No. 1, pp. 69–92.

Zaprulkhan, Z. (2018). Maqāṣid Al-Shariah in the contemporary Islamic legal discourse: Perspective of Jasser Auda. Walisongo: Jurnal Penelitian Sosial Keagamaan, Vol. 26, No. 2, pp. 445–472. doi:https://doi.org/10.21580/ws.26.2.3231

Zarqa, M. A. (1988). Islamic distributive schemes. Distributive justice and need fulfillment in an Islamic economy. The Islamic Foundation, Leicester, pp. 163–216.

Zauro, N. A., Saad, R. A. J., & Sawandi, N. (2016). The moderating effects of financial inclusion on Qardhul Hassan Financing Acceptance in Nigeria: A proposed framework. International Journal of Economics and Financial Issues, Vol. 6, No. 7S, pp. 143–148.

Zein, I. M., Al-Ahsan, A., & Zakaullah, M. A. (2008). Qur'anic Guidance On Good Governance. *Guidance for good governance: Explorations in Qur'anic, Scientific and Cross-cultural Approaches*. London: Palgrave Macmillan, pp. 9–37.

Zibago. (2015). Pakistanis give Rs 650b in charity every year: Study. https://defence.pk/threads/pakistanis-give-rs-650b-in-charity-every-year-study.383105/

Zuki, M. S. M. (2012). Waqf and its role in socio-economic development. ISRA International Journal of Islamic Finance, Vol. 4, No. 2, pp. 173–178.

Index